**THE AUTHOR**  Professor Robert Cole teaches Modern European History at Utah State University in America, and has lectured at British colleges. He has travelled extensively in France, and made numerous trips to Paris. His published books include *A Traveller's History of France* (in the same series), a history of British propaganda and European neutral countries in the Second World War, and an analysis of the writing of late British historian, A.J.P. Taylor. He has also reviewed extensively for a variety of academic history journals.

**SERIES EDITOR**  Professor Denis Judd is a Fellow of the Royal Historical Society and Professor of History at the University of North London. He has published over 20 books including biographies of Joseph Chamberlain, Prince Philip, George VI and Alison Uttley, historical and military subjects, stories for children and two novels. He has reviewed extensively in the national press and in journals, and has written several radio programmes.

The front cover shows a detail from *Boulevard Monmartre, Afternoon Sun* by Camille Pissarro (The Hermitage, St Petersburg/The Bridgeman Art Library, London).

*Other Titles in the Series*

# A Traveller's History of Paris

To everyone who is, has been, or ever wanted to be, a Parisian

# A Traveller's History of Paris

SECOND EDITION

## Robert Cole

Series Editor   DENIS JUDD
*Line drawings*   *JOHN HOSTE*

INTERLINK BOOKS
An Imprint of Interlink Publishing Group, Inc.
NEW YORK

First American edition published 1998 by

INTERLINK BOOKS
An imprint of Interlink Publishing Group, Inc.
99 Seventh Avenue
Brooklyn, New York 11215

Published simultaneously in Great Britain by The Windrush Press

**Library of Congress Cataloging-in-Publication Data**

Cole, Robert, 1939–
    A traveller's history of Paris / by Robert Cole. 1st American ed.
       p.      cm. — (A Traveller's history series)
    Includes index.
    ISBN 1–56656–228–7
    1. Paris (France)—History.   2. Historic sites–France–Paris–Guidebooks
I. Title.   II. Series: Traveller's history.
DC708.C573   1998
944'.36—dc20                                            94–7120
                                                             CIP


Printed in Canada

# Table of Contents

# *Preface*

This stylish and intelligent guide to Paris is an excellent companion to Professor Cole's earlier and very well received *A Traveller's History of France*. Very like their subjects, these two books are part of the same whole, complementary, but also full of contrasts and subtle differences.

As a city, Paris possesses one of the most clearly defined and instantly recognisable identities of any metropolis. In part this is a physical, or at least a topographical, identity. The Eiffel Tower is a universal icon of impressive, not to say phallic, power. It is also a reminder to those Anglo-Saxons who might otherwise choose to forget it, that nineteenth-century French technological expertise followed hard on the heels of its British equivalent; the French, too, were artificers of the modern industrialised world.

But the Arc de Triomphe, the Avenue des Champs Élysées, Montmartre and Sacré-Coeur, the Latin Quarter, Notre-Dame, the Louvre, the Opéra, la Place de la Concorde, the Bastille, the Moulin Rouge, the Hôtel des Invalides, Pigalle and the Pont Neuf all summon up images and associations that are enduring and accessible. One long vanished building, the Bastille, has provided the world with an immensely powerful metaphor for a sudden, successful and long overdue assault on privilege and tyranny. We all know what 'storming the Bastille' means, and, in general, approve. Indeed, the great Revolution of 1789 set the context and established much of the vocabulary for the next two centuries of political and revolutionary struggle, while the Parisians' reputation, both literally and theoretically, for 'manning the barricades' was boosted by the uprisings of 1830 and 1848, and especially by the traumatic period of the Commune in 1871 after France's unexpected and humiliating defeat by Prussia.

Long before Caesar came to conquer Gaul, a tribe of river people lived upon the islands of the Seine, the largest of which became the Île de la Cité. By 53 BC an important Roman administrative centre, *Lutetia Parisiorum*, was established there. Despite the intense regionalism of so much of French history, this foundation set Paris on the path to its national and international celebrity. By the sixteenth century de Montaigne was able to write, 'I am French only through this great city, great above all things and incomparable in its variety, the glory of France and one of the most noble ornaments of the world.'

Despite its complex, violent and frequently bloody history, Paris retains a dreamy, romantic reputation in the minds of many. The sentiments expressed in popular songs, like 'Springtime in Paris' or 'I love Paris in the springtime', reflect a universal perception of a beautiful city dedicated to romance and the ideal place in which lovers can indulge their fantasies. The older, grubbier, but once not inaccurate, image of Paris as the appropriate venue for illicit sex and the classical 'dirty weekend', has all but vanished in an age, at least in the Western world, of greater sexual freedom and the readily available 'blue' video tape.

There seems no likelihood of Paris losing its perceived primacy of place in terms of culture, romance, ideas or sheer physical beauty. For those who wish to begin a love affair with Paris, or simply to renew an old passion, Robert Cole's book should be essential bedside reading.

Denis Judd
*London, 1994*

# Pride of Place

Paris on the river Seine is the central point in the Paris Basin, a network of rivers and trade routes north of the Massif Central. The Seine's tributaries include the Marne, Aisne and Oise. All are navigable and contribute significantly to the economic importance of the Paris Basin, which, in addition to the industries of Greater Paris, includes the farms, orchards and vineyards of Beauce, Touraine, Champagne and Burgundy.

## When Paris sneezes. . .

The city is central to far more than the Paris Basin, however; it is also the centre of France. 'In so far as a French nation exists today,' observed historian Edward James, 'it is because of the relentless policies of centralization pursued by one Paris-based government after another.' 'When Paris sneezes,' goes the adage, 'France catches cold.' For example, the French Revolution of 1789 began in Paris, and to an important degree its success or failure depended upon what happened there.

Oddly enough, Paris became the centre of France as the result of royal whim. For most of the century after Hugh Capet became the first king of Francia in 987, Orléans, Soissons, Laon and Paris were economic and political equals, and also rivals. Then came Philip I, who favoured Paris, and subsequent monarchs lived there and built palaces, paved streets, and encouraged education and trade; the city never looked back. In the first century AD, the Roman settlement of Lutetia Parisiorum was a village of a few hundred inhabitants; twenty centuries later, Paris is a city of well over 2 million, at the centre of a conurbation that exceeds 12 million, nearly one-fifth of the population of France.

## The Creation of Suffering

Paris is the result of centuries of struggle, much of it with the rest of France, with which Parisians enjoy a love-hate relationship as a consequence. The Parisian view of the history of French civilization has resembled the axiom that 'all roads lead to Rome' in reverse: that is, all that is best in France began in Paris and spread outward. This perspective is the product of Parisian history, and of the Parisians who have written it. Since Julius Caesar first camped on the Île de la Cité in 53 BC, the city has been besieged, bombarded, invaded, occupied, looted, and decimated by plague. Meanwhile, its inhabitants have rioted, risen in revolt, stormed strongholds, massacred and contested, have been distinguished equally by wisdom and petty-mindedness, and have variously embraced monarchy, republicanism, reaction, radicalism, élitism, democracy, religion, anti-clericalism, liberality and bigotry. Parisians also have embraced great learning, philosophy, art, architecture, music, theatre and literature, on the way to making their city the cultural centre of France certainly, arguably of Europe, and perhaps even of the civilized world.

## 'Vain and Fantastical'

A 'pride of place' mentality has characterized Parisians for centuries. 'To be in Paris, is to be,' enthused an anonymous correspondent to diarist Jean de Jandun in 1323, and Michel de Montaigne, a visitor to Paris from Bordeaux in 1588, acknowledged that: 'I am a French man but by this great citie, great in people, greate in regard of the felicitie of her situation. . . .' Historian and Parisian Jules Michelet wrote in the nineteenth century that 'Paris conquered France: and France the world,' adding that 'the real France is northern France'. Geographer and Parisian Vidal de la Blache agreed. The Paris region was where 'national history essentially took place'. Meanwhile, an English journalist writing in 1929 observed that Paris

... is the Latin spirit expressing itself as Taste in a world already civilized, and conquering, not with man's will, but with feminine attraction. Paris will be the metropolis of modern civilization as long as culture appreciates elegance, as energy attains refinements, and as glory finds its complement in pleasure.

Present-day Parisians agree. They regard the city's 'beautiful people' as the only true representatives of the élite of French culture and civilization.

Such 'pride of place' can be, and often is, annoying to outsiders. Nevertheless, Paris is difficult if not impossible to ignore, and few have tried. That has not prevented criticism of the city and its inhabitants. Louis XIV disliked Parisians intensely, and 'could not bear people who liked Paris'. English cleric William Cole insisted in 1765 that the 'vain and Fantastical' Parisians should recognize the '*Petitesse*, the Littleness, the Nothingness of Paris in respect to the Beauty, Grandeur & Superiority of London...'; while Arthur Young, also English, when visiting the city between 1787 and 1790 complained of dirty and dangerous streets, poor lodgings and debilitating inequities of wealth. Nearly a century later, American writer and historian Henry James warned: 'You may not like Paris, and if you are not extremely fond of her you will in all probability detest and abominate her.'

## *Parisians*

Perhaps more than most cities, Paris is its people. Who are they? The answer is far from obvious. Historically, Paris has been a magnet for French provincials (after the First World War, nearly two-thirds of the population were from the provinces), and for visitors, artists, writers, composers, and exiles from revolutions and repression. Paris has been home to Jews, Catholics, Protestants and atheists, and with the dismantling of colonial empire, to Asians, Arabs and Africans. Are Parisians, then, simply those who reside permanently in Paris? Not in the opinion of a Parisian cab driver recalled by Richard Bernstein.

The cab driver, Bernstein wrote, lamented in the manner of an Evelyn Waugh reference to London many years earlier, that 'there are no Parisians any more,' only foreigners. Why did these Asians, Arabs and Africans – and perhaps he meant Jews as well – remain in Paris, he wondered. After all, they were not even French. In the cab driver's view, such people would be foreigners no matter how long they or their descendants resided in the city, how perfectly they spoke Parisian French, how patriotically they sang 'La Marseillaise' on 14 July (or disdained from singing it), or how bravely they had fought in France's wars. 'Not that I'm a racist,' he hastened to add. 'Not at all. I don't vote Le Pen.'

Far from being unusual, this cab driver voiced what many Parisians feel, if they do not always give it voice. Parisian 'pride of place' is the outcome of historic struggles to free the city from 'foreigners' fully as much as it is the result of achievements by the city's great men and women. The history of Paris, therefore, is the story of conflict between institutions, ideas, groups and individuals, and above all, between those who have favoured change and those who have resisted it: that is, between adherents of a *vieux Paris* and advocates of a *Paris nouveau*. As Bernstein's cab driver would be the first to agree, the process has rarely been sanguine, though often sanguinary.

# CHAPTER ONE

# *Lutetia and Paris,*
## 53 BC–AD 1000

### *Lutetia and Paris, 53 BC–AD 1000*

Paris began as a Celtic settlement on an island in the Seine River. The Romans gave it importance, and Frankish kings made it the capital of France, or rather of the Île de France, so called because it was an 'island' surrounded by the rivers Seine, Oise, Aisne, Ourcq and Marne. It is reckoned that the site of the present city was a stop upon an ancient trading route across Celtic Gaul between Marseille and Britain. If so, a community may have existed there even before the Parisii (boat people). The Parisii and other Celts occupied the surrounding hills from the seventh century BC, and the island since the third. The earliest likely settlements were on the various heights above and on both sides of the river, away from its marshy banks: Charonne, Menilmontant and Belleville in the east, Montmartre in the north, Chaillot in the west, and the Mont Sainte-Geneviève to the south.

### *Lutetia Parisiorum*

When the Romans arrived with Julius Caesar in 53 BC, they camped on the Île de la Cité, the central one of a small group of islands in the Seine near its confluence with the Oise and Marne, and occupied by the Parisii. The Parisii 'were remarkable neither for their numbers nor for the extent of their territory'. They were probably there because the Belgae had driven them from the north-east into Senones territory (which tribe gave Sens, south-east of Paris, its name), where they sought protection. The Senones granted the Parisii the islands and surrounding territory, and they began plying themselves to a very lucrative river trade.

The Romans remained on the island, and named their settlement Lutetia Parisiorum, which gave rise to a legend popular in the middle ages, that the city had been founded by Helen of Troy's lover, Paris. Lutetia was connected to both banks by wooden bridges.

## DRUIDS

Since they were Celts, the Parisii were most likely governed by Druidic religious practices, which were central to Celtic culture from Britain to the Rhine. The Druids were an élite class of priests who applied law and justice, supervised religious ceremony, and were the repository of traditional lore. The Celts held that sacred spirits lived in forests, streams and mountains. They also worshipped gods which Julius Caesar equated with the Roman deities Mercury, Jupiter, Apollo and Minerva. The Druids set the tone for religious practice, which included human sacrifice. The Romans were both fascinated and horrified, perhaps surprisingly in light of their penchant for slaughtering people in the arena. Pliny and Strabo described the Druids divining omens from humans ritually stabbed in the back, shooting sacrificial victims with arrows, impaling humans, and worst of all caging large numbers of victims in a huge wicker cage made in human shape, and setting the lot afire in order to create a sort of sacred holocaust. These Latin writers were mystified by the Druids' ability to convince people that it was an honour to die in so horrible a fashion.

Perhaps more important was the mistletoe ceremony, in which a white-robed Druid cut a branch of mistletoe from a tree with a golden sickle. As the branch fell it was caught on a white cloak, and then two white bulls were sacrificed. In the end, the Romans were not much impressed by Druidic practice. Moreover they thought, wrongly, that the Druids exercised a nation-wide political power. Certainly they were powerful, but in spiritual, cultural and social rather than in political terms. In any case, the Romans suppressed the Druids, by both force and decree.

## GALLIC WARS

In 53 BC the Senones and Carnutes refused to send delegates to Julius Caesar's Assembly of Gaul at Amiens. Considering this a rebellious act, he ordered the Assembly to the Île de la Cité, close to the rebellious tribes. The following year, Vercingetorix led the Celts in revolt across the country. The Parisii, under Camulogenus, joined him and took control of Lutetia, their army camping on Mons Lutetius on the Left Bank, the site of the Panthéon. Caesar ordered Labienus to crush them. He defeated a Gallic force at Melun, crossed the Seine and marched downstream to the Right Bank, his four legions camping approximately where the Cour Carrée of the Louvre later stood.

As Labienus approached, the Parisii decided that Lutetia was indefensible. They set fire to it and destroyed the bridges connecting the island with the mainland. Labienus then appeared and engaged Camulogenus in a short and devastating battle, appropriately on the site of the Champ-de-Mars and the École Militaire. Camulogenus and his army were slaughtered; thereafter the Parisii tribe was under Roman rule, as indeed was the rest of Gaul.

## ROMAN LUTETIA

The Romans rebuilt Lutetia and surrounded it with a wall. They also made the town the seat of the sailors' corporation (*nautae Parisiaci*), which erected a temple and altar in praise of Jupiter and the Emperor Tiberius on the present site of Notre-Dame Cathedral. 'Under Tiberius Caesar Augustus the Parisii sailors have publicly raised this altar to Jupiter, most good, most mighty,' read the inscription. There was a votive column as well which, interestingly, bore representations of Roman gods but also Gallic deities, Taran the thunderer, Teutates the protector, and Esus, god of battles. The *nautae* symbol was a ship, probably the forerunner of the ship with the inscription *Fluctuat nec mergitur* that appeared in the twelfth century as the Paris coat of arms. The *nautae* certainly foreshadowed the medieval guild *mercatores aquae Parisiaci*, the Paris hanse, the master of which held the title *Prévôt des Marchands*.

Roman Lutetia soon spread beyond the Île de la Cité to the Left Bank, to what came to be known as the Latin Quarter. By 200 AD

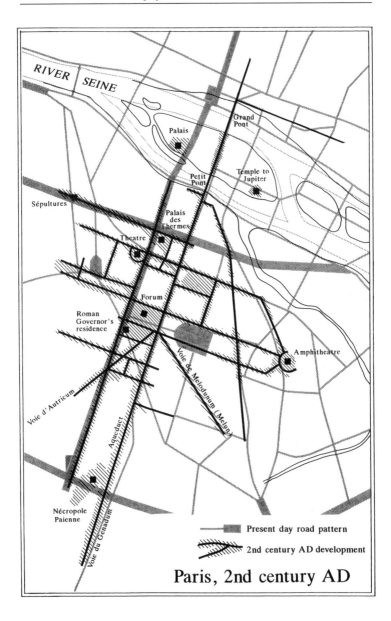

RIVER SEINE

Grand
Pont

Palais

Temple to
Jupiter

Petit
Pont

Sépultures

Palais
des
Thermes

Theatre

Forum

Roman
Governor's
residence

Amphitheatre

Voie de Melodunum (Melun)

Voie d'Autricum

Aqueduct

Nécropole
Paienne

Voie du Ocnadum

Present day road pattern

2nd century AD development

## Paris, 2nd century AD

visitors saw a town of some standing. Arches supported an aqueduct that brought water to the imperial baths and the public fountains from Rungis, Paray and Mont Jean, eleven miles to the south. The Roman garrison camp, a cemetery and a 10,000-seat arena, where Gallo-Romans enjoyed watching Christians being slaughtered, occupied Mons Lutetius. Near by, on the site of the Odéon, was a tiered amphitheatre; it also had porticoes where spectators could walk about and chat before performances and between acts. The Left Bank was also home to the imposing palace of the Caesars, to the forum, decorated

The Roman Arena built in the second century AD

with statues including an image of the Emperor, and baths, open to the public and free on certain days.

Crossing the wooden bridge (Petit Pont) to the Cité, visitors would have seen the prefect's palace and basilica, or hall of justice (on the site of the Palais de Justice), and the column and temple to Jupiter built by the *nautae*. Over the Grand Pont (Pont Notre-Dame) was the Right Bank with Mons Martis (Montmartre) in the distance, crowned by temples to Mercury and Mars and its sides dotted with villas. When mainland Lutetia suffered extensive fire damage about 280, the inhabitants abandoned the banks for the island. In due course they returned to the mainland to rebuild and the city expanded even more, becoming the hub of a Gallo-Roman communication system for northern Gaul. Avenue Renfert-Rocher is built over a Roman road, *via infer*, which relieved the traffic strain on the main road between Paris and Orléans, the capital of Roman Gaul.

Roman religion – Emperor worship, part of the purpose of Jupiter's temple, and worship of the gods of the state religion – was imposed over both Druidism and primitive Celtic rituals. Also, the cults of Isis and Osiris, and Mithras, came to Paris with the Roman legions. However, as the Gauls embraced these 'foreign' religions, they often conflated them with their own traditions. John Knapton observed that while the Gallic Mercury was recognizably Mercury, he had the appearance of 'an amiable Gallic peasant'. A truly Roman religion took root among the now Romanized Gauls only when Saint Denis and Christianity arrived in the third century.

## Saint Denis

Denis was ordered by the Pope to bring Christianity to the people of Lutetia. According to Gregory of Tours, he was 'sent to Gaul and made Bishop of Paris, suffered many torments for the name of Christ, ended his earthly life by the sword'. There was more to it than this cryptic comment allows. Denis came to Lutetia with two companions, Rusticus and Eleutherius, proselytized among the inhabitants, and was martyred. In the process he became a legend, owing to embellishments by medieval commentators long after Gregory, many of whom invariably confused him with Dionysius the Areopagite, who lived more than a century earlier.

As the story goes, Denis spent a long life converting people to the faith and founding many churches, during which hostile Roman authorities left him alone. Then, in 261, when he was more than one hundred years old and feeble, those authorities, determined to suppress Christianity, arrested him. He was beaten, placed on a grill in a furnace, given to hungry lions, and hung from a cross. Amazingly, he survived this abuse and was beheaded on Mons Martis, soon to be changed to Mons Martyrum in his honour, from which derives Montmartre. The night before his execution, angels administered the holy sacrament to him through his cell window, which seemed to endow Denis with unusual powers. The next day after his head was struck off, he rose, picked up the head and went with it to a stream where he washed it. That done, he proceeded a further five miles, to the village of Cato-lacus, the site of the present basilica of Saint-Denis, where he died.

Over the centuries first a church, erected by Sainte Geneviève, then a monastery, and finally the basilica were erected on the spot. He became the patron saint of France – though not of Paris, which honour was reserved for Sainte Geneviève – and in 1124 Louis VI marched off to war under the monastery banner, and with the battle cry 'Montjoye Saint- Denis!'

In a grassy square, Place Suzanne-Buisson, near the legendary stream where Denis washed his head, stands a modern and dignified statue of the saint holding his severed head in his two hands. The statue is sur-rounded by flowers, and a small fountain sprinkles water into a pool below it. Katherine Scherman saw dignity in the head. 'After all, it was chanting psalms.' For the true believer, this small memorial might be more illustrative of the saint's contribution to Paris than either Sainte Geneviève's church or Bishop Suger's twelfth-century Gothic basilica which, because of its many sarcophagi holding regal remains, is known as the 'royal necropolis'.

## *Julian*

Saint Denis brought Christianity to Paris. Julian, as governor, did much to secure Gaul from barbarian invaders, and made of Paris an important imperial city. He also repudiated Christianity, though with no lasting effect on Gaul or Paris. He had good reason for being an Apostate.

Julian was a nephew of Constantine the Great, who made Christianity the state religion of the Roman Empire. Constantine had also ordered the murder of most of Julian's male relatives, a fact of which he was aware. Moreover, at school in Athens, he read Greek philosophy, literature and mythology, and embraced the Classic ideal in art, all of which was at odds with the atrocious and brutal behaviour characteristic of Constantine and subsequent Christian emperors. Consequently Julian abjured Christianity in favour of the neoplatonic paganism popular among Athenian thinkers. However, in Gaul he kept his repudiation quiet in deference to influential bishops. Perhaps this, too, was in keeping with the outlook of the Greek thinkers of his day. In any case, it was only later that Christian writers condemned him as Julian the Apostate.

In 357, Julian was summoned to Gaul as governor and caesar (military commander). He was only 24, inexperienced at politics or war, and thought still as a student. He embarked on his campaigns with his baggage full of books. Paris was his capital, as it had been for Constantine and other caesars before him. Julian continued to call the town Lutetia, even though an imperial decree of 212 granting citizenship to all free inhabitants of the Empire resulted in Lutetia being renamed Paris, after the Parisii. Julian surrounded himself with philosophers and scholars, steeped, as one historian has put it, 'in the pleasant but misleading dream that the progress of the mystics and the tide of the faith could be turned'.

Life in Paris was happy for Julian. He left written commentaries which are illuminating with regard to the town and its surroundings. He wrote on one occasion:

> I had taken up my winter quarters in my beloved Lutetia, for that is what the Celts call the little town of the Parisii. You reach it from either side by a wooden bridge. The volume of water varies but little and is nearly always the same at every season. The water of the river is agreeable to look upon and excellent to drink.

He found the general circumstances of the region as agreeable as was the water. The weather, for instance: 'The winter is mild, which the Parisii attribute to the vicinity of the Atlantic and the warm effluvia borne by the breeze, for it seems that the water of the sea is hotter than fresh-water.' Round about Paris, 'the country is covered with good vines, and also fig-trees, which they take care to wrap round with straw or some other covering to protect them against bad weather'. Bad weather was indeed the condition in 358: 'This year the winter was exceptionally hard and the river was covered with ice.' Julian compared the ice with blocks of marble he had seen quarried in Phrygia. 'I cannot give you a better description of the enormous blocks of ice which float on the water, one after the other without ceasing, almost forming a bridge from one bank to the other. The inhabitants protect themselves against the cold in their houses by means of stoves.' At first Julian declined to use the stoves, which burned charcoal. On the occasion when he relented, he was nearly asphyxiated by the fumes and had to be revived by his physician. Centuries later, Parisian novelist Émile Zola was not so fortunate.

Julian's elevation to the Imperial throne in 361 followed his victories over the Alemanni and the Franks, and was enacted in a scene similar to that which had put Claudius (who was born in Lyon) on the throne many years before. In the old palais in the Cité, Julian stood before his legions, who were mutinous over being ordered to Persia. He urged obedience; in return they proclaimed him emperor, crowned him using a military collar as a diadem, and bore him in triumph through the streets. Julian accepted the honour, agreeing even to use force to take the throne if necessary. It is likely that, had he refused, his soldiers would have murdered him. In the event, he became emperor, and the legions went to Persia after all, where Julian was killed in battle in 363.

## *Barbarian Invasions*

Within a century of Julian's time, Roman Gaul again felt the weight of barbaric invasions. This time they would not be turned away. In the course of the fifth century, Franks from the north and north-east came to control most of Gaul. Some of them made common cause with

Attila the Hun, known among imaginative Roman Christians as the Scourge of God, who also sought to conquer Gaul. However, he ran afoul of the future patron saint of Paris.

## SAINTE GENEVIÈVE

About 422, a girl was born in the village of Nanterre, now a suburb of Paris, and named Geneviève. According to tradition, she inclined early towards the religious life, taking the veil at the age of fifteen. Her apparent zeal brought the young *religieuse* to the attention of Bishop Germain of Auxerre. A medieval chronicler recounted their meeting in this language:

> Among the people, Saint-Germain, from a sign given by the Holy Ghost, spyed out the little maid Sainte Geneviève, and made her to come to him, and kissed her head and demanded her name, and whose daughter she was, and the people about her said that her name was Geneviève.... [Her parents] came unto him, and the holy man said: is this child yours? They answered: Yes. Blessed be you, said the holy man, when God hath given to you so noble lineage, know you for certain that the day of her nativity the angels sang and hallowed great mystery in her, with great joy and gladness.

When her parents died, Germain helped Geneviève settle in Paris, where her frequent visions and unpalatable predictions annoyed the Parisians to the point that they came to hate her. There were rumours of attempts on her life. That is, until Attila invaded Gaul, burning and pillaging as he came.

The legend is that Geneviève 'saw' Attila approaching Paris, which indeed he was. When it was verified that the Hun conqueror had crossed the Rhine near Worms, south of Mainz, his ranks swollen by Alemanni allies as well as levies from the Hungarian plains, that Metz was in flames and Hun armies were at Verdun, Laon, Saint-Quentin, Reims and, finally, the banks of the Marne, then the Parisians recognized that the young nun knew what she was talking about. It was a terrifying moment. Floods of refugees from the east and north turned the city into chaos as they crowded on to the Seine bridges and camped in the streets, before pushing on to the south and west, much as the Belgians in the Second World War. Meanwhile the Roman administrators removed to Bordeaux (not the last time a French government would flee south before an invading army), where they made common cause with the Visigoths, who controlled Aquitaine and were Attila's primary enemy within Gaul. Panicked, the Parisians prepared to follow.

Then Geneviève, emaciated from fasting and prayer, urged them to stay, promising that they would be delivered from the Hun. 'Go on your knees and pray!' she exhorted. 'I know it, I see it. The Huns will not come.' In due course Attila, more concerned with Visigoths than with Parisians, turned away and made for Aquitaine. On the Champs Catalauniques near Châlons, a combined army of Visigoths, Armoricans, Franks and Burgundians commanded by the Roman general, Aetius, stopped their progress. Three years later, Attila died in Northern Italy, possibly murdered, possibly of natural causes, and possibly in the arms of a lady from the Danubian basin named Ildico.

Paris was saved and Geneviève got the credit. Thereafter her visions were irresistible, but not her defence of Paris. In 464 the Merovingian Childeric besieged the city on his way to other conquests. So, too, did his son, Clovis, who made Paris his capital in 508. Historians are unclear which Frank ruler Geneviève defied when she went up the Seine to Troyes with eleven barges to get food for the beleaguered city. Whichever it was, legend has it that many miracles accompanied her journey, and when she returned her barges were laden with corn for the starving city.

By such actions and a display of unrelenting Christian piety, Geneviève won the respect of even pagan rulers. In 475 Childeric gave her permission to build a chapel where St Denis was buried. She also figured in the conversion of Clovis to Christianity – though his Christian queen, the haughty Burgundian Clotilde, no doubt figured more – and persuaded him to build the church of St Peter and St Paul on Mons Lutetius. She was interred there when she died about 509, and the church was renamed Sainte-Geneviève-du-Mont. It is thought that her remains are presently in Saint-Étienne-du-Mont, next to the Panthéon, which replaced her original church. Paris honoured the *religieuse* who saved Paris from the Huns by making her their patroness.

## Paris and the 'Long-Haired Kings'

When its citizens first bent the knee to the Merovingians, known as the 'long-haired kings', Paris faced rulers whose style, language and culture were crude compared to their own. Educated, property-owning Parisians spoke Latin still, though in a form reflecting influence from outside. They were Christian (a Jewish population existed, as was true in most Gallic towns and cities, but was not large), albeit in the manner of adherents to a state church, wherein the bishop was an officer of the state. Parish churches were repaired Roman churches or, if new, simple and rustic by comparison. The Parisians' identity as Gallo-Romans was challenged as Franks and other barbarians brought with them differences in language, dress and manner. The lower orders were rough versions of the Gallo-Roman merchants and *patricii*, save that their language probably retained more of the Celtic, and their Christianity more vestiges of pre-Roman paganism. French, that is *langue d'oïl* as distinct from the Latinized *langue d'oc* of the south-west, developed after the Franks arrived in the Paris Basin. In time it became the language of Paris, and because of Paris the language of France. That transformation required another millennium.

Meanwhile, Paris continued as an important trading centre, its citizens as sophisticated as those in any Gallo-Roman city and more so than in most, and certainly more so than the *paysans* of the surrounding villages and countryside. The law code remained Roman until the Franks imposed the Salic Law, probably in the sixth or seventh century.

### THE CAPITAL

Clovis, who had been made a consul of Rome by the Byzantine Emperor Anastasius, entered Paris in the imperial manner, clothed in purple and escorted by priests and lictors. He made Paris his official residence as well as the seat of government, though he likely spent his time in hunting lodges in the congenial woodlands of the Paris Basin. His guard was quartered in the city, however.

The Salic Law required that property be divided among heirs equally; after Clovis, therefore, this essentially family enterprise became Austrasia, Neustria, Burgundy and Aquitania, leaving Paris as the capital of Neustria only. Thereafter, Paris played no great part in Merovingian, and even less in Carolingian, politics. It might be accurate to say that Parisians remained aloof from their royal residents after 508. After all, the Franks had treated them roughly, destroying much of Gallo-Roman Paris in the third century, which was rebuilt on a much smaller scale behind defensive walls. When they came to stay, the Franks used Gallo-Roman buildings as stone quarries, irrespective of Paris traditions.

Then there was Clovis. Even if he was a nominal Christian and the darling of Church propagandists, Clovis was a brute (at least by the Gallo-Roman standards of educated Parisians) who salved his conscience by building churches to honour the relatives he murdered to prevent them becoming rivals to his throne. Parisians looked with scepticism at such 'Clovian miracles' as a heavenly dove delivering the holy chrism with which he was anointed, a white doe showing his army the way across the River Vienne, and a white light guiding his army to victory over the Visigoths in Aquitaine.

## MURDER IN THE PALACE

Clovis was a typical Merovingian. This bloodthirsty family slaughtered one another as long as the dynasty lasted. He left four sons, and one famous instance of Merovingian brutality involved two of them, Childebert and Clothaire, and the three sons of their brother, Chlodomer, several years after Clovis' death in 511. Chlodomer had died, leaving his sons in Paris in the care of Clovis' widow, Clotilde, their grandmother. Childebert and Clothaire feared that Clotilde would proclaim the boys as rulers. The uncles took the boys prisoner and came to the grandmother with a proposition: would she prefer that their hair be cut or that they be killed? To have the royal locks shorn was a disgrace from which a Merovingian could never recover; certainly he would never afterward be allowed to ascend a throne.

Clotilde reputedly replied: 'If they are not to be raised to the throne, I would rather see them dead than shorn.' Clothaire was glad to oblige. He killed the elder child with a sword and the younger with a dagger, despite that child's pleading with Childebert to save him. A sorrowing Clotilde arranged burial for the dead boys in the Church of Saint-Peter and Saint-Paul (later renamed Sainte-Geneviève-du-Mont). Repenting the role she played in their death, the dowager queen spent the remainder of her life as a penitent, dressing in coarse robes, living on bread and herbs, and giving herself over to caring for the poor and sick.

The third son escaped his uncles, aided by palace servants. He later shaved his own head and entered holy orders. Eventually he returned to Paris and built a monastery in what became the village of Saint-Cloud, several miles from Paris. The name reflected his name, Clodoald.

## MURDER IN THE RUE SAINT-HONORÉ

Another typical Merovingian killing (though in this case it is difficult to find the victim particularly sympathetic) involved Brunhild, wife of King Sigebert of Austrasia. The king and Brunhild's sister were murdered by the Neustrians, and in turn Brunhild murdered the Neustrian ruler, Chilperic. She played kingmaker over the next three decades, orchestrating a number of further killings, and behaving despotically towards the Austrasian magnates. Finally they rebelled and betrayed her to the Neustrian king, Clothaire II, in 613. The chronicles relate that she was taken prisoner, 'reproached' with responsibility for the death of ten kings. She was then set on a camel for three days to be mocked and insulted by the army, after which she was tied to the tail of a horse 'which was lashed into a fury'. Soon all that remained of Brunhild was 'a shapeless mass of carrion', as Thomas Okey described it with something less than delicacy. Tradition places the execution at the corner where Rue Saint-Honoré meets Rue de l'Arbre Sec.

## MEROVINGIAN PIETY?

Acts of Merovingian 'piety' (other than churches built in honour of relatives they murdered) that applied to Paris include the church Clovis built for Sainte Geneviève, and Childebert's Church of Saint-Vincent, inspired by Germain (Germanus), bishop of Autun and of Paris, in 542 to house a relic of the true cross the king brought back from Spain. He and successor Merovingians were buried there. The church was renamed Saint-Germain-des-Prés when Germain was canonized in

754. Childebert's reign also saw the beginning of the basilica of Saint-Stephen next to the Notre-Dame sacristy on the Île de la Cité.

# *Dagobert*

Sometimes called the Great, Dagobert came to the throne in 628 and named as his principal minister of state Eligius, bishop of Noyon. Dagobert was the first Frank since Clovis to take the title King of all the Franks. He moved his court from Metz to Paris, where he lived a debauched life with numerous mistresses and an extravagant court. To meet the king's expenses, Eligius was quite creative in the raising and administration of taxes, so that upon Dagobert's death he fled Paris with a mob at his heels.

Dagobert was generous to the Church, even when he was also robbing it to pay for his excesses. He rebuilt the Church of Saint-Denis because, as a youth, he had discovered the neglected church raised by Sainte Geneviève in the village of Catolacus one day while hunting. Later, fleeing his father's anger, Dagobert was able to hide there, where he fell asleep and dreamed of the saint. Thankful for all of this, he had the church enlarged, beginning in 630, and embellished it with gold and gems.

Of course, refurbishment was not accomplished without a miracle. On the eve of the consecration, it was written, a leper went to sleep in an alcove of the church. He was awakened by a shining light and beheld Christ surrounded by the apostles, a crowd of angels, and Saint-Denis himself. This host consecrated the church, and when that was accomplished Christ instructed the leper to tell King Dagobert what had transpired during the night. As proof of His presence, Christ removed the leper's diseased skin and threw it against the wall. Apparently Dagobert was convinced, because the 'grisly memento', in Katherine Scherman's phrase, became a holy relic.

## DAGOBERT'S FAIR

On 9 October 635, Dagobert established the Fair of Saint-Denis to celebrate the saint's feast day. This became a famous occasion that Paris itself could not rival. The Saint-Denis fair contributed much to the ecclesiastical, economic and intellectual life of the early Middle Ages. Pilgrims, merchants, strolling players, and travellers of every other description, filled the Paris streets leading to Saint-Denis with lively activity. A new Grand Pont was erected to the Right Bank, and Paris expanded its centre westward from the Île de la Cité.

# The Carolingians

But first came the Carolingians. The line sprang from Charles Martel, 'the hammer', a wealthy Moselle Valley aristocrat who served as *major domus* (Mayor of the Palace), a magnate employed to manage the royal estates. By the end of the seventh century, the Merovingians had become decadent and largely useless, referred to as *rois fainéants* (do-nothing kings). Martel enjoyed a reputation as saviour of France from Islam (at the battle of Tours in 732); upon the death of Thierry IV, he simply set the monarchy aside. In 754 Martel's son, Pepin, was crowned king of the Franks at Saint-Denis by Stephen II, the first pope ever to visit Paris. Pepin's son was Charlemagne, during whose reign the Frank kingdom became the Frank Empire, and then the Holy Roman Empire. Charlemagne made his capital at Aix-la-Chapelle (Aachen), however, and for the time being Paris was out of the political mainstream.

One Carolingian action was important to Paris, however. The *major domus* was replaced by the office of count, whose duties were local government and administration. Hence the governor of Paris and the Île de France was titled the count of Paris, obliged to maintain the city and its region in the service of the emperor. In this manner Count Odo, and then his great-nephew Hugh Capet, rose to prominence.

## CAROLINGIAN PARIS

Charlemagne came to Paris once at Christmas, and once for the dedication of the Saint-Denis church, completed in 775 by Abbot Fulrad. His toleration of Jews throughout his kingdom was echoed in Paris, as was his policy of encouraging trade and commerce in the Empire. Strategically situated in the Île de France, Paris grew into a financial and commercial power, the 'market of the nations', even if it did lose political power. The annual Saint-Denis fair attracted merchants from Spain, Provence, Lombardy, Venice and Syria.

Otherwise, Charlemagne largely ignored the city. Twenty-one metropolises in France, Italy and western Germany received legacies in his will; Paris was not among them. 'Paris did not inherit so much as a chalice,' observed Maurice Druon, 'which makes it the more strange that the city saw fit to erect a statue to Charlemagne in front of Notre-Dame and one which does not even resemble the man it is supposed to represent.' The equestrian statue, raised in bronze in the Place du Parvis Notre-Dame, depicts a bearded medieval king, giant in stature and, by implication, noble and good-hearted. The real king-emperor was apparently pot-bellied, stoop-shouldered and clean-shaven, save for a long moustache worn in the Frankish manner. His biographer, Einhard

The Emperor Charlemagne

(775–840), recorded that he also spoke in a squeaky, high-pitched voice and, though a great patron of learning and letters, never mastered the art of reading or writing.

## THE CITY

By the Carolingian age, the pagan Gallo-Roman city of Lutetia–Paris had become the Christian Frank city of Paris. The Roman camp and cemetery were long gone from the Left Bank, and the caesars' palace and the amphitheatre were ruins, their stones and marbles long since taken for Frankish building projects. The basilica and abbey of Sainte-Geneviève now adorned Mons Lutetius. Saint-Germain-des-Prés and Saint-Julien-le-Pauvre were near by. A new Frankish city was developing on the Right Bank, marked by the abbey of Saint-Vincent-le-Rond to the west and that of Saint-Laurent to the east. Houses were spreading out from the four monasteries, and ancient villages slowly turning into suburbs.

Crumbling Roman walls still surrounded the Île de la Cité, and the Grand Pont and Petit Pont still bridged the Seine. The well-off descendants of Gallo-Roman merchants predominated on the island, travelling the streets in richly decorated ox-drawn chariots and no doubt haughty in the knowledge of their heritage. Gallo-Roman but also Christianized: the Church of Notre-Dame had replaced the temple to Jupiter, St Nicolas rather than Apollo was now patron of the guild of the *nautae*, and their votary to Mercury had given way to an oratorio erected to St Michel. Churches had been built for Saint-Gervais and Saint-Denis-de-la-Chartre, 300 nuns occupied the convent of Saint-Eleusius just west of Notre-Dame, and to the east the Hôtel-Dieu, founded by Bishop Landry (later Saint-Landry), cared for the ailing poor. Frank law and government were dispensed from the old Roman basilica and palace of justice, opposite the Hôtel-Dieu.

Churches and religious houses in Paris were as rich as the merchants, if not richer. The sixth-century abbots of Saint-Germain-des-Prés held nearly 90,000 acres of land in various provinces, including 42,000 in the Latin Quarter and environs, worked by more than 10,000 serfs, and huge annual revenues. By the ninth century, the lands of the abbey of Saint-Pierre-des-Fossés were so extensive that its properties shared

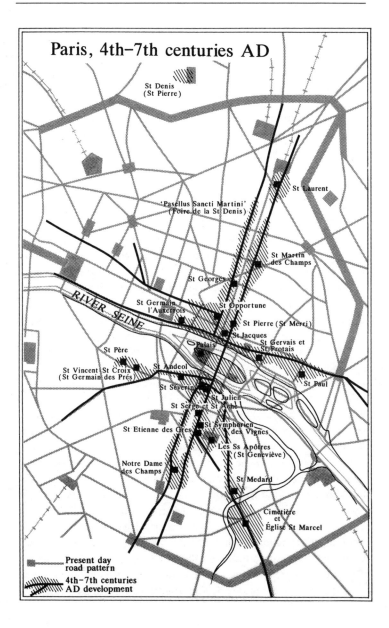

# Paris, 4th–7th centuries AD

St Denis
(St Pierre)

St Laurent

'Pasellus Sancti Martini'
(Foire de la St Denis)

St Martin
des Champs

St Georges

St Germain
l'Auxerrois

St Opportune

RIVER SEINE

St Pierre (St Merri)

St Jacques

St Gervais et
St Protais

St Père

Palais

St Vincent St Croix
(St Germain des Prés)

St Andeol

St Séverin

St Paul

St Julien

St Serge et St Aché

St Etienne des Grés

St Symphorien
des Vignes

Notre Dame
des Champs

Les Ss Apôtres
(St Geneviève)

St Medard

Cimetière
et
Église St Marcel

Present day
road pattern

4th–7th centuries
AD development

boundaries with those of ninety-four other domains. Of these, ninety were owned by ecclesiastical houses and only four by secular persons.

## *The Northmen*

One day, late in his life, Charlemagne was informed while dining that 'strange, black, piratical craft' had attacked a seaport on the coast of France. He is reputed to have said with tears in his eyes:

> Know ye my faithful servants, wherefore I weep thus bitterly? I fear not these wretched pirates, but I am afflicted that they should dare to approach these shores, and sorely do grieve when I foresee what evil they will work on my sons and on my people.

Such prophetic insights may be taken with a grain of salt, but the fact remains that those ships brought the infamous Northmen, the Vikings, who, beginning in the seventh century, were all over the lands which bordered the North Sea, raping, looting, pillaging and making a painful nuisance of themselves. 'God protect us from the fury of the Northmen,' prayed the monks at Lindisfarne. They were joined by brother monks along the Seine, including those of houses in and around Paris.

Paris was attacked and sacked by Vikings first in 845, and again in 852, 856, 858, 861 and 865. Each time the inhabitants fled as the Northmen ravaged religious houses, murdered priests and monks, and took away all the loot that they could carry. In this way the Abbey of Sainte-Geneviève and the church of Saint-Germain-le-Doré were sacked and burned, the latter losing its bronze roof. Saint-Germain-des-Prés was badly damaged on four occasions, despite having paid bribes. Only Notre-Dame, Saint-Stephen and Saint-Denis escaped; in their case bribery worked. Saint-Denis was fortified in 869 by order of Emperor Charles the Bald, which was almost his only display of concern for the sufferings of Paris. The Parisians looked to him to save them, but the emperor was more concerned with his own political ambitions, and ignored Paris while paying only scant attention to Viking incursions up the Seine Valley.

Charles's indifference resulted in a momentous shift in the history of Paris and of France. Ignored by their sovereign, the Parisians turned to

Robert the Strong, former Count of Toulouse, *missus* of Anjou and Maine and a warrior of great renown. The Northmen killed him in battle on the Loire in 866, but his sons carried on, including Odo who succeeded him as Count of Paris.

## SIEGE OF PARIS

A second series of raids in the Seine region began in 876 under Rollo the Ganger, 'a colossus so huge that no horse could be found to bear him'. He laid waste everything in his path, and to many monkish scribes recounting the deeds of this terror from the North, it seemed that Christian sanctuaries were ravaged, deserted and left to become the 'dens of wild beasts, the haunts of serpents and creeping things'. So reported Alan Barbetorte after having had to cut his way through thorns and briars to gain entrance to the Cathedral of Nantes. Such monks as he feared that all Christendom was doomed.

Trusting no one now but Count Odo, the Parisians restored and fortified the Roman walls around the Île de la Cité, and raised two constantly manned wooden *châtelets* (castles) to protect the approaches to the bridges. Meanwhile, little was done to rebuild the town on the left or right banks, since these settlements were virtually indefensible. Once again the city of Paris had shrunk to the twenty-five acres of the island.

## THE RAID OF '85

The greatest Viking siege of Paris, and the best recorded, began in the autumn of 885. Abbo, a monk of Saint-Germain-des-Prés, witnessed the event and decided to set it down on parchment. The siege opened when Siegfried, the Saxon leader of a mixed army of Viking raiders, demanded that the Parisians destroy the Grand Pont in order to give passage up the river to his ships. He promised to leave the city alone in return. Trusting Siegfried no more than they trusted Emperor Charles, the Parisians refused and the siege began. It lasted ten months. The defence was led by Count Odo, Bishop Gozlin and Abbot Ebles of Saint-Denis.

The Northmen entrenched their force around Saint-Germain-l'Auxerrois on the right bank, from where they assaulted the Grand

Pont with battering rams, siege engines, stone balls, flaming darts, which set fire to the *châtelet* and other wooden structures, and clouds of arrows. The siege continued into the winter, and Paris not only had to deal with the Northmen but with a flood which destroyed the Petit Pont. The high water enabled the raiders to climb up on to the *châtelet* which guarded the bridge. The defenders were offered their lives if they would surrender. When they did, they were immediately killed. 'These things I saw with mine eyes,' wrote Abbo.

A famine followed, which weakened the beleaguered Parisians, but not sufficiently to give the Northmen victory. Bishop Gozlin died, possibly from its effects; Odo lived and continued to provide heroic leadership. On one occasion he broke out of the city and galloped away to confront the new Emperor, Charles the Fat, who was even less helpful than had been his bald namesake. This Charles told Odo that he would offer the Northmen unmolested passage up the Seine – that is, through Paris – and into Burgundy to pillage undisturbed, if they would break off the siege. The count spurned this offer and fought his way back into the city, where, Abbo recorded, the Parisians cheered his resolution and prepared to continue the battle.

By this time the Northmen had apparently had enough, and rather than continue trying to force the Parisians to destroy the Grand Pont, they hauled their 700 ships out of the river, and dragged them on rollers through the fields to a point east of the Cité, where they were refloated, and the Vikings continued on their way to Burgundy. This was a remarkable feat, and, Maurice Druon observed, tongue-in-cheek, the only time in history that a battle fleet went on its way overland, in this case across the Champ-de-Mars, the plain of Grenelle and the fields of Saint-Germain-des-Prés. No doubt the Burgundians would have preferred it otherwise, because, the chronicles record, the Vikings inflicted upon them the worst winter that Burgundy had ever known.

## *Paris and France*

France came into being when the Imperial throne abandoned Paris. This western Frank kingdom of Neustria was referred to by the end of the ninth century as Francia, hence France. It had been ruled from

Paris, but when the kingdoms reunited under Charlemagne and the seat of power moved elsewhere, Paris became a provincial city, at least politically. Its governors were feudal dependants of the Carolingians, but were increasingly ignored by them. Over time, the Francians looked to these governors, rather than to Charlemagne's successors, for leadership. Hugh Capet emerged from the line which governed Paris and the immediate feudal territory of the Île-de-France. Though not strictly speaking the first king of France, Hugh founded the first royal dynasty to rule France.

## A KING FOR FRANCE, AND A PARISIAN AT THAT

The French monarchy grew in part out of disillusionment with the Carolingians during the Viking era. By the tenth century the bishops, counts and barons of West Francia had had their fill of Frank rulers. When Charles the Fat died without issue in 888, they agreed to break away and elected Count Odo of Paris as their king. His reign was not an unparalleled success, however. Viking raids continued, local magnates rebelled, and kingmakers and rivals to his throne provided constant distraction. Odo was followed in 898 by a restored Carolingian, Charles the Simple, who was king of West Francia only and never emperor, and he in turn by a succession of usurpers and others from various parts of Francia.

## HUGH CAPET

Finally, in 987, Hugh Capet, grandson of Robert the Strong, ascended the throne. With him the corner was turned; the Robertians and Paris triumphed within the kingdom of West Francia. To be sure, as the royal domain was limited to the Île de France this triumph was scarcely noticed by the rest of Francia. Hugh was crowned in Reims Cathedral by Archbishop Adelbéro, setting a tradition that lasted until the Revolution of 1789, and was revived – briefly – in 1824.

It is speculated that there had been collusion between Hugh and Adelbéro to make the count into a king. When Lothaire ascended the throne in 954, Archbishop Adelbéro opposed him, and after the accession corresponded with Hugh Capet and others in a manner suggesting a plot. Lothaire learned of this and ordered the archbishop to appear before an ecclesiastical assembly at Compiègne. Hugh appeared instead, at the head of an army which dispersed the assembly. Soon after Lothaire had his son, Louis V, crowned as co-regent. Upon Lothaire's death, Louis simply took up where his father left off, and laid siege to Reims in an effort to bring Adelbéro down. The archbishop offered to argue his case in front of any assembly Louis wished to call, in order to spare the people of Reims. Louis could not refuse, and so called an assembly, again at Compiègne.

On the day the assembly opened, Louis went boar hunting, an old Carolingian tradition, in the course of which he was killed. Whether by accident or by design will never be known with certainty; what is known is that Hugh Capet immediately took over the leadership of the assembly, and arranged for Adelbéro, his position as defendant conveniently forgotten, to address the group. Adelbéro did, and so persuasively that those present agreed to take no action on anything until the great nobles convened to choose a successor to Louis. This meeting took place at Senlis, where the archbishop was in complete control. He told the nobles: 'The throne is not to be taken by hereditary right, and we must put at the head of the kingdom a man who is distinguished not only for his physical nobility, but also for his qualities of mind, a man whom honour recommends and magnanimity supports.' They agreed, and Hugh was elected.

Hugh Capet made Paris his capital, but moved regularly between Paris, Étampes, Sens and Orléans. In Paris he resided on the Île de la Cité, in the renovated palace of the old Roman governors on the site of the present Palais de Justice. He had little actual power, but much sacerdotal prestige. Being anointed king, he assumed a moral stature above that accorded to territorial aristocrats, no matter how great their political, economic or military power. Above all, Hugh was shrewd and understood the limitations of his position, interfering in local affairs only when asked. Otherwise he reigned rather than ruled.

All the same, King Hugh gave Paris a position within Francia that was perhaps less than it enjoyed when Julian sat as Roman governor and made Paris his capital, but was certainly more than the city enjoyed under Clovis or any of his successors. It was a good beginning.

# CHAPTER TWO

# The Medieval City,
## 1000–1461

### The Millennium

Medieval Christianity treated even the most symbolic Biblical texts quite literally. Consequently, Europeans were convinced that the world would end with the end of the first millennium; and in Paris, as this day approached, political and social life was paralysed, churches bulged with terrified penitents, and donations poured into ecclesiastical coffers in record amounts. Of course nothing happened, and on the morning of the second day of the second millennium the sun beamed down brightly upon an unscathed city. Kings and clerics alike began decorating Paris with sacred houses, in gratitude that prayer had averted destruction. As the chroniclers recorded, Christendom 'seemed to thrill with new life; the earth cast off her out-worn garments and clothed herself in a rich and white vesture of new churches'.

Paris came into its own between 1000 and 1483 as the political, intellectual and theological metropolis of France. The monarchy grew slowly but steadily in power and influence from its Parisian base, the University of Paris emerged as the principal centre of learning in Europe, and the Church not only expanded in numbers of foundations, but established standards in style and decoration that have rarely been equalled since. Of course, this growth was accompanied by conflict, sometimes open and sometimes covert, between individuals and institutions, foreign and domestic, striving for influence or outright domination.

# The First Capetians

Hugh Capet's successors were the first French monarchs both to rule from and reside in Paris, more or less continuously. Otherwise, until Philip II, they were notable mainly for weakness, indolence and sexual excess.

## ROBERT II, 'THE PIOUS', 996–1031

One early Capetian, Robert II, was at least interesting if only because he blended piety with romance, and established an important, if curious, royal tradition. He was the first French king credited with curing scrofula by touching. Legend has it that a blind man approached the king as he washed his hands in preparation for an Easter feast. Startled, Robert threw the basin of water in the blind man's face, whereupon he recovered his sight. Word spread that the king had performed a healing miracle; it was a small step from throwing water to laying on hands.

Robert was called 'pious' because he was known as a theologian, musician and mystic who composed psalms and 'could sing the office better than a priest', and because his reign coincided with the great expansion in Paris church building, to which he contributed generously. In and around Paris alone fourteen monasteries and seven churches were built or rebuilt during his reign, including Saint-Germain-des-Prés and Saint-Germain-l'Auxerrois; and the old Roman basilica and palace in the Cité were replaced by a new, much grander palace and hall of justice, and a royal chapel dedicated to Saint-Nicolas. Robert also gave generously to charity, and troops of poor and ailing Parisians followed him whenever he went about the city.

His piety notwithstanding, Robert was a typical French monarch in his relations with the Church. On the one hand, he presumed a royal right to appoint bishops of his own choosing throughout the realm. On the other, he set aside his first wife, Rosala of Italy, to marry Berthe of Burgundy, a widow and his fourth cousin. Neither eventuality pleased the pope, who charged the king with incest and excommunicated him. His subjects, fearing God more than the king, turned their backs on him. However, he clung stubbornly to Berthe until, as a chronicler recorded, 'there remained to him only two wretched servants who prepared his food, and even these looked with abhorrence on the vessels the king used for eating and drinking and threw the remains of his meals on the fire'.

Finally, after five years of being a pariah, Robert sent Berthe away and married Constance of Arles. Papal blessing was bestowed upon the match (indicating that setting aside Rosala had not been the problem); tranquillity was not. Constance reputedly nagged and tormented the king, and filled his court with plotters, thieves and debauchees. He was shocked by the vain and frivolous troubadours brought from the queen's native Aquitaine, who with their licentious songs, lascivious music and dissolute lives, were a 'corrupting influence on the simple manners' of the Parisians, and said so. To no avail. Curiously, the king's inability to defy his tyrannical consort actually enhanced his reputation for piety.

If Constance liked debauchery, she disliked charity, at least in the open-handed manner practised by her husband, and he was forced to dispense it behind her back. On one famous occasion, she had the royal lance decorated with silver, and Robert got a beggar to help him remove it, then slipped him out the back with the silver before Constance could discover what had happened. Meanwhile, the queen complained whenever Robert admitted the poor to his table, which made persisting in this form of generosity a constant torment. That, too, enhanced his pious reputation.

## FEUDAL PARIS

Robert reigned over a feudal society of which serfdom was an integral part. Usually associated with rural society, serfdom extended to medieval Paris because wealthy monasteries and secular lords owned both land and serfs in the city and its environs. Serfs existed to serve and had few rights: church-owned serfs, for example, gave evidence in law courts for their master, and represented him in the event of a judicial duel. Religious houses exchanged them as chattel, and they could marry only with permission of abbot or bishop, who retained the right of disposition over issue from the marriage. Upward mobility was rare for any serf; if a female serf married a freeman, their children were automatically serfs.

Artisans and merchants of the city were little better off, for they owed a part of their produce to Church landlords and other seigneurs. In the eleventh century, the bourgeoisie and Jews, as well as serfs, were sometimes sold, exchanged or bequeathed in wills by seigneurial masters, both ecclesiastical and secular. One historian wrote, 'The story of medieval Paris is the story of the efforts of serf and burgess to win their economic freedom.'

Easier said than done, of course; serfdom was part of the divine order. The only recourse for a serf – or a bourgeois, for that matter – was rebellion. One such revolt, in the early eleventh century, provided France with its first record of a revolutionary song:

> We are men such as they,
> We have limbs such as they,
> We have bodies as tall,
> We can suffer as much;
> We lack only the heart.

Robert did nothing to aid the Parisian bourgeoisie, Jews or serfs in their search for economic freedom and social justice. It never would have occurred to this pious prince. The Parisians seemed to have liked him all the same, for if he made no contribution to social liberation he did provide some innocent fun. It is said that Parisians often remarked with amusement upon the king's feet, which were so supple that, as he rode through the streets, his big toe almost met his heel around the stirrup.

## Paris and a Russian Queen

Anne of Kiev, queen of Henry I (1031–60), wrote long, despairing letters to her father, the ruler of Russia, regarding the limitations of eleventh-century Paris. The bishops of Soissons and Meaux had led her to believe that her betrothed was a combination of Clovis and Charlemagne, and that Paris was Byzantium West. Anne arrived to find a 45-year-old boor who mumbled poor Latin and reigned over, rather than ruled, a country dominated by contentious feudal nobles. She believed that she was descended from Alexander the Great. Marriage to the prince of this minor western kingdom was something of a come-down, particularly as her Kiev rivalled the splendours even of Constantinople, having copied its elaborate architecture, arts, imposing ceremonials and profusion of wealth and luxury, while Paris was a city of 'gloomy houses, ugly churches, and revolting customs'. It is no wonder that her letters home, written in perfect Greek, contained strong hints that she had been sold into a kind of slavery. She was not the first royal female to be thus served, and would not be the last.

## PROVING SAINT DENIS

Anne's letters did not dwell much on those parts of their heritage which made Parisians proud, such as the abbey church of Saint-Denis, resting place of various kings of France and the patron saint himself – or so it was thought. In 1053 the priests of Saint-Ermeran at Ratisbon asserted that one Gisalbert had spirited Saint Denis' remains from the abbey in 892, and that Saint-Ermeran now possessed them. This was disturbing news if true, and King Henry at once organized a refutation of the claim. He assembled abbots, bishops, including the archbishops of Reims and Canterbury, princes and large numbers of Parisians in the abbey church, who watched while the silver coffins, kept in a vault under the high altar and which contained what was reputed to be Saint Denis, two companions, a nail from the true cross, and a piece of the crown of thorns, were opened. Saintly remains and holy relics were then borne in procession, and placed exposed on the high altar, where they remained for fifteen days. The priests of Saint-Ermeran sniffed at the demonstration as a cheap trick and maintained that they still had the body. They maintained alone, for the rest of France, especially Paris, seemed persuaded that Saint Denis was where he was meant to be.

## ABBOT SUGER

A century later church and saint were in the care of Abbot Suger, who also served as minister to Louis VI (1108–37) and to his son, Louis VII (1137–80). It may be said that rarely have such mediocrities been served by so competent a steward. Suger was a frail man with an iron will, who had charge of ecclesiastical affairs throughout the realm even while he sat on the Royal Council. Neither role was easy.

The French Church was then winding a tortuous path through a maze of popes and anti-popes, nunneries in which the sisters 'lived in open sin', and abbeys where un-Christian behaviour was commonplace, such as at Sainte-Geneviève, where canons, their servants and papal officers once brawled over possession of a carpet upon which the pope had knelt, during which even the king suffered a blow. While dealing with such situations as these, Suger also looked after royal finances and administration, which on one occasion, when Louis VII was on crusade, required him to thwart an attempted coup by the king's brother. This was the last straw for a weary Suger, who wrote an admonishing letter to the king: 'The disturbers of the kingdom have returned, and you, who should be here to defend it, remain like a prisoner in exile.... You have handed over the lamb to the wolf, and the State to its ravishers....'

Louis took the hint and came home. Suger handed him the kingdom intact. Two years later, exhausted from his labours, the abbot died.

## SUGER THE BUILDER

Royal administrator though he was, Suger first and foremost was a cleric, a keeper of relics, and a defender of the faith. As abbot of Saint-Denis he looked after the remains of the patron saint, France's most holy relic, and the abbey symbol, the Oriflamme (golden flame), which supposedly had been sent directly from heaven to Saint Denis himself. It was made of silk in the form of a gonfalon (a banner hanging from a crossbar), done in red and gold worked into a flame pattern, and suspended from a gilded lance which Suger once handed to Louis VI when the king was preparing for battle. The Oriflamme decorated the royal standard from then until it was replaced by the fleur-de-lis.

Saint-Denis was famous for its annual fair on the saint's feast day, which drew great crowds of traders, but also of pilgrims intent upon seeing the holy relics, sometimes with tragic results. Suger described such a tragedy in this language:

> Those who entered the church could not get out and strove in vain against the crowd at the doors. Within the church no one could walk; women were pressed as in a winepress, shrieked as though in childbirth. Many were

carried out with extreme difficulty to the monks' meadow but expired there. Others, to escape death, walked on the heads of men as on a continuous floor. The religious who showed the relics were so crowded that more than once they were obliged to escape by the windows with their precious burden.

Clearly, the existing abbey church was inadequate. In 1136 Suger set himself the task of changing that. The choir was constructed first; it was the architectural grandparent of such later cathedrals as Chartres, Reims, and especially Notre-Dame of Paris, begun in 1163 by Maurice de Sully, bishop of Paris, who like Suger did not live to see his undertaking completed. This was to be expected for, as Victor Hugo remarked of Notre-Dame: 'Great buildings, like great mountains, are the work of centuries.'

The basilica of Saint-Denis was the church that made the transition from the Romanesque, characteristic of monasticism, to Gothic, the concept of a Church linked to the outside world. The outside world included the illiterate masses, such as the mother of Goliard poet, thief and rake, François Villon. She understood her faith from the decorations of the Gothic church. Villon put these words in her mouth: 'I am a poor, old woman who knows nothing, who cannot read. But in the church I see Paradise painted, and Hell where the damned boil.'

## Philip II, 'Augustus', 1180–1223

This monarch made Paris the centre of medieval European civilization. He was known as Philip *le Dieu-donné*, or gift of God, because he was born in the twenty-eighth year of Louis VII's reign, by when nearly everyone had given up on a royal heir. One story attributes the name to a pair of old women, who, on the day of Philip's birth, supposedly informed an English student in Paris that 'God has given us this night a royal heir, by whose hand your king shall suffer shame and ill-hap'. He began his regal career at the age of fifteen, after setting his senile father aside, and was only twenty-one when he spent Christmas at Gisors with the ageing Henry II of England, for the famous meeting immortalized and treated with some historical licence in the film *The Lion in Winter*.

Philip II who made Paris the centre of medieval Europe

As French kings went, Philip was a success. He manipulated marriages and alliances, waged wars with sufficient skill to expand royal power against both foreign rulers (the Plantagenets of England, notably) and his own contentious vassals, and was loyal to the Church so long as it was loyal to him (such as when French bishops backed him against the papacy over his divorce from Ingeborg of Denmark and remarriage to Agnes de Meranie), though he allowed no extension of ecclesiastical power. He approved the bestowing of a charter on the University of Paris and codified university studies, built churches and laid down rules of conduct for Paris clergy, extended the city walls, paved the streets, made Paris even more of a commercial centre, and reorganized state administration. Upon his death in 1223 the royal lands were three times as extensive as when he ascended the throne, and the monarchy had never rested upon a surer foundation.

## 'AUGUST' BUILDINGS

Between 1181 and 1183, Philip built Les Halles, two large warehouse-markets for drapers and weavers at the old market at Champeaux. At Les Halles merchants could sell their wares within the protection of a roofed stall, which could be locked at night. Unhappily, the first heretics to be executed in Paris were burnt at the stake here, at Philip's orders. '*Beni soit le Seigneur en toutes choses*' (Blessed be the Lord in all things), intoned the most pious chronicler, Pigord, when he described the fate of these and other heretics.

Philip erected a château on the right bank, opposite Saint-Germain-l'Auxerrois. He had outgrown the palace of the Cité, or thought that he had. This palace, called the Louvre, would serve as royal residence, fortress, treasury and prison. It is said that Philip liked to look out from a window upon the waters of the Seine flowing below, and muse upon the burdens of state. The Louvre was expanded, modified and lived in, off and on, by subsequent monarchs, until Louis XIV abandoned it altogether for the Château of Versailles in 1682.

With Philip's blessing and sometimes his aid, Paris entered a frenzy of building. Work continued on Notre-Dame, Sainte-Geneviève was rebuilt, and the Saint-Honoré, Saint-Pierre (St Pères) and les Mathurins districts, all named after churches or monasteries, date from his reign. Three royal hospitals and three aqueducts were built, as well as fountains to provide fresh water in place of Seine river water, which was becoming polluted. The Parloir aux Bourgeois was also created in response to the important role Philip assigned to the Paris bourgeois while he was on crusade. Its function presaged that of the later Hôtel de Ville (city hall) from which the municipality would one day be administered.

### PHILIP'S WALL

The old protective wall, part of which dated from Gallo-Roman times, encompassed twenty-five acres of the Cité. Philip expanded it to include 625 acres, or nearly a square mile, of the Cité and the Left and Right banks. The wall took twenty years to build and was completed in 1211; it was eight feet thick (2.5 metres) with twenty-five gates and as

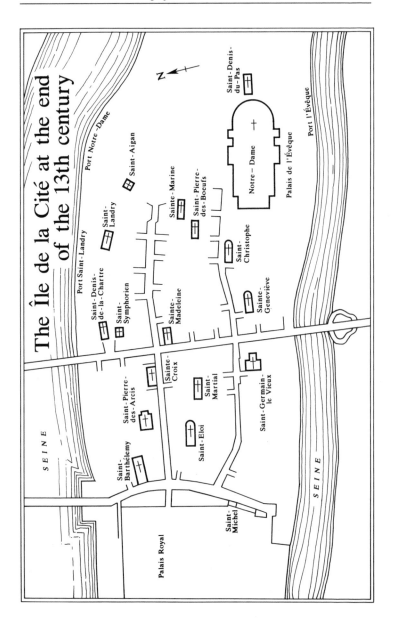

The Île de la Cité at the end of the 13th century

many as 500 towers. Chains, supported by boats and connected to towers on the banks, blocked entrance to the city by river from east and west; the eastern chain crossed the tip of the Île aux Vaches (Île Saint-Louis).

Using present urban geographical terms, the wall began on the Right Bank near the end of the Pont des Arts, passed through the Louvre quadrangle, continued northward along the line of the Rue Jean-Jacques Rousseau, and crossed the Rue Montmartre before turning east. It curved in a south-easterly direction to the Rue des Francs Bourgeois, which it followed to the Rue Saint-Antoine. It finished at a river tower on the Quai des Célestins. The wall resumed on the Left Bank at the Quai de la Tournelle, turned south-west inside Rue des Fossés Saint-Bernard, and proceeded west above Rue Clovis enclosing the abbey of Sainte-Geneviève. It followed Rue des Fossés Saint-Jacques, doubled outward to include the Parloir aux Bourgeois near the south end of Rue Victor Cousin, and started west again at the end of Rue Soufflot. It crossed Boulevard Saint-Germain, continued on within the Rue de l'Ancienne Comédie, and followed a more or less straight line back to the Tour de Nesle on the river.

That tower became legendary. Jeanne de Bourgogne, wife of Philip V (1316–22), supposedly entertained herself by having scholars tied up in sacks and flung from the tower into the Seine. François Villon claimed that Jean Buridan, who claimed that an ass placed equidistant between two equally attractive bundles of hay would starve before it could decide which to eat, was saved from this fate by falling into a straw-filled barge placed beneath the tower by his students.

## PHILIP'S PAVEMENT

If Paris was inclined to 'lift her proud head above the rest', as Champagnais traveller and chronicler Gui de Bazoches put it, a major reason likely was in order to elevate Parisian noses above the nauseating odour produced by soil with an unusually high sulphur content, and streets which were both passageways and a sewer system. Animals added to the mess, threatening citizens of all degrees into the bargain. Louis VI's eldest son was killed when his horse shied at a herd of pigs in the neighbourhood of Saint-Gervais. Thereafter pigs were banned, save those belonging to the monastery of Saint-Antoine which were required thereafter to wear bells. Other animals remained at liberty, however, contributing authenticity to such ancient street names as Rue Merderais.

Then Philip, standing one day at his Louvre window, decided to do something about the stench. He ordered the *prévôt* to pave at least the main streets running east and west and north and south: Saint-Martin and Saint-Jacques, Saint-Antoine and Saint-Honoré. Sandstone blocks three feet square were laid down in these streets, from which derives the expression *être sur le pavé* (to be down and out). The king also formed a sort of police force, truncheon-armed guards who protected him from assassins when he went for a walk on his newly paved streets.

## PHILIP AND THE JEWS

In Paris, as elsewhere, Jews were considered foreigners, and contemporaries were also startled when Bernard of Clairvaux was 'kind even to the Jews'. Paris Jews lived in a ghetto, the district around the Rue de la Pelleterie, until Philip expelled them from the city in the early thirteenth century after first confiscating their property. He gave the synagogue in Rue de la Juiverie (now Rue de la Cité) to the bishop of Paris, who consecrated it as La Madeleine de la Cité church. He also paid for going on crusade by making the Jews purchase their freedom.

# Louis IX, 'Saint-Louis', 1226–1270

Louis IX also did much for Paris. After his death he came to be known as 'Saint-Louis'. However, this may have been the result of Joinville's hagiography more than of biography. The Sire de Joinville's Louis IX is the king of popular imagination, sitting in the Cité palace garden, or in the bois de Vincennes under an oak tree, and listening to the entreaties of his humble subjects. This Louis was tall, spare and graceful, with a sweet face and 'the eyes of a dove', a man with a sense of humour who loved a good story and possessed a certain wit. Joinville wrote that the king once remarked to his chaplain, Robert de Sorbon, that: 'It is a bad thing to take another man's goods, because to make restitution [*rendre*] is so difficult, that even to pronounce the word makes the tongue sore by reason of the r's in it.' He was stern with blasphemers, undertook his children's religious and royal education personally, and, like Philip before him, regarded Jews as a ready source of monetary plunder.

## THE REAL LOUIS

Louis's behaviour suggests that he was also one of history's great neurotics, always on a quest for salvation, possibly inspired by his pious mother's injunction that she would rather see him dead than commit a mortal sin. Louis's regimen consisted of fifty genuflections and Ave Marias before retiring to bed; two masses upon rising in the morning and further offices said at the hours of tierce, sext, nones, vespers and compline; wearing a hair shirt; having the most scabrous beggars from the street brought in to dine with him; and trying to wash the feet of all the abbots in Paris. Taken as a whole, such zealousness does not argue a stable personality.

## SAINTE-CHAPELLE: RELICS AND BOOKS

It was supposed that the pious Saint Louis built Sainte-Chapelle to hold the holy relics he had purchased from certain Venetian merchants. In reality the chapel preceded the relics. Across a courtyard from the Cité palace, Sainte-Chapelle was constructed because Louis wanted a convenient place in which to indulge his obsession with prayer and worship. Naturally enough, when he had his relics, a crown of thorns, a piece of the true cross, the blade of the lance that pierced the side of Christ, and the sponge with which the vinegar was applied to His lips, he housed them there, in the upper chapel. On solemn occasions they would be put on display.

Louis also collected books and documents. Books on philosophy and theology were kept in Sainte-Chapelle, where they were available to students and scholars, with whom the king sometimes sat and read. In the palace next door he maintained an archive of royal acts, titles to property, treaties, customs of various fiefs, charters of towns and guilds, and edicts and judgements, all carefully catalogued and preserved. It was the first such archive in France, and was created, so Joinville claimed, in order that Louis 'might know the rights of all men, and thus give enlightened justice'.

The intricate interior of Sainte-Chapelle built by Louis IX

## THE PIETY AND CHARITY OF SAINT LOUIS

Louis's piety and charity were legendary. In the first instance, he settled six monks from Mount Carmel, brought back when he returned from crusade, in a house near the Quai des Célestins, and built churches for the orders of the Carthusians, Augustinians, Dominicans, Franciscans (known as Cordeliers because of their corded belts), Holy Cross, Saint-Antoine, and the Sisters of Saint-Bega (Béguines). In the second, he established such hospitals as the Quinze-Vingts (15 + 20) for blinded knights, and later beggars as well, was benefactor to the Hôtel-Dieu, opened a home for prostitutes, the Filles-Dieu, and a house in the Rue Coupe-Gueule for 'sixteen poor masters of arts' working for their doctorates in theology. This house became the Sorbonne and was the model for other colleges that became part of the University of Paris.

# Paris: the Centre of European Learning

In the middle ages, cathedral school and private tutor were the customary paths to literacy for male and female alike. However, only males attended university. In the eleventh century it was Montpellier for medicine, Chartres for logic and Laon, Anselm's school, for theology. In the twelfth century Paris overtook them all. In E.R.Chamberlin's words,

> the wandering student, passing from Laon to Chartres to Angers, or to some obscure monastery made temporarily famous by a new teacher, would come at last to the banks of the Seine.... There he would seek out, or drift to one master or the other. There, as often as not, he stayed.

## PETER ABÉLARD

So came Peter Abélard, scion of a noble family of Nantes, to Paris. He gave up his inheritance in order to seek knowledge, a not uncommon phenomenon. Thomas Aquinas, also an aristocrat, would do the same, and in Paris. Abélard first sat at the feet of Guillaume of Campeaux at Notre-Dame, whom he confounded in 'one of those disputations which was the academic equivalent of the tourney'. That ended his association with Guillaume and Notre-Dame. He crossed the river to Mont Sainte-Geneviève, taking crowds of Guillaume's students with him. Abélard was brilliant, a rhetorical craftsman of rare skill, and poetical; he was also handsome, and the master of *versi d'amore,* 'which he would sing with a voice wondrously sweet and supple'. At that point Héloïse entered the picture.

## HÉLOÏSE

This niece of Canon Fulbert of Notre-Dame was intelligent, beautiful and charming, and found Abélard irresistible, even though she was twenty-two years younger than the philosopher. Soon Héloïse found herself in Abélard's rooms in the Rue Chanoinesse near Notre-Dame, where they alternated between study and love-making. Canon Fulbert came to know of this and ordered Abélard to leave Paris. Abélard left, but he took Héloïse, now pregnant, with him to Brittany, where she gave birth to their son, Astrolabe. Intermediaries persuaded the Canon to have compassion and the couple returned to Paris. They were married in his presence, but secretly so that Abélard could continue in the Church; in return, the couple promised to be celibate.

It was a promise not kept. Fulbert found out, was incensed at the couples' cavalier disregard for his efforts on Abélard's behalf, and publicized the marriage in order to ruin Abélard. Héloïse placed herself under the protection of the nuns at Argenteuil, from where she denied that there had been a marriage. This was more than Canon Fulbert could bear, and he arranged for a barber and several Paris ruffians to castrate Abélard. That proved a mistake for all concerned: the canon's property was confiscated by an ecclesiastical court, which also condemned his hired ruffians to suffer the *lex talionis* (having done to them what they did to him), and to have their eyes put out as well. As for Abélard, when he had recovered he persuaded Héloïse to take the veil, and himself entered holy orders at the abbey of Saint-Denis.

It was not easy for them thereafter, though it made their historical reputations. Héloïse was deprived of the man she loved, but she wrote the letters that made her famous. Some were philosophical, while others 'prove that the flame burning within her was anything but spiritual'. Abélard began the works that proved his singular genius: *Introductio ad Theologiam, Dialectica, De Intellectibus, De Generibus et Speciebus, Norce Te Ipsum* and, greatest of all, the rationalist *Sic et Non.* However, he was frequently charged with heresy and his writings were burned. Bernard of Clairvaux, once described as a mere pamphleteer in the service of God, could do little better than produce scurrilous diatribes against Abélard. 'We have in France a monk without a rule . . . a prelate without solicitude, an abbé without discipline, a tortuous adder creeping out of his hole, a new hydra who grows seven heads for every one cut off . . .' was one of his efforts. Finally Abélard was called to account at a council in Sens, where Bernard read out seventeen condemnatory propositions and refused to argue them. Abélard stormed out of the council and retired to Cluny. He died there a few years later and was buried at Paraclete, where Héloïse joined him when her time came.

# *The University of Paris*

The name Latin Quarter derives from Roman times. Nevertheless it was an apt name, for all medieval scholarship was in Latin, and it was to this portion of the Left Bank that students and masters began to come in the twelfth century. The university emerged accordingly.

University was then a loose term which meant a body of masters who developed rules of behaviour which they could impose upon those licensed to teach – in other words, a guild. As the university evolved, the masters formed a governing body with a chancellor, or secretary, who actually granted the licence, with the masters' consent. The statutes governing university, or guild, behaviour were first written down in 1208, and included such rules as that masters must dress in plain black robes reaching to their heels, follow the 'accustomed order' in lectures and debates, and attend the funerals of all deceased masters.

The main branches of study were theology, medicine, canon law and the arts; they became distinct faculties in the course of the twelfth century, receiving official status between 1200 and 1244. Theology, medicine and canon law remained tied to the Cathedral Chapter of Notre-Dame, however; only the arts faculty was established on the Left Bank, on Mont Sainte-Geneviève. Organized by nationality – French, Norman, Picard and English – it was the largest, the most junior and the most contentious faculty. It also became officially the University of Paris after Philip II and Pope Innocent III extended recognition of the charter, in 1200 and 1210.

There was no campus as such, and the colleges (residences for scholars) came later. At first, each licensed master rented a room and taught what he knew, in Latin, to student-scholars who came to him for that purpose. The first college, the Dix-huit, was founded in 1171 by Jocius of London, who was appalled at the living conditions available to most masters and scholars. It was later absorbed into the Sorbonne, founded in 1253 by Robert le Sorbon. Cardinal Lemoine College followed in 1302, and by 1400 forty colleges existed. Three hundred years later that number was about sixty-five. Few of these colleges survive in the present university, the Sorbonne being a notable exception. The Sorbonne is so famous, in fact, that the name is often used to mean University of Paris.

A collegial note of interest: on 19 June 1781 the Jesuit Louis le Grand College awarded 600 livres to a young *boursier* from Arras for 'twelve years of exemplary conduct and of success in examinations and competitions'. His name was Robespierre.

## THE SCHOLARS

Students were eligible for university at the age of sixteen. They could live wherever and under whatever conditions pleased them or they could afford. Initiation rites for new scholars were not always in the best taste nor conducted with an eye toward physical safety. Regulations were sometimes enforced by beatings. The scholars worked hard, but they also played, at which they much resembled their modern counterparts. Activities ranged from staging mock marriages between tavern signs, such as The Sow and The Bear, to committing acts of thievery and brawling in wine shops.

'Town against gown' battles were frequent, brought on by the conviction among law-abiding citizens that the scholars were debauched, degraded, licentious thieving vagabonds, and by an equal conviction among the scholars that the stuffy, ignorant, narrow-minded bourgeoisie were naturally inferior to them. Sometimes the law was involved: in 1200, the *prévôt* and armed citizens scuffled with German students who had abused an innkeeper for insulting their servants. More often the scuffling was unofficial, much of it taking place on the Petits Prés des Clercs, or clerks' meadow, where in 1192 scholars were assaulted for being insolent to local residents, in 1278 were attacked for tearing down a wall meant to keep them out of the meadow, and in 1345 fought with monks from Saint-Germain-des-Prés over fishing rights on the nearby fosse.

## SCHOLARSHIP

All the same, Paris became *the* centre of learning in this epoch. 'Never before in any time or any part of the world, whether in Athens or in Egypt, had there been such a multitude of scholars,' wrote Guillaume of Armorica in 1210. Between 1100 and 1400 Paris saw the likes of

Abélard, Peter Lombard, John of Salisbury, Thomas Aquinas, Duns Scotus, Robert Bacon and Albertus Magnus. Aristotle's logic and argument, particularly from his writing on ethics and the natural sciences, entered the schools in Paris in the thirteenth century and provided the philosophic framework, termed scholasticism, within which learned men debated 'realism' (the real existence of abstractions) and 'nominalism' (abstractions useful only as intellectual devices for speculation).

Scholastics often put themselves at odds with Rome, and the Church frequently threatened them. Benedetto Caetani, later Pope Boniface VIII, warned: 'You Paris masters at your desks seem to think that the world should be ruled by your reasoning. It is to us that the world is entrusted, not you. I truthfully declare to you that, rather than go back on its word, the Court of Rome would destroy the University.' Brave words, but during the Schism between Avignon and Rome, with the transfer of the papal see to Avignon, which began six years after Pope Boniface's death in 1303, it was the University of Paris that 'pronounced upon the legitimacy of popes', not the other way around.

## Society and Economy

I am in Paris [wrote Gui de Bazoches about 1190], in that royal city where abundance of natural wealth not only holds those who live here, but also attracts those from afar. Just as the moon outshines the stars in brilliance, so does this city, the seat of the monarchy, lift her proud head above the rest.... The Grand Pont ... is the scene of seething activity; innumerable ships surround it, filled with merchandise and riches. The Petit Pont belongs to the dialectitians, who [abide] there in deep argument. In the island, by the side of the King's palace that dominates the whole city, is seen the palace of philosophy, where study reigns as sole sovereign in a citadel of light and immortality.

Paris grew steadily in population (200,000 in 1200 and 300,000 in 1300), if not in refinements; new religious houses appeared, including Guillaume of Champeaux's abbey of Saint-Victor, the churches of Sainte-Geneviève-la-Petite, Saint-Jacques-la-Boucherie and Saint-Pierre-aux-Boeufs, and a nunnery on Montmartre. Marshes were drained and fields taken out of cultivation to provide land for new buildings. The city spread east and west along both banks, absorbing villages as it went.

TRADE

Hay, grain, wood, wine, coal and salt, unloaded onto wharves at the Port of Paris on the Quai de Grève (later the Quai de l'Hôtel de Ville), made their way to the victualling district around the Grand Châtelet. This area was the centre of Paris trade life throughout the middle ages and beyond, as indicated by streets named after trades: the rues la Grande Boucherie (butcher's shop), la Pierre à Poisson (fish), de la Tuerie (slaughterhouse), de l'Écorcherie (knacker's yard), Pied de Boeuf (ox foot) and L'Araignée (spider), among others ('L'Araignée' referred to the butcher's four-branched meat hooks, which resembled a spider). Rue Val d'Amour (street of love) and Rue Pute-y-Muce (whore-in-hiding) indicated another lively trade in the region; rue Pute-y-Muce later became Rue de Petit-Musc.

Buying and selling at the goldsmiths' stalls

Each section of the city boasted particular trades. Apothecaries were in the Cité, parchment sellers, scribes, illuminators and bookmen occupied the Latin Quarter, money changers and goldsmiths worked the Grand Pont, and victuallers were near the Châtelet. Hawkers proliferated. '*J'ai bon fromage de Champaigne; ou Fromage de Brie!*' (I have good cheese from Champagne or Brie) called the cheese seller, while near by the fruit seller cried out: '*Figue de Melités sans fin, j'ai raisin d'outre mer*' (figs from Melités without end, I have grapes from overseas).

The *taille* rolls of 1292 indicate a city with 352 streets, ten squares, eleven crossroads and more than 15,000 ratepayers. They also list twenty-six proprietors of public hot baths, which suggest that people bathed more often than has sometimes been thought. And hot they were, if the hawkers were honest, crying out 'the bath is hot, and I lie not'.

## ÉTIENNE BOILEAU AND THE GUILDS

Trade, commerce, the training of artisans and draughtsmen, were regulated by guilds. The guilds sometimes interfered in urban politics – or at times they *were* urban politics. A charter of 1134 speaks of the 'ancient establishment of butchers', an indication that guilds began very early. Louis VII (1137–80) soon after confirmed the *marchands de l'eau de Paris* with a monopoly on river trade and the right to levy tolls on all goods carried by river into the city; this guild surely dated in some form from Roman times. The title and power of *prévôt des marchands de l'eau de Paris* were associated with the river guild, which the monarchy had made an ally. In 1261 Louis IX appointed Étienne Boileau to the post; as *prévôt*, he was virtually a royal urban major-domo, looking after and regulating guild activities. Boileau went further than his predecessors, however, examining the statutes of all the city corporations, and revising them wherever he thought fit. He also published all manner of information about the city and its economy in the *Livre des Métiers* (Book of Trades), a document for thirteenth-century Paris not unlike the Domesday Book for eleventh-century England.

## MASTERS AND APPRENTICES

Boileau catalogued 120 corporations with 5,000 members; appren-

ticeship and examinations for master were a vital part of their operations. 'Whosoever wishes to practise the craft as master, must know
how to do it in all points, by himself, without advice or aid from
another, and he must therefore be examined by the wardens of the
craft,' was the rule. Mastery began with apprenticeship: apprentices
paid a premium of 20–100 sous, and remained in their position from
four to twelve years depending upon the skills required by the particular trade. That was the theory; in practice, while an aspirant remained
an apprentice he or she offered no competition for the master. Terms of
apprenticeship differed little from slavery. Apprentices could be bought
and sold, and runaways were returned by force. Brutal treatment was
commonplace, even though it was officially disapproved and abusers
paid heavily when discovered. In one recorded instance, a master struck
his apprentice with a set of keys and made a hole in his cheek; in
another, Jean Bruières treated Isabelle Béraude so viciously that she
died.

QUALITY OF LABOUR

Guilds covered every enterprise from knife-making to brocading
tapestries. Even thieves, assassins, beggars and vagabonds formed guilds.
As trades evolved, so did sub-trades, such as the knife trade dividing
between those who made handles and those who made blades. This
explained why the number of corporations Boileau described had
doubled half a century later. Strikes occurred, though they seldom
degenerated into violence. This was due to an attitude of mind which
dictated that in Paris the artisan worked as little as he or she could get
away with, and quit work at the end of the day earlier rather than later.
Contemporary commentators disapproved, and of the lax morality
which seemed to accompany it: 'The innkeepers and wine merchants
secretly mix water with their wine, or bad wine with good. The
innkeeper charges for a bad candle at six times its value. . . . Wretched old
women water the milk. . . . Butchers blow out their meat . . .' and so on.

# *The Social Order*

Paris contained every social class: beggars in church doors and on

bridges, peasants from the country buying and selling, artisans, craftsmen, students, schoolboys, hawkers, merchants, jongleurs, mounte-
banks, monks, friars, canons, professors, courtiers, heralds, knights,
nobles, and ladies taking the air in litters; there were also pilgrims en
route to Saint-Denis or Sainte-Geneviève, and prisoners being taken to
the Grand Châtelet. One might also see the judges who had sent them
there, and on occasion even the king. 'Paris was then, as now, an
epitome of the life of France,' wrote Joan Evans.

## THE BOURGEOISIE

'Bourgeois' first appeared in a royal ordinance of 1134, not in the
writings of Karl Marx as some undergraduates seem to think. It referred
to the free burghers who did not fit into traditional social categories.
Paris being his principal city, Philip II gave a special and separate status
to the Paris bourgeoisie. When he went on crusade in 1190, he created
a council of territorial lords to look after the realm, and another of Paris
bourgeoisie to keep an eye on them. The bourgeois council included
Ébrouin the Moneychanger, Othon of the Grève, Robert of Chartres,
Thiboud the Rich, Baldwin Bruneau and Nicolas Boisseau. These six
controlled the treasury and the Great Seal, and issued their diplomas
with the formula 'under the witness of our bourgeois'. Of course Philip
had no intention of sharing power with townsmen, and these diplomas
were revoked upon his return. All the same, a social class was recognized thereby, shouldering aside, as it were, the ancient idea of society
classified simply as those who worked, those who prayed, and those
who fought.

## THE HAUTE BOURGEOISIE

This new class soon evolved its own divisions, and they were not much
removed in practice from those which characterized territorial France.
Urban serfs belonging to territorial lords or the Church were at the
bottom, lesser folk of street and alley were near them, free or partly free
tradesmen and artisans were further up, and the wealthy free burghers
were on top. In the thirteenth century these had become the '*hauts
bourgeois*'. Renart le Contrefait wrote:

> To be a free burgess is to be in the best estate of all; they live in a noble
> manner, wearing lordly garments, having falcons and sparrow-hawks, fine
> palfreys and fine chargers. When the vassals are obliged to join the host, the
> burgesses rest in their beds; when the vassals go to be massacred in battle, the
> burgesses go to picnic by the river.

Clearly, they had a good deal.

*Le Ménagier de Paris*, written between 1392 and 1394 by an *haut*
bourgeois for his young wife, describes their outlook, clearly indicating
standards that admittedly ape the aristocracy but do not presume
equality with them. It also indicates that a woman's place was to be
decorative, domestic and subordinate, a position neither new nor
unusual then or later. A proper wife, according to *Le Ménagier*, tended
roses and violets, wove garlands, and practised dancing and singing
among friends and equals. She also recognized the social gap between
the bourgeoisie and the nobility, never appearing at feasts of lords 'too
great for us, for that would not be fitting to your position, nor to mine'.
Her regimen included rising daily at the same time, dressing well but
not pretentiously, and going into the city or to church with her duenna
always in attendance. She was to walk 'with head up, eyes lowered and
be quiet and looking straight before you at the ground, regarding
neither man nor woman and stopping to speak to no one in the street'.
At home she supervised the household, garden and servants. Her
steward chose day labourers and trades people while her duenna
advised her about domestics. She had also to see that the kitchen was
kept clean and the meals well prepared. Perhaps Max Weber was right
to identify the Protestant ethic with the middle classes, for this *Ménagier
de Paris* has a curiously Calvinist ring, a century and a half before Calvin.

## Parisians on the Fringe

City ordinances described false beggars, false pilgrims, counterfeiters,
thieves, cutpurses, prostitutes, and others who flocked to Paris from all
over France, in sometimes alarming language. For example, this
description of false beggars 'sporting open wounds, sores, scabs, swel-
lings; smearing themselves with salves, saffron, flour, bloody, and other
false colours, and dressing in muddy, filthy, evil-smelling and abom-

inable garments even when they go into churches...'. But for every false beggar there were a dozen real ones, from mendicant monks to blind residents in the Quinze-Vingt.

## THIEVES

The crowds in Les Halles or at the fair of Saint-Denis offered golden opportunities for thieves. The records indicate that they stole with equal enthusiasm from rich, poor and every stage in between. Novelist Victor Hugo's view of Paris in *Notre-Dame de Paris (The Hunchback of Notre-Dame)* was drawn from Henri Sauval, who wrote in the seventeenth century and probably overemphasized the Cour des Miracles (Court of Miracles) as a centre for Paris criminals. Thieves were everywhere; for many it was their only means of survival.

## ADAM CHARRETIER

The Châtelet prison housed thieves, murderers and other criminals, but also debtors who remained there until they could pay up. They were the 'honest prisoners', who paid for their lodging and food: for a count ten livres; an ordinary knight five sous; a Jew eleven sous; and a humble citizen eight deniers. Of course payment depended upon the debtor having means despite his or her indebtedness.

There was no such treatment for the likes of Adam Charretier, however. He was a typical Paris criminal, who had been imprisoned at the Châtelet in 1391 as a cutpurse; he was probably a professional pimp as well. Charretier claimed that he was a pastry chef by profession. Being boastful, he claimed to have stolen fifty purses in Les Halles alone, and bragged that he had lost count of his other thefts. In the Châtelet he slept on straw or bare stone. Had he been a prisoner of the ecclesiastical courts, he would have occupied an oubliette, a cell at the bottom of a steep shaft: subterranean, dark, with water standing in it, and called an oubliette because to be put there was to be forgotten. The most common exit was a fatal bout of pneumonia. Charretier and others like him were tortured, fed on bread and water until their trial, after which they would be hanged or something worse. On the positive side, if that is the appropriate word, punishment was meted out quickly once confession had been extracted on the rack. Bigamists had their heads shaved, counterfeiters were thrown into boiling cauldrons, and thieves and burglars were hanged. Those convicted of political crimes were beheaded, and their heads and limbs displayed on pikes, while their torsos were left on the gibbet to rot. This went on in Les Halles; the exact site was probably quite near the abattoir.

## PROSTITUTION

This crime created special problems. First, prostitutes were numerous; second, their clients frequently included the clergy, which gave Church condemnation of the practice a hollow ring; third, punishments for women were restricted to burning, being buried alive, or the pillory, and two of these were more extreme than fitted the crime. Consequently the inclination of prostitution law was to 'contain' rather than punish. For example, Louis IX restricted prostitutes to certain streets and limited the hours in the day they could work. They were also forbidden to wear bourgeois dress; a streetwalker could be arrested for wearing gilt buttons, pearls, lavishly embroidered belts, shoe buckles, furs and the like. The effect of 'containment' was minimal, as demonstrated by the steadily increasing number of complaints from honest citizens that their streets, churches and locales were being taken over by prostitutes.

## MARGOT ROQUIER

Most prostitutes were probably forced into the profession. Margot Roquier seemed typical. A country girl, she came to Paris when she was eighteen to learn the embroidery trade, and lived in distressing poverty with her brother and sister-in-law. After a time her sister-in-law, Catherine, introduced Margot to Jean Braque, a royal chamberlain, who offered her thirty francs to become his mistress. Margot resisted, but without success. Catherine helped Braque force her into his bed, and then waited for it to be over. When it was, the chamberlain gave Margot two gold francs, which she gave to her sister-in-law. Thereafter Braque used Margot regularly at half a franc each time. Catherine as pimp collected the money and beat her sister-in-law if she tried to avoid the work.

Justice was done in the end, however. When the pair was caught out, the law was directed against Catherine rather than Margot: she was condemned in the *prévôt*'s court, exposed in the pillory, and then burnt.

## MEDICINE

The Paris fringe usually lived short lives, ended by disease. The more fortunate ones found themselves in the Hôtel-Dieu, a hospital for the aged and the sick, founded in the ninth century and expanded and enriched in the thirteenth, which was also the teaching hospital for the University of Paris. It provided clean sheets and the wards were scrubbed daily. Water from the Seine was piped in and heated; regrettably, after it had been used, it was dumped back into the river. The physicians there had read Hippocrates and Galen, and knew much of the Arab medicine introduced into Europe through the great medieval medical centres at Salerno and Montpellier. They understood herbs, poultices, boils, purgatives and diets, had experimented with surgery, and were never sure why one treatment worked and another did not. They likely knew as well the Hippocratic adage: 'Life is short and art is long, time and chance sharp or sudden, experience fallacious and dangerous, judgement difficult.'

## DAILY LIFE

Life was clearly better for affluent Parisians than for those on the fringe; however, all Parisians lived with filth in the streets. Poor neighbourhoods allowed rubbish to pile up, since there was no penalty for not removing it, while the affluent hired a drayman for the job, who inevitably spilled part of his load along the way. Rubbish was not removed from Paris so much as relocated to other streets. As to personal hygiene, Paris had public urinals for common people – one near Notre-Dame even had running water. The bourgeoisie had privies in their back garden; they also had a plentiful supply of Seine water. Not so the poor, which greatly complicated the basics of their home life.

Parisians ate well if they had any resources at all. Gillebert de Metz described booths throughout the city with cooked eggs, venison and chicken. Pâtisseries and charcuteries provided pork, fowl and eel patés, cheese tarts, pigeon, goose, and various kinds of pudding. Bread came in many kinds and qualities, as did cheese and fruits. Wine shops were plentiful but closed early, which may actually have encouraged patrons to overindulge. Finding one's way home after dark in an unlighted city, with a bellyful of vin ordinaire, must have been a unique experience.

## Philip IV, 'the Fair', 1285–1314

Joan Evans called Philip's reign an 'era of change'. To a certain extent it was. He made the *Parlement* of Paris a legitimate court with constitutionally established judicial, fiscal and political functions, encouraged trade, added to bourgeois privileges, and regulated the Saint-Denis fair. However, his reign was challenged by economic and social crises brought on by expensive wars, bad weather and worse harvests. Food shortages were acute in Paris in 1305 and subsequent years; in 1317, a procession of barefooted, practically naked supplicants made their way to Saint-Denis to pray to the saint for relief. Philip sought to deal with economic conditions by manipulating the currency and by seizing the wealth of the Templars. They were charged with heresy, arrested throughout France, and their property transferred to the Hospitallers, who were made to pay Philip huge sums for it. The Paris temple was suppressed and the principal leaders, including Grand Master Jacques de Molay, burnt.

Philip would appear to have been a king without scruple. Early in his reign he had favoured the Templars and even took refuge in the Temple from riotous Parisians. Perhaps on that occasion he had a glimpse of the Templars' treasure and decided, when the time was right, to help himself.

## The Hundred Years War

Then came the English to claim the French throne by force. It was not a happy time for France or Paris: the flower of French chivalry was slaughtered at Crécy, Poitiers and Agincourt; the English scourged the countryside in a series of *chevauchées* ('scorched earth' campaigns); the Black Death claimed probably a third of the French population in 1348; and, driven by suffering beyond endurance, the people rose up in frequent *jacqueries* (popular rebellions), including in Paris. It was all because Philip IV's grandson, Edward III of England, believed that he had a better right to the French throne than Philip VI, which the *Parlement* of Paris denied.

## ÉTIENNE MARCEL

In 1355 Étienne Marcel, a rich merchant from an *haut* bourgeois family and a member of the powerful drapers guild, was elected *Prévôt des Marchands*. He asserted himself from the start. First, he moved the seat of municipal administration from the Parloir aux Bourgeois to the Maison aux Piliers (later the Maison des Dauphins) on the Place de Grève. Then he forced the Dauphin, Charles, who was regent since his father King John II was a prisoner in England, to accept a species of constitutional reform which made Marcel virtual dictator of Paris and the prince a virtual prisoner. Thereafter Charles was treated with less than respect, on one occasion being forced to watch two loyal friends being murdered. However, the bourgeoisie backed the *prévôt*, and formed a Committee of National Defence under his leadership to organize the defence of the city. Marcel seized the Louvre and set 3,000 labourers to work extending the city walls. Most of it was complete a year later when Charles, who in the meantime had escaped into the Île de France where he raised an army, turned up with it at the city gates.

Marcel attempted to win to his cause Charles of Navarre, an unpleasant man who had murdered the Constable of France and made secret deals with the English. However, Navarre addressed the Parisians from the walls of the abbey of Saint-Germain-des-Prés with such skill that they elected him captain of Paris. A certain jockeying for position followed, ending with Marcel attempting to seize Navarre's treasure which was stored at the abbey fortress of Saint-Denis. He was thwarted by Jean Maillart, once the *prévôt*'s friend, who had been swayed by Navarre's oratory. When Marcel arrived at Saint-Denis, Maillart was already there. They exchanged angry words, after which Maillart mounted a horse, seized a royal banner, and galloped away calling out 'Montjoye Saint-Denis!' to those loyal to the crown, urging them to come to the aid of the dauphin.

Meanwhile Marcel went to the bastille of Saint-Antoine, where Maillart and the royalists found him. When Maillart demanded an

explanation, the *prévôt* replied that he was guarding the city. They
fought, and Marcel was killed by a blow from Maillart's axe. His body
was dragged to the church of Sainte-Catherine-du-Val-des-Écoliers,
stripped naked and publicly displayed. The next day Charles, having
made his peace with Navarre, entered Paris. Marcel's followers were
brought to the Place de Grève and executed. All of this is according to
the chronicler Jean Froissart.

A few years later, Charles mounted the throne as Charles V, 'the
Wise' (1364–80). He was a builder, of sorts, who turned the Louvre
into a sumptuous palace for himself and his court; he built gardens, a
tennis court, and a 'Hôtel des Lions' where he kept a zoo. A library was
added, and the king built or restored a number of palaces along the
Right Bank, known collectively as the Hôtel Saint-Paul. He also
completed Marcel's wall. Much of this was the work of Hugh Aubriot,
whom Charles appointed *Prévôt de Paris*. This was an important change.
Aubriot's role was to serve the king, and in that capacity he usurped the
powers of the often contentious and sometimes seditious *Prévôts des
Marchands*, whose role had been to serve the bourgeois.

## PARIS IN TURMOIL

Charles VI (1380–1422) came to the throne as a minor in 1380. Royal
uncles vied for power as regent, and an uprising in Paris, or the
appearance of one, followed. Twenty thousand armed citizens gathered
at the wall to greet the boy-king and his uncles upon their return from a
victory against the Flemings, their arms displayed to indicate willingness
to fight for the king. They were told that the display upset his majesty
and that they should go home. They obeyed and paid dearly for it. The
king and his 12,000 soldiers entered the city, and arrested the president
of the *Parlement* and other civil officials along with 300 prominent
bourgeois. The executioner was busy for several days thereafter. The
crown then assessed Paris an enormous fine, curtailed its liberties, seized
the Maison aux Piliers and imposed heavy taxes. The following year the
Bastille, begun in 1380, was completed. This fortress-prison would play
a sinister role in the imagination of Parisians for four centuries.

This was a time of troubles. Charles faced factional fighting between
the Armagnacs, followers of his brother, the duke of Orléans, who had

urged the king to stand up to his uncles, and the Burgundians, to whom the uncles turned when Orléans succeeded in persuading the king to defy them. There was the question of Charles's heir. The uncles had married him to Isabella of Bavaria. She had no compunction against sexual misalliances and put it about that he was not the father of their sons. On the night of 12 November 1407, Orléans was murdered in Paris by Burgundian ruffians. Witnesses saw Burgundy's son, Jean *sans* Peur, lantern in hand, gaze down upon the corpse and mutter '*C'est bien*'. Appropriate conclusions were drawn and civil war resumed between Armagnacs and Burgundians. For five years Paris was treated to a steady parade of atrocities as each side committed murder and mayhem upon the other. Charles, none too stable or intelligent under the best of circumstances, deteriorated rapidly under the strain.

ENTER THE ENGLISH

The Burgundians made an alliance with England. To forestall the consequences, the count of Armagnac seized the now demented Charles and his son, and prepared to defend the capital. In 1418 an ironmonger on the Petit Pont opened the gate at Porte Saint-Germain, through which poured a Burgundian army. By dawn the next day 1,500 Armagnacs had been slaughtered, including the count, a strip of whose skin was carried through the city and waved in mockery of the white-scarf Armagnac symbol. The Burgundians took charge of the king, though some Armagnacs managed to escape with the dauphin in tow.

Treachery begets treachery. Jean *sans* Peur sought a reconciliation with the Armagnacs in 1419. The dauphin was with the Armagnac delegation, and when Jean knelt to greet him he was struck from behind with an axe and then stabbed. In 1521, a monk of Dijon showed Jean's skull, complete with axe-induced hole, to King Francis I. 'Sire, it was through this hole that the English entered France,' he explained.

Not quite. Jean *sans* Peur was a Burgundian, after all, and the English ruled France in alliance with Burgundy. Ironically, Henry V, who brought it all to pass by imposing the Treaty of Troyes upon Charles VI shortly before his death, died himself before he could actually ascend the throne. He left an infant son to do it for him.

## *Paris under the English, 1420–1436*

Paris was tied to the English in ways the rest of France was not. Parisians had to swear allegiance to the English House of Plantagenet. Charles VI's widow, hated by the Parisians, was allowed to live on in the Saint-Paul palace until she died. The duke of Bedford, regent in Paris for Henry VI, lived in lordly fashion in the Palais des Tournelles, surrounded by a library of rare manuscripts and a garden of equally rare birds. Life was hard in a city which had to 'beg help from England as its own resources dwindled'. Discontent was expressed through frequent rebellions against the occupiers, though as Armagnac–Burgundian factional quarrels continued, not all riotous behaviour in Paris was directed against the English. Even so, everyone from guild leaders to the meanest street hawkers were made to swear oaths of good behaviour, if not actual loyalty, to the English, as a defense against acts of resistance.

Paris under the English was a medieval city under siege throughout this epoch, because Charles VII, the legitimate king of France who kept himself at Bourges, continued to make war against the Anglo-Burgundians. The countryside around was so wasted by war that shortages were endemic, and in cold weather wolves prowled Paris faubourgs looking for food. Carelessly buried corpses gave them an appetite for human flesh, causing Parisians to be on the alert if they ventured beyond the walls. Within the walls, beggars who once had lived off of the generosity of bakers and fishmongers, who threw stale bread and tubs of unsold fish to them in the Grande Boucherie, now were joined by bakers, fishmongers and other starving citizens in fighting with herds of pigs for cabbage cores and the dregs from barrels of apple cider.

After more than a decade and a half of English rule, Paris was liberated by Charles VII. The chronicler Thomas Basin wrote movingly of the joyous outpouring which followed, from a people who had lived under perilous and degrading conditions for years:

> It was sweet for them to see the woods and fields, however dry and barren these everywhere were, and to rest their eyes on the green meadows, the springs, the rivers, the brooks – things that many of them, who had never left the enclosure of their walls, had only known by hearsay.

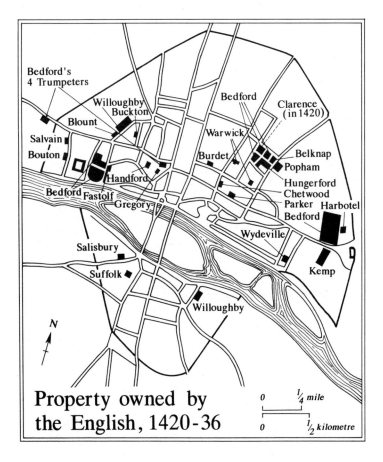

Bedford's
4 Trumpeters

Willoughby
Buckton

Blount

Salvain

Bouton

Bedford Fastolf

Handford

Gregory

Bedford

Salisbury

Suffolk

Willoughby

Bedford

Warwick

Clarence
(in 1420)

Burdet

Belknap

Popham

Hungerford
Chetwood
Parker

Bedford

Harbotel

Wydeville

Kemp

N

**Property owned by
the English, 1420-36**

0     ¼ mile

0     ½ kilometre

## JEANNE D'ARC

Jeanne d'Arc played a remarkable role in liberating France from the English. She delivered the city of Orléans, and brought Charles VII to Reims for his coronation. However, she appeared in Paris only at the storming of the Porte Saint-Honoré in 1429, where she was wounded and taken to a house in Place du Théatre, as it is now known, which lay outside the city wall. Otherwise her contribution to the liberation of Paris was limited to having given Charles sufficient courage to act for the good of all France, including Paris.

# CHAPTER THREE

# *A City in Turmoil,*
## 1461–1661

### *Paris and the Renaissance*

The Renaissance is often defined as the revival of interest in the classics abetted by the advent of printing and expanding European economies. It was a time of turmoil in the arts, learning, trade, politics, religion and society generally. Paris was no exception. The city was characterized in this period by rapid growth, expanding bureaucracy, flourishing trade and commerce, and stress among workers and the poor, to which religious warfare contributed not a little.

#### LOUIS XI, THE 'UNIVERSAL SPIDER', 1461–1483

Louis XI followed his father, Charles VII, on the throne, at once the last medieval and first Renaissance king of France. More than any predecessor, he imposed royal government on France and French interests upon Europe. Louis's tactics presaged Machiavelli and earned for him the sobriquet, 'the universal spider'. He regarded Paris as central to his regime, and characteristically the Parisians responded to him with a mixture of enthusiasm, scepticism and outright resentment. Louis was crowned at Reims, and proceeded to Paris, where great crowds jammed the route from Porte Saint-Denis to Notre-Dame Cathedral to watch a royal procession as characteristically Renaissance as that enjoyed later by Francis I.

Six scarlet-clad Parisians held a canopy of blue satin adorned with fleurs-de-lis over the king's head as he processed on horseback. Along the route, Louis was entertained by a fountain from which flowed milk and wine, by men and women dressed as 'savages' who wrestled and

A view of fifteenth-century Paris

'made countenances' on a scaffold, and by three naked young women disporting themselves as Sirens in an artificial pond. A chronicler was moved to write that to look upon each lovely breast, '*droit, séparé, rond, et dur,*' was a sight '*bien plaisant*'. No doubt Louis felt the same.

The king took up residence at the Hôtel des Tournelles rather than in the Louvre, from which he undertook the endless task of securing his throne against such insurgent noblemen as the dukes of Brittany, Bourbon and Orléans, and the counts of Charolais and Dunois. At first, Paris was unsupportive of the king. The post-coronation show notwithstanding, Parisians were resentful that Louis did not extend to them privileges accorded other cities. 'Coarse gibes and satirical songs and ballads' against the king made the rounds of the Cité and the Palais. However, 'the Spider' won over his council of six members each from the bourgeoisie, *Parlement* and university with 'grace of speech' and banquets at the Hôtel de Ville, and they agreed to draft citizens to bear arms in defence of city and king. This did not go over particularly well with those eligible for this levy, and Louis's relationship with his capital thereafter was always somewhat strained.

Nevertheless, Louis took it as read that Paris was the key to his kingdom. He taxed the city, made it endure a siege on his behalf (July–November 1465), gave it a central role in enhancing national trade, and incarcerated his enemies in the Bastille or executed them in the Place de Grève. When in Paris, Louis attended mass daily at Notre-Dame and continued his early practice of dining with members of the bourgeoisie. However, he preferred country living, and spent his last hours at Plessis-lès-Tours in the Loire Valley rather than in the Hôtel des Tournelles.

PRINTING

Louis's most significant contribution to the life of Paris was the introduction of printing into the city. Two booksellers, Fust and Schöffer, brought printed books to Paris in 1463. Fearful of competition from this new art, the powerful scribes and booksellers guilds had the books confiscated. Louis paid Schöffer 2,500 crowns in compensation, and made it clear this also was a reward for introducing printed books into the capital. In 1470, Guillaume Fichet and Jean de la Puin of the Sorbonne invited Swiss printers to set up a press in Fichet's college rooms, and three years later two Germans, Peter Kayser and Johannes Stohl, were printing books in the Rue St-Jacques at the sign of Saint Soleil d'Or.

They printed in German Gothic script; however, Roman letters regained dominance in the reign of Francis I because he and his intellectual sister, Margaret of Angoulême, favoured them. Paris printing and publishing generally took off in Francis's reign, as indicated by the fact that 300 books were published there in 1530 alone.

# *The Sixteenth-Century City*

Michel de Montaigne described Paris as the 'glory of France and one of the most noble ornaments of the world'. This curious hyperbole was produced by a sixteenth-century sceptic who was in Paris only briefly, and who wrote it while Paris was being torn by bloody religious strife. It referred to a city whose inhabitants feared plagues and each other, and who lived in narrow, crooked streets covered with garbage and ashes, smelling of rotten meat, human and animal effluvia. Some Parisians held bouquets of flowers or perfumed cloths to their noses to fend off the odours.

Still, the city was lively and growing. In 1515 the population was 170,000, and 450,000 by 1600. Travellers described the Right Bank, the mercantile centre of the city, as a beehive of activity: streets jammed with people on foot, in carts, or riding horses or mules, and shops and eating places filled to bursting. Notre-Dame Cathedral was also crowded, though not necessarily with worshippers. Thomas Platter, a Swiss student, described prostitutes and pimps soliciting in the choir, abandoned infants displayed in a special stall in the hope that someone might take them in, and the masses of people who wandered through the nave gossiping, or else using it as a passage on their way elsewhere.

The Left Bank was dominated by the university, with its fifty colleges and thousands of students who, when not at their studies, swam in the Seine and engaged in sports – javelin throwing, calisthenics, high jumping and wrestling, among others – in the open fields of the Prés des Clercs near the Porte de Nesle. It was also the centre of a lively book trade. Outside the walls various faubourgs, or suburbs, many of which consisted of hastily and shabbily built hovels, were expanding along with the population. The typical 'faubourgeoisie' was a lesser artisan or a market gardener growing vegetables to sell in the city. There were exceptions, such as Faubourg Saint-Germain-des-Prés, large, stable and as wealthy as the city within the walls, and Saint-Marcel, where lived the family Gobelins, founders of the famed tapestry works. However, in this period Les Marais within the city on the Right Bank remained the preferred district for the rich and famous.

## WEALTHY PARISIANS

Paris was a consumer, a producer, and an *entrepôt* dominated by the wealthy *hauts* bourgeois. They owned 40 per cent of the food-producing land around the city, sold food to the city, exported food produced in the Paris basin, and took a share of the value of goods of all kinds passing through the city. They were mercantile middlemen who shipped Paris-produced luxury items – fine woollens, haberdashery, books, jewellery and bibelots – as well as French-produced grains, plaster of Paris, building stone, wine, salt and other products, to markets outside the country. Through the efforts of such entrepreneurs, and because it was the intersection of major transportation routes connecting France with northern and western Europe, Paris emerged in the sixteenth century as one of the premier European commercial centres. Only in banking did it lag behind such cities as Lyon.

The *haute* bourgeoisie of Paris invested their profits in land, annuities, and royal offices for themselves and their heirs. In the sixteenth century most high officials in the Hôtel de Ville were bourgeois officers of the king, who aped noble values and life-styles. They built great mansions and spent far more lavishly on clothing and entertainment than did their medieval predecessors. They imported fine silks, furs, spices and sugar from around the world, but also cheap, less durable silks from Florence and Genoa because, as an Italian observer noted, 'the French became bored if they had to wear the same clothing too long'. Conspicuous consumption kept a large number of skilled craftsmen and artisans employed; it also provided evidence of a widening gap between the *haute* bourgeoisie and the lower classes of Paris.

## THE GUILDS

Apart from this élite of royal office-holders, the Paris social order was still determined by the guild system, which was dominated by the Six Corps of drapers, grocers, hosiers, mercers, furriers and jewellers, also an élite. Wardens of the Six Corps were almost the only merchants elected to civic, as distinct from royal, office. They were consulted on all matters involving city trade, monopolized offices dealing with charitable and parish functions, and – a mark of their privileged status – they carried the ceremonial canopy whenever dignitaries made formal entry into the city. Their domain was the Consular Court, established in 1563 to settle commercial disputes. Six Corps élites were wholesale merchants, whose standing was a matter of wealth, but also of a generally-held assumption that they had wider experience and broader vision than mere shopkeepers.

Well down the guild ladder socially, and organized on the basis of skill and experience as well as money, were the artisans' guilds. During a century when prices rose but wages did not, contracts between masters and journeymen, the latter beginning to resemble rudimentary trades unionists, produced rising tension. Disputes frequently resulted in strikes, protests, 'unruly behaviour' and violence. Striking journeymen would arm themselves with sticks, daggers and swords, and threaten the masters and journeymen who did not strike.

## WOMEN AT WORK

While women remained on the fringes of guild society, there were exceptions. Some women-only guilds included the *lingères*, who made handkerchiefs and linens, and the *chapelières de fleurs*, makers of floral crowns for religious feast days. Men and women were accorded equal status within a few guilds, others allowed widows to carry on their husband's trade provided they did not remarry outside the guild, and occasionally married women belonged to guilds other than their husband's. Charlotte Guillard ran her late husband's printing business, which employed twenty-five to thirty journeymen, and Marguerite Bury was in the grain trade while her husband was a baker.

Within guilds or without, women were a vital part of the Paris workforce. They ran shops and worked in them, sold fish along the Seine, peddled flowers, vegetables, butter and eggs in Les Halles, and provided the bulk of menial labour as domestic servants, washerwomen and water-carriers. Sometimes they were found working shoulder to shoulder with men as day labourers on public construction projects.

## *BIEN PUBLIQUE*

In the middle ages, 'Christian charity' perceived the poor as God's special children and therefore deserving of alms. In sixteenth-century Paris the poor were viewed as merely layabouts who preferred to live off public welfare. Meanwhile bad harvests, plagues, inflation and religious war increased their number dramatically. Public begging was outlawed in 1536, and in 1551 laws were enacted which limited eligibility for public assistance and forbad women to have their children in tow when selling candles outside churches. To do so, went the rationale, evoked sympathy from prospective customers, which proved that such women were really only begging. In 1544 the Grand Bureau des Pauvres was created with the task of organizing public welfare; its function was to examine public welfare rolls and to try to get as many poor people off them as possible.

This was all negative treatment of the problem of poverty. On the positive side was a parallel effort to improve the public hospital system. The Hôtel-Dieu was enlarged in 1535, and the Hôpital Enfants-Dieu and the Hôpital de la Trinité were opened to care for orphans. During Henry II's reign (1547–59), the city bought a disused lepers' house from the abbey of Saint-Germaine-des-Prés, and established a new hospital for the 'incorrigible poor' which in time became an old peoples' home. These were public organizations; they were supplemented by private ones, such as the Quinze-Vingts home for the blind, and Sainte-Catherine's and Les Filles-Dieu for homeless women.

## CITY GOVERNMENT

In an age of turmoil, keeping public order was problematic, but more than ever a crucial function of urban government. Parisian government was a blend of royal and bourgeois authority. Royal authority was exercised through the *prévôt de Paris*, headed by a high noble of the court, and the *Parlement* of Paris, which was part of the Curia Regis. The Bureau de la ville, the chief officers of which were the *prévôt des marchands* and four *échevins* – roughly a mayor and aldermen – represented the bourgeoisie. The Bureau collected taxes, constructed ports and roads, and raised the militia when needed. The *Parlement* served as a law court which ratified royal legislation, regulated roads, bridges, quays and public health, controlled the price of bread and other commodities, guaranteed the supply of corn and fuel, fixed work hours and wages, penalized shoddy workmanship, and intervened in academic and religious affairs throughout northern France. These institutions played a co-operative role in maintaining public security in Paris, by providing forces to guard city gates, keeping order in public squares during times of crisis and among crowds watching public executions, and defending the city generally against threats from within or without. Royal and bourgeois co-operation was much needed in the sixteenth century, as the traditional balance within the social system was threatened by rising conflict between Catholic and Protestant.

## *Francis I, 'Renaissance prince', 1515–1547*

A Renaissance prince was an absolute ruler, to the extent that absolutism was possible. 'We owe obedience to the king and it is not for us to question his commands. All authority comes from the king,' wrote Cardinal Antoine Duprat, Francis I's chancellor and archbishop of Sens. In fact, the *Parlement* of Paris sometimes refused to register royal enactments, and filed remonstrances against them with the king. When the *Parlement* persisted, the king was compelled to summon them to a *lit de justice* (literally 'bed of justice') and personally supervise the registration. However, otherwise there was little limitation the *Parlement* or others could impose upon the monarch. Absolute monarchy was as close to being absolute as tradition, law and day-to-day instruments of control would permit.

As a Renaissance prince, Francis I projected the image of a patron of the arts and scholarship, and master of ostentatious display. In 1520 he met Henry VIII of England, also a Renaissance prince, at Val Doré (the Field of the Cloth of Gold) near Calais. The French king's tent was covered with cloth of gold, and topped by a life-size statue of Saint-Michel carved in walnut. Entertainments included banquets, dances, mummings, joustings and, as both Francis and Henry regarded themselves as athletes, even a royal wrestling match. This was display of the most ostentatious sort.

Francis's display when he entered Paris following his coronation at Reims was equally ostentatious. The *prévôt des marchands* and *échevins*, guild wardens, *Parlement* members and others met the king at the abbey of Saint-Denis and escorted him into the city. The *gens de ville* went first, and then the *gens du roi*, wearing various royal insignia, and the marshals of France, the grand master and the gentlemen pensioners, all decked out in cloth of silver and gold. The great seal followed, accompanied by Chancellor Duprat. Pages, musicians and heralds led four gentlemen bearing, in turn, the king's hat, cloak, sword and helmet, followed by various of the royal household. Finally there was the king himself, on horseback, wearing a suit of silver cloth and a bejewelled white hat, and throwing gold and silver pieces to the crowds lining the streets. Needless to say, they cheered. Two companies of the *Cent gentilshommes* (household troops) and 400 archers followed the king.

The procession culminated at Notre-Dame where Francis attended a thanksgiving mass. In the evening a great banquet, with dancing and other entertainments, was held at the palace, followed by several days of jousts and tournaments held in the Rue Saint-Antoine. The festivities finally ended on 11 March 1515, when the *Bureau de la ville* presented Francis with a gold statue of his patron saint, and he could settle down to the task of ruling an increasingly troubled land.

## PATRON OF THE ARTS AND LEARNING

Francis I was well equipped for that part of his Renaissance prince image which required him to be patron of the arts and letters. Guillaume Budé described him in *L'Institution du Prince* as 'educated in letters ... and also possesses a natural eloquence, wit, tact, pleasant manners; nature, in short, has endowed him with the rarest gifts of body and mind....' Francis was responsible for a great deal as patron of arts and letters. Among other things he renovated the Louvre and a number of châteaux around Paris, most famously Fontaineblue; brought the likes of Leonardo da Vinci, Andrea del Sarto, Jean Clouet and Benvenuto Cellini to Paris; made Budé master of the royal library, the foundation of the present Bibliothèque Nationale, which might explain Budé's glowing description of the king; established the *lecteurs royaux* – regius professorships – at the university of Paris (though he did not at the same time provide their holders with an income); encouraged humanism in theology and letters; and encouraged intellectual freedom – up to a point – which made possible Rabelais's humanistic satires, *Gargantua* and *Pantagruel*, and Marguerite of Angoulême's *Miroir de l'âme pécheresse* (Mirror of the Sinful Soul). This work, critical of Catholic dogma, was censored by the Sorbonne until Francis intervened. Here was a true royal patron; moreover, he could argue with the masters in Latin.

## CELLINI

Benevenuto Cellini, Florentine sculptor, goldsmith, diarist who took himself at his own valuation, and among the most difficult of Renaissance artists, deserves special mention. Francis brought him to Paris on two occasions, the second in 1540. Arrogant, bombastic and intemperate, Cellini made many enemies in Paris during the next five years, including the *prévôt de Paris* and the king's mistress, the duchess of Étampes. A shameless sycophant, Cellini ingratiated himself with the king, who gave him the Petit Nesle on the Left Bank opposite the Louvre in which to live. Unfortunately the *prévôt* already lived there. Cellini armed himself, his servants and two apprentices, and threw him out. Subsequently efforts were made to throw Cellini out in turn, and he was attacked in the streets and sued in the courts. The duchess did everything she could to poison Francis against him, even to trying to sabotage the artist's work. Despite all of this, Cellini prevailed, leaving Paris with a number of outstanding sculptures, justifying at least somewhat the king's faith in this exasperating Florentine.

## FRANCIS AND THE PARISIANS

Francis I understood that Paris, the royal city, represented wealth, power, prestige, honour and, ultimately, legitimacy for the crown. Paris was proud of being the royal city and Francis was proud of Paris. However, he and his Parisians had their ups and downs.

The king always needed money. In 1522 he introduced a system of public credit called *rentes sur l'Hôtel de Ville de Paris*, through which he raised loans for his Italian wars from the Paris public, at a rate of 8.5 per cent. Parisians found the scheme suspect, even though the loans were regularly repaid. In 1523, when an English army approached and Francis was in Lyon, the panic-stricken city sent to him for help. He replied that he would give his life for Paris, and if he could not come in person would send the queen and his children. He did not appear, and the English army retired of its own accord. Parisians thereafter charged that the king was aggrandizing himself in Italy with their money, while leaving Paris defenceless. It did not help when he was captured by the Spaniards in 1526 and had to be ransomed, or that in his absence the queen mother, Louise, did not protect Paris from 'hordes of disbanded and unpaid troops converging on the capital', or that his sister, Marguerite of Angoulême, appeared to have Protestant inclinations – a reference to the beginnings of the religious turmoil that soon would tear Paris and France apart.

Parisians were not slow to make Francis aware of their displeasure. When word came that the king had recovered from an illness contracted as a prisoner in Spain, Parisians disguised as royal messengers rode through the streets proclaiming that he had died and that the queen mother, his regent, was concealing the truth for ulterior reasons. Soon afterward, a woman emerged from the cloister of Notre-Dame riding an imitation horse drawn by persons got up as devils, and surrounded by others in masters' gowns on which the name 'Martin Luther' was prominently displayed – a warning to Francis that his sister's Protestant heresy would not go unchallenged.

Such liberties could be dangerous. On one occasion a certain Monsieur Cruche, a poet and playwright who performed morality plays and novelties in the Place Maubert, included a satire on the love affair between Francis and *Parlement* councillor Lecoq's daughter. A group of courtiers disguised as bourgeoisie treated Cruche to supper at a tavern in the Rue de la Juiverie, and invited him to perform the scene for them. He did, they set upon him, nearly beat him to death, and prepared to drown him in the Seine. Cruche escaped, so the story went, only because he persuaded his attackers that he was actually a priest.

Francis and the Parisians went on arguing about money, religion and the security of the capital virtually until the day of his death.

## Paris and the Protestant Reformation

The Protestant Reformation began when Martin Luther challenged Church orthodoxy in 1517 at Wittenberg, and was excommunicated as his reward in 1521. The Sorbonne condemned Luther's views in 1519, and in 1523 the *Parlement* seized Lutheran books from Paris booksellers. In 1526 the queen mother, Louise, ordered that the 'evil and damnable heresy of Luther' be driven from France straightaway. Then in 1534 Ignatius Loyola assembled six fellow students from the College of

Sainte-Barbara, including Francis Xavier, in the crypt of an old church on Montmartre; there he founded the Society of Jesus (Jesuits). Then Jean Calvin published *Institution of the Christian Religion* in 1536, which paved the way for Protestants, called Huguenots, to proliferate in France, and the war was on. Paris humanist Louis Le Roy, writing in mid-century, judged the spread of venereal disease to be preferable to the spread of religious sectarianism.

# *'A Most Catholic Capital'*

Historian Barbara Diefendorf has concluded that '... civic pride, monarchial loyalism, and Catholic belief were conjoined in sixteenth-century Parisian life'. The festival of thanksgiving organized on 8 April 1559, following the peace with Spain, was characteristic. On that day delegations from every parish, monastery and church joined officials from the Hôtel de Ville for a massive mid-morning parade from Notre-Dame to Sainte-Chapelle and back. The mendicants were first, then the parishes, banners, crosses and relics held high; next came the Notre-Dame and Sainte-Chapelle chapters, and finally city officials. Notre-Dame provided an image of the Virgin and a jewel-bedecked reliquary named for Saint-Sébastien, to which was added a reliquary of the True Cross, protected beneath an elaborate canopy and surrounded by torches, for the return from Saint-Chapelle. Scarlet-robed magistrates from the *Parlement* joined the procession at the Palais de Justice, which then circled the Île de la Cité before returning to the Cathedral for a mass of celebration. The tragedy of the Catholic–Protestant war that held Paris in its grip for most of the sixteenth century was under-standable, if hardly forgivable.

## HERESY AND THE SORBONNE

The Sorbonne was the repository of religious orthodoxy in Paris from the start. Noël Béda, faculty syndic, described heresy as any deviation from Sorbonne teaching, and blamed Martin Luther whenever it happened. Parisian bookseller John Froben recorded that, early on, Luther's attacks on the sale of indulgences were 'read even at the Sorbonne', where 'they met with everyone's approval'. This changed

The Sorbonne today

when Luther's assault spread to include the basics of Roman doctrine. By 1523 the Sorbonne directed the *Parlement* of Paris in censoring books, ordering students' rooms searched, and arresting those accused of heresy. King Francis disapproved of Luther but, like such humanists as Desiderius Erasmus, objected. The Sorbonne persisted all the same, censoring even royal librarian Guillaume Budé, and condemning Henry VIII of England for claiming that his marriage to Catherine of Aragon violated canon law. Meanwhile, Parisians periodically demonstrated in favour of the violent suppression of Lutherans, defined in popular imagination as anyone who ate meat on Friday.

In 1533 Budé was banished to Mont-Saint-Michel and his writings seized. The same year, Collège de Navarre students staged a play depicting Marguerite of Angoulême preaching heresy at the bidding of a fury named Mégère. The name was a pun, that is a conflation of her first name with that of her almoner and an accused heretic, Gérard Roussel. Marguerite's 1529 poem pleading for religious open-mindedness among the doctors of the Sorbonne was now published in response to the Navarre students:

> I beg you that these fractious debates
> About free will and liberty be left
> To the great scholars who, having liberty, have it not:
> So pressed are their hearts by their inventions
> That Truth can no longer find its place...
> Be assured that you are free indeed
> If you have the grace and love of God.

## THE AFFAIR OF THE PLACARDS

Catholic–Protestant relations, tense from the beginning, heated up considerably after Church-bound Parisians discovered, on the morning of 18 October 1534, that during the night the city had been decorated with Protestant propaganda on 12 × 15-inch placards or broadsheets. They were printed in Gothic script and entitled: '*Articles véritables sur les horribles, grands & importables a buz de le Messe papall*' (True articles on the horrible, great and insufferable abuses of the papal mass). That is, the mass falsely claimed to duplicate the sacrifice of Christ on the Cross, falsely implied the real presence of Christ in the Host, contradicted Scripture with reference to the Real Presence, pretended to be a miracle when it was really only a memorial service. The message was the work of Antoine Marcourt, an exile who later become a Huguenot minister. It was smuggled into Paris by Guillaume Féret, a servant of the royal apothecary.

The response was electric. Hysteria fed by rumour swept the capital: Heretics planned to sack the Louvre! Churches would be burnt! The faithful would be massacred at mass! All foreigners were suspect, and one unfortunate Flemish merchant was lynched by a mob. The *Parlement* rounded up everyone remotely suspect and ordered a general procession of 'reparation'. The royal court, the main corporate bodies of Paris, sovereign courts, university, religious orders, municipal government and trade guilds participated; the famous Sainte-Chapelle relics were brought out, including what was claimed to be the Crown of Thorns, at sight of which 'people's hair stood on end', or so it was reported; and the Blessed Sacrament was carried by the bishop of Paris beneath a canopy borne by three royal princes, and Francis himself walked along behind, bareheaded – a gesture of considerable humility. The procession made its way to Notre-Dame for high mass, and in the afternoon the king publicly denounced all heretics. The day ended with six supposed heretics being burned at the stake. It was a remarkable outpouring of religious orthodoxy.

## PUNISHMENT OF HERETICS

Punishments for crimes in the sixteenth century included mutilation, torture, hanging, and drawing and quartering, with the monarch sometimes looking on. Counterfeiters were boiled alive, and robbers and assassins broken on the wheel. But the worst was reserved for heretics.

If they were lucky, they got off with imprisonment or exile and having their books burnt. After the Affair of the Placards, however, attitudes hardened and the odour of both burning flesh and burning paper permeated the Place de Grève. Louis de Berquin's writings were incinerated on order of the *Parlement* in 1523; he followed them five years later. In 1535 an edict warned that those who sheltered heretics would be punished with them in like manner, and offered a reward for anyone who informed on them. Between 1541 and 1544, some sixty-five books banned by the Sorbonne and dozens of others were burnt outside Notre-Dame, and of six Paris booksellers or printers prosecuted, one was tortured and two sent to the stake. The *Parlement*'s prisons filled with victims of purged religious houses, and the fires burned with greater frequency as Francis I lost patience with heresy. The 'Burning Chamber', as the Place de Grève was being called, claimed thirty-nine victims between 1547 and 1550, and that was only 7 per cent of the 557 suspects investigated.

Chancellor and Archbishop Duprat thought heretics got off lightly with the stake, and devised *l'estrapade*, from which the condemned was suspended by iron chains over the fire, and raised and lowered into it. This greatly prolonged the agony and, perhaps, the archbishop's enjoyment.

## *Religious Wars*

After Francis I died in 1547, Henry II, Francis II, Charles IX and Henry III reigned in turn until 1589 – a half-century of religious war, with Paris squarely in the middle.

### RELIGIOUS FANATICISM IN PARIS

Parisian Catholics, fanatical in their faith, were prepared to fight, persecute, and commit murder in its name. So, too, were Parisian Huguenots. The Huguenot prince of Condé threatened Paris with an army in 1562, and the city sent militia units to Faubourg Saint-Jacques to reinforce the Catholic duke of Guise. The city register boasted that the units were 'so well equipped that they excited the admiration of the Swiss and other soldiers in the king's pay'. How they would have actually performed is unclear, since Condé did not attack. Then, in 1567, Huguenot armies caused great economic hardships by blocking entrance to Paris, until Paris mobs ventured out to attack the Huguenots, and managed to relieve the starving city.

Public opinion remained staunch against compromise. In 1569 Huguenot leader Admiral Coligny was hanged in effigy in the Place de Grève, and then condemned by the *Parlement* and sentenced to be drawn, hanged and strangled. This was a gesture, as he was not in Paris at the time, and in any case Catherine de' Medici, the queen mother, who was doing her best to achieve a balance between Catholics and Protestants, would not have approved the *Parlement*'s judgement. Parisians had to settle for the effigy.

Meanwhile Huguenots within the city were subject to persecution. Placards, this time Catholic in content, urged that Huguenots be 'killed without qualm'. One placard exhorted its readers:

> Hang and strangle them,
> So that death can strap them in,
> And dissolve them into the earth,
> Because they haven't wanted to live
> According to the Church of Saint Peter.

## ST BARTHOLOMEW'S DAY MASSACRE

On 22 August 1572 an attempt was made on the life of Admiral Coligny, possibly orchestrated by the Guise family in revenge for the assassination of the duke of Guise in 1563 by Huguenots. Wounded only, the admiral elected to remain in Paris where he placed himself under the protection of King Charles IX. His followers remained as well, and, outraged at the attempt on their leader, talked of taking vengeance. The talk spread, was blown out of proportion, and the Catholic populace was soon in uproar. The Huguenots planned to 'cut the king's throat, kill his brothers, and pillage the city of Paris,' they claimed. It was to prevent such an eventuality that the events of 23 August were set in motion.

The king himself seemed convinced. He summoned *prévôt des marchands* Jean le Charron to the Louvre, told him that the Huguenots were plotting a coup, and ordered him to arm the militia, call up the city artillery and close down the gates and river traffic. Le Charron did as he was told. That evening, a contingent of Swiss guards broke into Coligny's quarters, killed the admiral and his protectors, and hanged his corpse by rope out of a window. Afterwards, the duke of Guise galloped through the city shouting: 'Kill them, kill them all; for it is the king's command.' This was the basis for claims later that Charles ordered Coligny's murder; there is no supporting evidence, however.

The massacre of Huguenots on St Bartholomew's Day began. The slaughter took more than 3,000 lives in Paris, and 8,000 in other cities. It started in the Saint-Germain-l'Auxerrois and Louvre quarters, and spread south and east through the city. Civilians joined militia in a frenzy of murder and looting that started with Protestant nobles. Prince Henry of Navarre was nearly one of them. This future king of France and a Huguenot was in Paris to celebrate his marriage to King Charles's sister, Marguerite. He saved himself only by promising to return to the Church, a promise he recanted as soon as he was safely away.

Others soon followed. Mathurin Lussault, jeweller, for instance, was killed in his home, and his son struck down in the street when neighbours refused to give him sanctuary. Lussault's wife died from being dragged through the streets by her hair and having her hands cut off to get at her gold bracelets. Such behaviour was typical of the frenzied Catholic mobs, and while the more gruesome accounts of the slaughter may have been written by Protestants for propaganda purposes, the truth was bad enough.

There was much jubilation over the event when it had finished. Masses were celebrated in thanksgiving for the massacre, Joachim Opser, a Swiss student at the Jesuit Collège de Clermont, wrote that, as he died, Admiral Coligny 'swept a crowd of heretical nobles into hell with him', and Parisians generally seemed pleased with themselves.

## THE SIXTEEN

Saint-Bartholomew's Day in 1572 touched off a religious war that raged through France for a decade and a half. In Paris the result was economic deprivation, which merely confirmed the Parisians in their religious fanaticism. They had been, in their view, 'abandoned by God, their king, their employers, and their customers'. In the 1580s a subversive movement of monks, priests, artisans, merchants and some judges took power away from the *prévôt*, the officials of the Hôtel de Ville and the *Parlement*. They were led by a clandestine council called the Sixteen. Since 1585 the Sixteen, together with the Catholic League which represented uncompromising opposition to Protestantism, had carried on a propaganda war, first against heretics and then against Henry III, who was derided as a puppet prince. The channels included the press for the literate, and placards, engravings, posters and paintings for the rest. The Sixteen also published the papal bull which excommunicated Henry of Navarre and the prince of Condé. Various *coups* were plotted against the king because he persisted in seeking a compromise with the Huguenots, though none succeeded; that is, until the Day of the Barricades.

## THE DAY OF BARRICADES

On 7 May 1588 Henry III ordered suspect houses searched throughout Paris, and replaced suspect militiamen with others of proven loyalty. On 9 May the duke of Guise entered the city with a small retinue, despite orders not to do so. Henry took precautions. Parisians awoke on the morning of 12 May to find the king's soldiers occupying positions on the bridges, at the Louvre, and in the Latin Quarter. Finding their liberties thus threatened, the citizenry rose in revolt. Barricades of barrels and chains were erected throughout the Latin Quarter, on the Île de la Cité, and around the Louvre. The king's forces found themselves threatened with muskets and arquebuses. Every street was like a besieged town, commented a military adviser to the king. Henry wisely withdrew from his capital without a shot being fired.

## Henry IV, 1589–1610

In August 1589 Henry III was assassinated, and Henry of Navarre proclaimed himself King Henry IV, the first Bourbon ruler of France. It was one thing to have the throne; it was another matter to sit on it. To be king in both fact and theory, Henry must have Paris; that objective eluded him for five years.

### THE SIEGE OF PARIS

Henry IV was still a Huguenot when he mounted the throne. As such he made war against the Catholic League, handing it a major defeat at Ivry in 1590. To fervent Catholics it appeared that a Protestant might gain France without abjuring his heresy. This made the League all the more determined, and they controlled Paris. 'God would never permit a heretic king to walk their streets,' they said, and when Henry attacked the city in May they stopped him outside Faubourg Saint-Martin.

The king then laid siege to the city, waiting in classic fashion for conditions to deteriorate sufficiently for the citizens to sue for peace. It nearly worked. By July starving Parisians had finished off horses, donkeys, rats, cats, dogs, grass, tallow and skins, and were starting on humans. However, they hung on, the walls manned by monks and Catholic diehards, while women were said to swear they 'would prefer to eat their children than to surrender for lack of food'. Meanwhile the duke of Parma, commander of armies in the Spanish Netherlands, set out to rescue Paris. Henry knew his forces were inferior to Parma's and he was forced to withdraw. The city was saved and fed, its citizens remaining both unconquered and convinced of their righteous cause.

## 'PARIS IS WORTH A MASS'

This is what Henry is supposed to have said when, after three more years of fighting, he accepted that he would never have Paris so long as he remained a Huguenot. In 1593, in the Basilica of Saint-Denis, he was received into the Catholic Church, 'Roman and Apostolic', heard mass and knelt among the tombs of his many predecessors. Soon after, he was crowned and anointed with holy oil at Chartres Cathedral. Then he headed for Paris.

There were Henrician supporters in the city, and they left two gates open for his troops. Early on the morning of 22 March 1594 the king entered Paris. Would the Parisians accept his conversion and acknowledge his kingship? He rode slowly towards Notre-Dame cathedral. There he heard a Te Deum while his followers ran through the streets proclaiming peace and amnesty for everyone. Then Henry appeared and came down to mix with the crowds who jammed the streets. '*Vive le Roi!*' someone shouted, and the cry was taken up by the multitude. Henry was now king in fact and the war was over, at least so far as Paris was concerned.

## RENOVATING PARIS

Henry IV did not talk about the divine right of kings; he simply was an absolute monarch, taking direct control of the police, criminal courts, press and pulpit, both assuming and exercising the power to trample on merchants, clergy and any other institution that stood in the way of putting things to order. Henry worked through such competent *prévôts* as Jean Séguier and François Miron, and royal ministers such as the duke of Sully. Renovation of a city devastated by years of religious and civil turmoil was high on his agenda. 'No sooner was he master of Paris,' reported the journal *Mercure François* in 1610, 'than the masons were at work.' The Hôtel-Dieu, the Hôpital de la charité, the Arsenal, the Pont-Neuf and the Louvre were transformed, the last because Marie de' Medici, whom Henry married in 1600 after divorcing Marguerite de Valois, complained that the palace was dark, full of 'vile' furniture, and altogether too medieval. Meanwhile more streets were paved, and aristocrats returned to the city and built elegant town houses in the Marais. Two squares, Place Vendôme and Place Royale (now called the Place des Vosges), were built, and Place de France was begun, though not finished until after Henry's death. The Rue Dauphine and Place Dauphine were developed between the Pont-Neuf and the Porte de Buci, with instruction from Henry that Sully should emphasize the Renaissance architectural order in the new buildings that still characterize parts of central Paris.

## Neighbourhood Builders

Mansions built in the Marais were *hôtels* – a sort of urban *château* – rather than houses. Not so those built in the Place Dauphine and the Place Royale. Houses there were called *pavillons*: less expensive than *hôtels*, but more elegant than a typical bourgeois house and symbolized, as

One of the mansions built in the Marais, the Hôtel de Sully

aristocratic *hôtels* did not, 'some commitment to urban life and at least a tolerance for neighbours'. In these quarters and because of the *pavillons*, the 'neighbourhood' was introduced. Residents walked under the same galleries, shared gardens, and could glance into each other's windows. They also followed occupations that placed them generally within the same social strata. Constructing in the neighbourhood style meant expanding residential building, something Paris had not seen for two centuries. The crown both encouraged and backed it financially.

## THE ÎLE SAINT-LOUIS

The Île Saint-Louis is an example of royalty-sponsored 'neigbourhood building' in the seventeenth century, though in this instance as many *hôtels* as *pavillons* were constructed. In 1611, a year after the death of Henry IV, his successor, Louis XIII, gave engineer and bridge-builder Christophe Marie the backing to construct a bridge and housing development on the Île aux Vaches ('island of the cows'), immediately to the east of the Île de la Cité. The canons of Notre-Dame owned the island and immediately objected. Lengthy negotiations followed, after which the island was sold to the crown, which gave it to Marie and his backers. They were ordered to build quays around the Cité and get on with developing the Île aux Vaches.

Work began, but it was years before it amounted to anything. The western side of the island was divided into irregular tracts and sold by 1622, but not even a bridge had been constructed. Meanwhile Marie went bankrupt, and a new group of financiers, headed by one La Grange, took over. Île aux Vaches was renamed Île Saint-Louis in honour of the king's patron and ancestor, Louis IX. Five years later the only completed structure was a bridge to the Cité, and that just in time for another financial crisis. Finally, in 1635 the Pont-Marie to the Right Bank was finished, and after that much building was done. *Nouveaux-riches* tax farmers and judges – members of the *noblesse de la robe*, which is to say the bureaucracy – begged and borrowed to build splendid *hôtels* on the eastern half of the island. Jean-Baptiste Lambert, son of a *procureur des comptes*, was typical. The *hôtel* built in 1642 which still bears his name was designed by Louis Le Vau, who later worked for Louis XIV at Versailles.

Building continued westward along the new quays, and often equalled the *hôtels* of the east side in interior splendour. However, they were more restrained and bourgeois on the outside, in keeping with the idea of the *pavillon* and the neighbourhood life-style.

## THE LEFT BANK

Meanwhile Louis Le Barbier was hard at work developing the Latin Quarter. He began with lands between the Rue de Seine and the Rue du Bac stretching south to the Rue Jacob and the Rue de l'Université, once owned by Marguerite de Valois. Le Barbier worked financially and entrepreneurially – including the fact that he also went bankrupt – in a manner similar to Marie and his successors on the Île Saint-Louis, save that Le Barbier built houses first and *then* sold them. Some were elegant in the *hôtel* manner, others were described as *maisons*, which would suggest more modest dwellings. He also built a grain market to encourage merchants to settle in Faubourg Saint-Germain. Le Barbier's Latin quarter development was for people of varied wealth and social standing, not, however, including those for whom even merely pleasant housing was beyond their means; that described a significant portion of the Paris population.

## THE RIGHT BANK

Le Barbier also developed the Quartier du Palais-Royal, in co-operation with Louis XIII's powerful minister, Cardinal Richelieu. It was organized around the cardinal's *hôtel* (Palais Cardinal) in the Rue Saint-Honoré, north of the Louvre. Faubourg Saint-Germain attracted merchants, other Latin Quarter areas' judges and members of the *Parlement*, and Île Saint-Louis financiers. The Quartier du Palais-Royal became the neighbourhood of such royal ministers as Jean-Baptiste Colbert who, whatever their origins, possessed both great wealth and aristocratic style. Between 1630 and 1680 this quarter was synonymous with the political history of seventeenth-century France. Richelieu, Cardinal Mazarin, Anne of Austria and Colbert were only a few of its politically powerful residents. *Hôtels* in this quarter were the standard for aristocratic style and taste for the period. The best painters decorated their ceilings, and their libraries, medals, statuary, tapestries and furni-

ture now fill museums around the world. In 1642 the playwright Pierre
Corneille wrote of Quartier du Palais Royal in this language:

> A whole complete city, built with pomp,
> Seems by miracle to have come from an old moat,
> And makes us presume, from its superb roofs,
> That all the inhabitants are Gods or Kings.

## BUILDING FOR THE THIRD ESTATE

No new neigbourhoods of Third Estate (lower-class) housing were
developed in the seventeenth century: a new house here and there, and
expansion of the numbers of houses within existing quarters, but that
was all. Rather, artisans and merchants remodelled old houses, cut large
single apartments into two or three smaller ones, added a storey, or cut
up a garden into tracts for building new dwellings. In this way Paris
absorbed a steadily rising working population without expanding its
area to any significant extent. All the same, there were designs for new-
start lower-class housing. In 1647 Pierre Le Muet published *Manière de
Bien Bastir pour Toutes Sortes de Personnes*, a handbook of housing designs
comprehensible even to the semi-literate. A set of thirteen designs with
very specific instructions enabled a mason to save money by constructing a house without the aid of an architect. Few such houses were
actually built, but the concept was the ancestor of the terrace house
style famous in London suburbs.

# The Assassination of Henry IV

No French monarch survived more attempts on his life than Henry IV:
at least twenty-three. One close call was in 1594, when a Jesuit law
student stabbed the king, his dagger narrowly missing Henry's throat
and breaking one of his teeth. In 1610 an attempt finally succeeded: the
king was stuck in traffic in the Rue de la Ferronnerie when François
Ravaillac, a strong, red-haired man, leaped into the royal coach and
stabbed him three times. Ravaillac was seized and later tortured, but he
would not confess that he was part of any conspiracy; rather, he was
simply a fanatical Catholic who could never forgive Henry for having
once been a Huguenot.

The assassination of Henry IV

Parisians were heartily sick of religious turmoil by this time and feared that this event might trigger renewed civil war. They took out their frustration on Ravaillac himself. He was burned with sulphur, red-hot pincers, molten lead, boiling oil and resin. Then his arms and legs were attached to horses pulling in different directions. After an hour and half he died and, according to Nicolas Pasquier,

> the entire populace, no matter what their rank, hurled themselves on the body with their swords, knives, sticks or anything else to hand and began beating, hacking and tearing at it. They snatched the limbs from the executioner, savagely chopping them up and dragged the pieces through the streets. One woman ate some of the bits.

Apparently, though Parisians were sick of religious war, they were not sick of vengeful violence.

# *'The Last Heroes'*

Violence was a way of life in seventeenth-century Paris. The poor were driven to it by hunger and taxes, but for the nobility, historically a warrior class, it was the basis of a life-style which the religious turmoil of the age simply encouraged. When the religious wars ended, violence did not. Rebellions of one sort or another, including that led by the count of Soissons in 1642 which ended abruptly when he accidentally shot himself while using the muzzle of his pistol to lift the visor of his helmet, plagued the reign of Louis XIII.

Meanwhile Richelieu, Mazarin, King Louis and his successor, Louis XIV, made war and conquest an ideal, and assumed privilege within society for the nobility virtually above the law. Their very style of dress was calculated to set them apart. Women wore low-cut dresses with tight bodices and flared hips, and both men and women wore velvet, silk, furs, fancy hose, plumed hats, enormous wigs, gloves, perfume and jewellery. Poets, philosophers, artists and writers glorified their behaviour, as in Corneille's plays, wherein, as Orest Ranum phrased it, the nobility 'reached great heights of intensity, obsession, even madness, stemming from jealousy, power, love, devotion, hate, incest, and pride which simply could not be attained by ordinary men'. This was the 'heroic' style of an aristocracy both violent and self-serving.

BELOW THE SALT

The Paris population in 1637 was estimated at 415,000 living in 20,000 houses, which means an average of twenty-one per dwelling. About 10 per cent of Parisians, including the *haute* bourgeoisie, were sufficiently wealthy, educated or of an attitude of mind to appreciate and live in the aristocratic style. The other 90 per cent lived within their corporations and guilds, child following parent generation after generation. This, more even than the city itself, was the locus of their individual identity. These Parisians ate bread and cheese, occasionally fish and rarely meat, and lived in crowded conditions. Their occupations were porter, carter, water carrier, wood carrier, baker, butcher, carpenter and shopkeeper. In short, the Parisians 'below the salt' continued to live much as they had in the middle ages, and, as they had in the middle ages, they rioted from time to time in the name of taxes, hunger, or any threat to their security from outside, such as the Fronde.

## The Fronde

The Fronde was a series of rural rebellions that finally reached the capital. The Frondeur was not a peasant or artisan, but a member of the privileged class in opposition to royal policy, frequently tax policy, out of fear that it might negatively affect his own wealth and position. When Louis XIII died in 1643, Louis XIV was only five years old. Cardinal Mazarin ran the government for his mother and regent, Anne of Austria (to whom Mazarin may have been secretly married). Soon the great nobles, the *gentilshommes* idealized by Corneille and others, were in rebellion.

These Frondeurs and their supporters occupied the streets of Paris from 1648 to 1653, and treated the citizens with less than kindness and good manners. Mobs pelted government officials with stones, and on 4 July 1652 set fire to the door of the Hôtel de Ville while the council was sitting. Nobles brought down anarchy, violence, death, starvation and the destruction of property upon the city. The Paris death rate doubled while the birth rate dropped; armies marauding through the Île-de-France left the city almost without food, and seriously disrupted its trade, which resulted in a dramatic increase in prices. For a time Parisians flirted with the prince of Condé, the principal leader of the Fronde, to the extent of acquiescing when he drove Mazarin and the royal family from the city. But they soon tired of this Frondeur who was the author of so much of their suffering. When Mazarin and the boy-king Louis XIV entered Paris in 1653 behind an army raised by Mazarin himself, they were warmly received.

## The Regime of Cardinal Mazarin and Nicolas Fouquet

Cardinal Mazarin restored order in Paris at the head of an army arrayed against the Frondeurs, and which enjoyed broad popular support. Or, to put it in the language of an anonymous English agent in 1655: 'As for

Paris the population detests the present government and yet has subjected itself to it voluntarily. . . . [I]n Paris the people desire calm and do not wish to listen to any more bickering.'

Until his death in 1661, Cardinal Mazarin co-operated with Superintendent of Finance Nicolas Fouquet, a wealthy member of the bourgeoisie who had risen to prominence through a purchased place in the *Parlement* of Paris. Together they ruled in a consummately corrupt manner, and the *Parlement* was too frightened of anarchy to oppose them. They skimmed millions from public revenue, which they spent on great houses and on anything of artistic note that they could get their hands on. Mazarin housed his treasures in the Hôtel Mazarin (now the Bibliothèque Nationale) between Rue de Richelieu and Rue Vivienne, and Fouquet his in a great palace at Vaux-le-Vicomte, southeast of Paris, which was remarkable even by the standards of the times. Le Nôtre designed it, Le Brun did most of the interior, and it was frequented by such Fouquet patronees as Corneille, Molière, La Fontaine and Lully. Three villages were removed to make space for the palace and grounds. The *hommes des finances* who served Mazarin and Fouquet, and rivalled them in corrupt practices, lived equally well and built massively. The Hôtel de Sully, built by Henry IV's great minister, was modest compared to the mansions they constructed.

Louis XIV felt he owed everything to Mazarin. Fouquet, faced in 1661 with a suddenly assertive young monarch and his new, reforming superintendent of finance, Jean-Baptiste Colbert, was not so fortunate.

# CHAPTER FOUR

# *The Glitter and the Gloom,*
## 1661–1789

In 1670 Paris theatre critic Chappuzeau observed that, 'regardless of where one turns, Paris was never so fine nor so stately as it is today'. True enough; but at the same time Paris had never had more poverty, crime, disease or vagabondage, and Parisians were as dissentient and violent as they had been in the Fronde epoch. Glitter and gloom equally characterized Paris in the seventeenth and eighteenth centuries.

## *Louis XIV, 1643–1715*

Louis XIII and Queen Anne were rarely intimate, and rarely spent the night in the same palace, never mind bed. Getting an heir had become problematic. Then one night in 1637 Louis was prevented by a storm from leaving Paris for Saint-Maur. His captain of the guard and the Visitandine, Sister Angélique, a nun of the Order of the Visitation of Our Lady (with whom Louis was once in love), persuaded him to stop the night at the Louvre. Anne was in residence, and her four-poster was the only comfortable bed in the palace. She proved willing to share, and Louis XIV was born nine months later.

### THE MAN IN THE IRON MASK

Or was he? There was a prisoner of state in the Bastille from 1698 until his death in 1703, who was brought to Paris wearing a black velvet mask (which rumour transformed into iron) to hide his identity. No one knows why. Was he Louis XIV's bastard? Queen Anne's bastard and elder brother to Louis XIV, as Voltaire insisted? Or was it the disgraced Nicolas Fouquet? The Alexandre Dumas *père* version presented in his novel, *The Man in the Iron Mask*, is the most fun: the mask concealed the real Louis Bourbon, whose twin brother Philip had usurped the throne. Of course Philip ruled as Louis because, though the real Louis was Evil whereas Philip was Good, Philip was the younger twin. Dumas was the very model of a Romantic novelist.

## *'Grandeur and Magnificence'*

Louis XIV entered Paris on 16 August 1661 with his new bride and queen, Maria Teresa, daughter of Philip IV of Spain. The procession began at Vincennes and moved to Place du Trône (Place de la Nation) outside Porte Saint-Antoine. There, on thrones set on a large platform, they received leaders of the Paris corporations, the *prévôts* of the University of Paris and the guilds, and other city officials, all of whom welcomed them with elaborate and long-winded speeches. When that ordeal had ended, the king and queen proceeded on to the Louvre, through a series of allegorically decorated triumphal arches raised for the occasion. The keynote was peace after a quarter of a century of warfare. Louis clearly was the hope of the future.

### THE SUN KING

'It is now time that I govern ... myself,' Louis announced when Mazarin died. To assist him, he made Jean-Baptiste Colbert, who had also served Mazarin, superintendent of finance. Colbert was to have no illusions regarding his place, however; Louis's style was absolutist, as explained by Bishop Jacques Bénigne Bossuet in 1670: 'Royal authority is sacred [and] absolute.... The prince need render account to no one for what he orders....' Thus, when the superintendent argued with the king over a Navy matter, Louis warned: '... [D]o not risk vexing me again, because after I have heard your arguments ... and have given my opinion on all your claims, I do not wish to hear further talk about it, ever.'

### THE KING AND PARIS

Louis had bad memories of his boyhood in Paris, including being threatened by Frondeurs, and looked forward to moving to Versailles.

Jean-Baptiste Colbert

During the 1670s he gave the Tuileries to various dependents, and the Palais-Royal to his brother, the duke of Orléans. The king chose to spend little on Colbert's plan to renovate the Louvre, in favour of massive renovation and expansion, directed by Le Vau, of the old royal château and park at Versailles. In the course of his reign Louis spent only 9,643,301 livres on the Louvre and Tuileries combined, but 65,651,275 on Versailles. After 1680 he came to Paris rarely and only on ceremonial occasions, such as in 1687 when he dined with city officials in the Hôtel de Ville following a thanksgiving mass at Notre-Dame for his recovery from a serious illness.

## THE ACADÉMIE FRANÇAISE

The Académie Française, founded by Cardinal Richelieu in 1634 and central to the reputation of both France and Paris, held its meetings in the Louvre. Louis became its patron in 1672, just in time to intervene in a controversy over chairs. Up to that time only the director rated an armchair, while everyone else sat on armless cane-bottomed chairs. Then gouty and infirm Cardinal d'Estrées was brought to an Académie session one day in an armchair. There were immediate protests that, by this action, the cardinal had destroyed the academic equality of the members. Louis settled the dispute by providing armchairs for everyone. To this day there are always as many armchairs as there are members.

## COLBERT AND THE NEW ROME

Paris entered the seventeenth century as an essentially medieval city, surrounded by walls and governed by an administration formed in the High Middle Ages. Louis XIV's reign saw much reform and modernization, for which Colbert could take much of the credit. Neither Cardinal Mazarin nor Superintendent Fouquet had recognized the importance of Paris to the well-being of France. Colbert did. 'Paris being the capital of the kingdom and the residence of the king,' he wrote, 'it is certain that it sets in motion the rest of the kingdom; that all internal affairs begin with it.' And again: 'You know that the example set by the city of Paris should do much to assure success in the rest of the kingdom.'

The son of a wealthy Paris bourgeois, Colbert was creative, a genius at administration, a visionary who wanted a well-ordered, monumental and prosperous Paris. He was also a classicist, whose ideal was the Roman Empire with the city of Rome its centre, the font of power, justice, style and cultural greatness. He drew the analogy of Paris as the equivalent centre of an imperial France, a sort of 'new Rome', and on this basis argued for the physical and cultural reconstruction of the city. He patronized architects, painters and sculptors, all directed to build, paint and sculpt in the classical manner. He patronized humanists and academicians, whose work on classical texts and knowledge of classical styles could add to the Romanization of Paris. Colbert reorganized the Academy of Painting and Sculpture, with Charles Le Brun as master, and charged it with training young artists. Meanwhile he also shed his light on such royal manufactories as Gobelins and Savonnerie, which were to be guided by the Academy in producing painting, tapestries, furniture, sculpture in marble and bronze, that would fit Colbert's classical ideal.

## PARIS SCHOOLS

Regrettably, the superintendent did not shed his classical light upon the Paris educational system. The *petites écoles* which provided elementary education under the medieval administration of the Grand Chantre of the Cathedral Chapter of Notre-Dame remained in a generally sorry state, as did the poorly-paid teachers, who were bound by the rules of their guild and had to pay the Grand Chantre 32 livres annually. The populace demanded alternatives and the *Parlement* agreed. However, the Grand Chantre was intractable and while dissatisfaction with the old system was clear, a solution was not forthcoming.

Meanwhile the university was losing its place as the centre of European learning. Reports on the colleges by royal officials referred to 'great disorders' and 'the need to restore discipline', as in the case of three *boursiers* (recipients of financial aid) of the Collège de Montaigu 'who having come into money have fallen into the corruption and contagion of riches'. In theory, a Faculty of Arts student studied in college for ten years, including two years of philosophy, to earn a bachelor's degree. In reality, most students came to the university only to take the two years of philosophy before being granted the *baccalauréat*, followed soon after by the *maîtrise ès arts* (Master of Arts). Moreover, the university allowed only its own graduates on the staff, who were poorly compensated compared to lawyers and medical doctors. Understandably the more capable minds often chose these professions over the arts and philosophy.

Louis stayed well out of educational controversies, doing his bit for the New Rome by stocking the 'pestiferous waters' of the Seine with exotic white swans, so that courtiers would have something nice at which to look while travelling to Versailles. It was a miracle that the swans survived, given the polluted river. They did symbolize the reforming of Paris more or less in line with Colbert's ideal of a New Rome, however, for like the swans this New Rome had much to do with grace, beauty and symmetry.

## ROYAL CONTROL OF CITY ADMINISTRATION

Colbert wanted his reformed Paris all at once. Incorruptible himself, he showed the *hommes de finances* that he could not be bribed, and added insult to this injury by persuading Louis to institute an Extraordinary Chamber of Justice (led by notables such as Chancellor Séguier and President of the *Parlement* Lamoignon), charged with suppressing false titles of nobility, illegal ecclesiastical privileges, illegal rents, and tax-farming contracts. The *Parlement*, nobility and bourgeoisie opposed the Chamber, but Colbert got round them by exploiting public opinion, which supported his determination to control rents and mortgages and the divisions within the guilds and corporations. Of course he also had the backing of the king.

As the reign progressed, Paris merchants and members of the bourgeoisie looked more and more to the crown and its ministers for aid in solving their problems. City administration became royal administration, and until his death Colbert personally selected the *prévôt des marchands*. As for the *Parlement*, Louis himself took it in hand. 'Everyone knows all the troubles that have been caused by the assemblies of Parliament,' he scolded them, as early as 1655, adding that, for the future, 'Monsieur le Président, I forbid you to allow any assembly whatsoever.' For the next sixty years, the *Parlement* of Paris was largely a tool of royal government.

## THE TRIAL OF NICOLAS FOUQUET

Nicolas Fouquet was arrested in 1661 by a now ageing Captain of Musketeers, d'Artagnan, on charges of corruption. He was not tried until four years later, during which time he became a 'martyr'. The Paris bourgeois, the bureaucrats, and the riffraff of the streets all supported him, which was very odd when it is considered that he truly was corrupt, without conscience, and indifferent to the suffering of those who paid the *taille* and other taxes from which he had skimmed in order to build his palace. There was also evidence that he had conspired against the Crown. The trial went forward, despite protest and calls for Colbert's dismissal, and Fouquet was convicted. He was not executed, however, which was just as well as Paris would likely have erupted in rioting and rampage. Instead his property was confiscated and he was exiled to Pignerol.

The trial was symbolic. On one level, Fouquet represented that corruption which the régime meant to reform. On another, his supporters numbered both victims and profiteers of that corruption. Parisians on the fringe – beggars and artisans – saw him as the victim of a tyrannical and corrupt royal justice; those who had profited from corrupt government saw in his fall a threat to themselves. These Parisians '[called] for Colbert's disgrace from their magnificent *hôtels* built with government funds'.

REFORMING THE ADMINISTRATION

Paris was governed from the Hôtel de Ville and the Châtelet. The former housed the *prévôt des marchands* and the *échevins*, who ran an inefficient bureaucracy of officials in nominal charge of the 16 *quartiers*, 64 *cinquantaines* and 256 *dizaines* into which the city was divided and subdivided. The Châtelet was the province of the *prévôt de Paris*, representative of royal authority in Paris. Louis's problem with these institutions was twofold: they were historically at odds with one another, which led to all manner of jurisdictional disputes and therefore to the city becoming what Nicholas Delamare described as 'a Sewer'; and many of their officials had participated enthusiastically on the rebel side in the Fronde. The king's response was to impose the royal hand on Paris, through Colbert.

In 1666 Colbert established the *Conseil de Police*, which he dominated through the chairman, Chancellor Séguier. Its role was to examine everything from public security to street cleaning and suggest improvements. The council's recommendations were passed to the Royal Council, wherein royal decrees and ordinances were enacted. The recommendations were accompanied by Colbert's warning that Louis himself 'intended to walk the streets personally' to see that new directives were observed.

The most important change in the status quo was the office of Lieutenant General of Police, created in 1667. It was directed by Gabriel Nicolas de La Reynie, the scion of a Limoges family of judges and bureaucrats.

## LA REYNIE

La Reynie was a most conscientious director. He personally reviewed investigations, visited prisoners, oversaw grain merchants and the price of bread, and censored libellous or pornographic materials. His office had jurisdiction over an impressive list of activities: it arrested law-breakers, including the insane; suppressed prostitution, abortion, gambling and vagabondage; kept watch over foreigners, spies and habitual duellers; oversaw street lighting and cleaning, fire-fighting, flooding and water distribution; and enforced the regulation of guilds, markets, food importation, medical services and barbers. Like Colbert, La Reynie acted always in the king's name, and like Colbert he understood that the best way to maintain public order in a disorderly city was to convince the Parisians that the king and his ministers were mainly concerned with their welfare.

The police minister used the phrase *'l'opinion publique'*, and practised censorship of novels or plays which were judged likely to influence it wrongly. This was never – or rarely – done openly; the preferred fashion was to 'suggest'. On an occasion in 1690, when a burlesque was per-formed with political overtones which 'His Majesty does not deem it proper to tolerate . . .', Chancellor Pontchartrain instructed La Reynie to approach the performers and 'ask some of the actors to give you the play to read, after which you yourself and on other pretexts will tell them not to perform it . . . .' However, this was a negative approach to swaying public opinion and La Reynie had greater success when he was able to thwart corrupt inspectors, hoarders, counterfeiters, speculators and other scoundrels who were taking economic advantage of the populace.

Parisians were notoriously hard to convince, however, particularly when the reforms of La Reynie and Colbert appeared to be responsible for consistently high taxes. In fact, high taxes were the fault of Louis's military ambitions, which over three decades came near to bankrupting both Paris and France. All the same, these royal administrators were blamed, and when Colbert died in 1683, the 'object of undeserved scorn and anger', in Orest Ranum's words, the funeral mass and pro-cession were held in the evening and protected by armed guards, in order to lessen the danger that Paris riffraff might defile his remains.

# *The Social Order*

Paris was a city in transition. Not only was it being reformed administratively, the role of wealth rather than birth as the basis of class was being redefined, as was the guild system.

## THE RICH

The rich in Paris were very rich, especially the *hommes des finances*. Samuel Bernard, for example, was said to have amassed a fortune of 60 million livres. As Ranum noted, the *hommes des finances* 'assumed an independence and intransigence which infuriated the public and perhaps explains the attitudes of even twentieth-century French functionaries'. They lived in the still fashionable Marais, and in Montmartre which was the 'residential Wall Street of its day'. Residents of this quarter included the likes of Antoine Crozat, a notorious financier; Poisson de Bourvalais, whose *hôtel* cost 250,000 livres; the count of Evreux, a blue-blood who married Crozat's daughter for her money; Delpech and Lelaya, both farmer-generals; Aubert, *receveur des finances* for Caen; Heuzé de Vauloger, treasurer of Alençon; and architects Pierre Bullet and Jules Hardouin-Mansart, who made fortunes designing *hôtels* and *châteaux*.

Meanwhile, the *beau monde* was crossing the river to the Faubourg Saint-Germain. By 1716 this quarter, with fifty-four *hôtels* belonging to great notables, outranked both the Marais with thirty-one and Montmartre with twenty-seven. Moreover, only the 'best people' lived there, which did not include the *nouveaux riches*. In any case, all three quarters offered the rich what they wanted: uncluttered streets and relatively clean air compared to the centre of the city, in addition to a grand and magnificent life-style.

## THE SIX CORPS

Many *hauts* bourgeois guild merchants had evolved into bankers and, in turn, into *hommes des finances* and become part of the *nouveaux riches*. Many came from the Six Corps, which ranked just behind the institutions of city government in importance. In the seventeenth century Six Corps members termed themselves *maîtres marchands fabricants*, so as not to be confused with mere artisans or small merchants. They paid high taxes, bought privileges and favours like any *homme des finances*, and differed from those individuals only in that they were sure to be native Parisians who placed their guild association above almost any other consideration. So jealous were the Six Corps of their exclusivity that they waged a legal battle for 300 years to keep the wine merchants guild out. This guild, the wealth of its members notwithstanding, was associated with socially unacceptable tavern and cabaret keepers.

It is estimated that in the seventeenth century over 200 Paris merchants possessed capital of more than 500,000 livres each, and that most of these belonged to the Six Corps.

## GUILDS AND WORKERS

Most Paris guilds fell well below the level, socially and materially, of the Six Corps. There were approximately 70,000 guild members in 1650, 20,000 masters and the rest apprentices and journeymen. As few as 7,500 of these belonged to the Six Corps. The basic guild structure had not changed from the middle ages, the member working his or her way from apprentice journeyman, and if the requirements were met, to master. However, a great deal had changed within this structure.

Apprentices now had to be sponsored by parents or guardians, and registered at the Châtelet. This was for the protection of both apprentice and master. Many apprenticeships were prohibitively expensive (300 livres per year, in some cases), and the time required to finish an apprenticeship, and the nature of work imposed, were often determined by the ability to pay. Seventeenth-century masters seemed less concerned with teaching their apprentices than with using them as servants (pastry apprentices often hawked their masters' wares around the city). Consequently, according to a police ordinance of 1678, they were ' "corrupted" by vagrants and cutpurses', and 'learned nothing of their trade'.

Conditions also changed for journeymen. By 1600 there was every possibility that a journeyman might spend his or her life as a simple worker, as the masters sought to limit competition. In Louis XIV's time, some guilds stipulated that only the children of masters could become masters. Others simply maintained a double standard for the

*chef d'oeuvre* (masterpiece) by which a journeyman became a master:
one standard for the unprivileged journeyman and another for the
children and relatives of masters. In either case the effect was to create a
social and economic hierarchy not unlike that which existed in the
upper strata of Parisian society. In Faubourg Saint-Germain, for
example, 'unprivileged' bakers were required to 'convert the equivalent of 36 bushels of wheat into 20-ounce units of dough which then
had to be baked down to precise 16-ounce loaves of white bread'. The
masters' offspring needed only to convert a small amount of wheat into
bread, with no strict standard. Workers had little recourse, since royal
authority continued to support the role of the guilds in the social
ordering of Paris.

The manufacturing district of Faubourg Saint-Antoine managed to
defy the system. Saint-Antoine was a 'protected area', meaning that it
was under the rule of the Church, in this case the abbess of Saint-
Antoine, who could lay down whatever rules for work she chose. She
chose to do without guilds, and her successors followed suit. A contemporary described the district as 'crowded with quantities of artisans
and journeymen who work without *maîtrise*'. When Saint-Antoine
workers were ordered to join city guilds in 1644, a legal battle ensued
which the abbess won. In 1675 Louis again ordered the workers to join
the guilds, and again the abbess seemed to have won the day, for the
records indicate that city guildsmen continued to be outraged.
Thereafter Saint-Antoine journeymen were being elevated to master
without reference to guild guidelines. Saint-Antoine defiance gave
others ideas, and by the end of the century journeymen workers were
defying their masters in the same way trades unionists would later
challenge factory owners.

## VAGABONDS AND BEGGARS

However poor and oppressed they might be, workers were still
respectable. Not so the hordes of beggars and vagabonds, often refugees
from rural pauperization, 'the most troublesome social ailments
afflicting Paris in the age of Louis XIV'. The *Parlement* tried to control
the problem with harsh legislation: in 1596 vagrants were given
twenty-four hours to leave the city 'under penalty of being hanged and

strangled without benefit of trial'. The effect was minimal, and a half-century later one-tenth of the Paris population, about 40,000, were vagrants. These thousands symbolized the misery that lay behind the 'glittering façade of the Grand Siècle'. Infanticides averaged 500 annually, and in the exceptionally harsh winter of 1708–9, 2,525 infants were abandoned in doorways or in front of the Hôtel-Dieu, from which hundreds of corpses were taken nightly for burial in mass graves. After 1656, upwards of 10,000 vagrants at a time were incarcerated in the Hôpital-Général, a sort of prison for vagrants cleared off the streets by a police force associated specifically with the institution.

How was the problem to be dealt with? Attempts at expelling vagrants proved hopeless, as did efforts to distinguish between vagrants and the 'honest poor'. Charity, and what we would term 'social assistance', provided what solution there was. Louis XIV gave money to Trinité and Saint-Esprit, the two best of many orphanages in Paris, 800 livres a year to Quinze-Vingts, the hospital for the blind, and 60–80,000 livres to be divided among the faubourgs for doling out to the needy. He also spent large sums on bread for Parisians in hard times, which generosity was much praised. Contemporary engravings depicted crippled children reaching out to receive their bread quota. The engravings did not also indicate the impact of profiteers and hoarders on the distribution process.

Public assistance included the *atelier public* (public works projects), and the Grand Bureau des Pauvres. Established to administer aid to the poor, both were run by the Hôtel de Ville and paid for by city taxes. The Church disapproved of this secularization of charity, but it was in keeping with the spirit of the times otherwise. Being badly-run bureaucracies, the *atelier public* and the Grand Bureau fell well short of expectations, which gave the Church reason to say 'we told you so'. In fact, the *charités* organized by zealous Catholics and the Hôpital-Général were far more effective. Unfortunately, many Parisians believed that Hôpital police kidnapped children off the streets to ship out to French colonies in America. To be sure, vagrants were shipped to the colonies, often as indentured servants; it is not clear that they were regularly forced.

In any event, success in dealing with vagabondage was limited. At the end of his reign Louis XIV was still ordering the rounding up and incarceration of armies of beggars and vagabonds from the streets of Paris.

## THE UNDERWORLD

For every vagabond and beggar there was also a footpad and cut-throat. 'Day and night, they rob and kill here,' complained Dr Guy Patin. His evidence included the exploits of one Sieur Aubry, a 'thrill killer' who once murdered a somnolent vagabond on the Pont-Neuf, '[from] gaiety of heart,' the police report said.

La Reynie imposed a number of hopefully corrective changes. A police force was organized at a cost of 120,000 livres per year and paid for by the king, to supplement the *guet* (night watch). The *guet* were also reorganized: their numbers increased along with their pay, they were provided with blue uniforms, and they began patrolling the streets of Paris on a regular schedule. The new police force, meanwhile, actually investigated crimes and arrested people.

Meanwhile it was made illegal to manufacture, sell, store or carry weapons without authorization. The bourgeoisie protested that they had held the right to such weapons since the fourteenth century. They need not have bothered. The police force was pitifully small, and in practice the ordinance was enforced mainly among the lower orders. The Cour des Miracles, a hang-out for thieves, cut-throats and vagabonds behind the Convent of the Filles-Dieu, was ordered to be destroyed (its name derived from the 'miraculous recovery' the crippled and diseased inhabitants made, as soon as they returned to the court after a day of begging and petty thievery). A street-lighting system was introduced in 1667. *Allumeurs*, paid from local rates, lighted 6,500 oil lamps each night, an improvement over the gloomy past at least in those streets where the system was installed. Citizens felt at least marginally safer walking the streets at night.

All of this was little enough, Leon Bernard has pointed out, for the rot which created the Paris underworld set in long before Colbert and La Reynie. Moreover, their improvements were hampered by Louis XIV's double standard for 'blue-blooded thugs'. Noble lawbreakers were targeted because they set a bad example for the populace; but, where ordinary people were incarcerated or hanged or otherwise slaughtered on the Place de Grève, noble lawbreakers were often simply exiled temporarily.

## THE ENVIRONMENT

A bourgeois, his nose offended once too often, petitioned Louis in 1680 to place public water closets in the Louvre, the Palais de Justice, and other much-frequented sites around the city and in the suburbs. '[O]ne sees a thousand ordures,' he wrote, 'one smells a thousand intolerable stenches.' Apparently little came of it, and if it had the effect would have been limited, for human waste was only part of the problem.

Paris was plagued, as always, by unpleasant odours from many sources. The area of the Hôpital de la Miséricorde alone contained the Bièvre, a stream that served as public sewer and a waste dump for the Gobelins factory, a pig farm, a neighbourhood tanner, a starch maker, and an abattoir which emptied blood into the street. Paving had not yet covered up all the infamous and stinking Paris mud, and even paved streets were filthy owing to a chronic urban water shortage. In 1660 the average daily per capita consumption of water was about a litre, which did not leave much for street cleaning.

The cemeteries were the most offensive. Nurses at the Hôtel de la Miséricorde complained for forty years about the odours which resulted from the careless burial practices of the Hôtel-Dieu cemetery in Clamart. On one occasion, Clamart buried 13,000 bodies in a mass grave designed for 3,000. The decomposing bodies soon pushed aside the covering earth and reappeared. The Cemetery of the Holy Innocents adjacent to Les Halles was even more notorious for both its procedures and its smells.

Serious effort was made to effect change. La Reynie organized street sweepers and tumbrel operators to pick up refuse, and dumping areas for 'corruptible' refuse, meaning human waste, and 'non-corruptible', meaning animal waste, were provided outside the city. These efforts fell short of expectations. Parisians had always thrown waste indiscriminately into the street (more than one passer-by had been drenched by the contents of chamber-pots launched from first-floor windows), and that continued despite La Reynie's efforts. On the bright side, as an English visitor noted, Paris produced excellent mushrooms grown in beds of 'Horse Dung 2 or 3 feet thick'.

IN SICKNESS AND IN HEALTH

Syphilis, a disease at least one physician thought was a new form of leprosy, was on the increase in the seventeenth century. Treatment for it and other diseases was dispensed usually in the patient's home by physicians of the university, surgeons of the Collège de Saint-Côme, barber-surgeons or apothecaries, depending on the size of one's purse. A doctor charged three livres a visit, affordable by the bourgeois and aristocracy but not by the poor, who had to rely on the rare free clinic, or on quacks who pretended to medicine in the streets. Quality of treatment, however, was questionable for everyone. Paris possessed only one hospital in the modern sense, La Charité in the Faubourg Saint-Germain. The care was excellent: one patient per bed, and each patient seen daily by a house doctor accompanied by a surgeon, an apothecary and an attendant. This was far superior to treatment in the Hôtel-Dieu, once the principal Paris hospital and a teaching hospital for the Faculty of Medicine of the University of Paris. The Hôtel-Dieu was now called the 'most extensive, the largest, the richest, and the most frightful of hospitals'. In 1678–9 the death rate at La Charité was 14 per cent, while at Hôtel-Dieu it was 28 per cent.

## *Modernization*

Colbert believed that a great city is a modern city. The medieval wall went, replaced by such tree-lined boulevards as the Champs-Elysées. Its gates became triumphal arches, two of which, in Rue Saint-Denis and Rue Saint-Martin, still survive. That was only the beginning.

GETTING AROUND TOWN

Paris was a continuous traffic jam. Thousands of carriages clogged streets that had been designed for feet, hooves and the occasional wagon wheel. There were eight carriages in Paris in 1594, owned by the very rich. By the 1630s there were 4,000; Faubourg Saint-Antoine

Porte Saint-Martin, built in 1674

alone had 3,000 in 1656, and by the end of the century 20,000 carriages were trying to make their way about the city. By then they had became a status symbol. The German Neimitz wrote in his travel guide that '... gentlemen cannot go about Paris on foot'. Promenading in carriages in the Bois de Boulogne, Vincennes, the Luxembourg, and at various fairs and in villages around the city, was popular among the rich. Carriages were also trysting places, or as transportation to trysting places such as the Moulin de Jarel, notorious as a 'factory of pleasures and the shame of bourgeois families'.

A public omnibus system was introduced in 1662, with seven colourfully painted coaches bearing the Paris coat of arms and with liveried drivers. The price was deliberately set too high for the working populace, which was warned not to make trouble about it. Naturally the warning had the opposite effect. On opening day mobs shouted insults and threw stones at the coaches; many were arrested, which deterred no one when another line opened a few weeks later. The project was soon abandoned, to be revived only in 1828. Meanwhile more streets were paved, which made carriage travel easier.

Consistently marked and identified streets made a postal system possible for the first time. Lazare Patin bought the postal monopoly for Paris in 1672, for l.7 million livres per year. By 1700 one could drop a letter at the Bureau Général de la Poste, in the Rue des Déchargeurs near Les Halles, or any of eight other letter-boxes around the city, for delivery to any European city 'west of and including Germany and Austria'.

## THE PRESS

The first Paris newspaper, *La Gazette*, was started in 1631, and challenged the public information monopoly held by the town-criers guild. In 1672 the first daily, *Le Journal de la ville de Paris*, began publication. Advertising sheets also appeared, though François Colletet failed in his effort, launched in 1676, to combine advertising with news. The problem was the government: such schemes as Colletet's were quashed because the régime remained committed to the guild system, and thought public advertising violated guild philosophy and rights.

# Building and Rebuilding

Modernization also meant buildings. The Hôpital de La Salpêtrière near the Bastille, designed by architects Le Vau and Libéral Bruant, was used variously to house paupers, prostitutes and insane women. The Savonnerie carpet factory was added to the Manufacture des Gobelins, and between 1667 and 1672 Claude Perrault built the Observatoire just south of the Luxembourg Palace and gardens, Bruant the Hôtel des Invalides on the Left Bank, near where the École Militaire would be constructed in the next century.

## CHURCHES

Louis's reign saw a great deal of church building and renovating. The principal examples included: Saint-Nicolas-du-Chardonnet, east of the Sorbonne; Saint-Louis-en-l'Île, on Île-Saint-Louis; Notre-Dame-de-l'Assomption, off the Rue Saint-Honoré, built in 1670 as a convent for widows; Saint-Thomas-d'Aquin, in the Faubourg Saint-Germain; the Église-de-la-Minimes, near the Place Royale, dedicated in 1679; Saint-Denis-de-la-Chartre on the Île de la Cité, restored and redecorated; Saint-Eloi, rebuilt in 1703; and Notre-Dame, redecorated beginning in 1699, during which the remains of the Roman altar to Jupiter was discovered.

## NEW – AND OSTENTATIOUS – SQUARES AND OPEN SPACES

The Carrousel, just north of the Grande Galerie of the Louvre, in which stands the Arc de Triomphe du Caroussel, was named for an 'equestrian extravaganza cum masquerade' held on the site in 1662. But that was nothing compared to the Place des Victoires, a square where Rue des Petits Champs meets Rue Étienne Marcel, which was inspired by the duke of La Feuillade in 1680. The duke was 'poor in everything except noble ancestors and bravery in battle', but wanted to thank Louis for his pensions and honours. The square was subsidized by the marquis of Louvois, superintendent of buildings after the death of Colbert, designed by Hardouin-Mansart, and decorated with a colossal statue of Louis XIV, ten metres high including the base.

Place des Victoires was followed by Place Vendôme between Rue de Castiglione and Rue de la Paix, also designed by Hardouin-Mansart, and also with a giant equestrian stature of the king, sculpted by Girardon. In 1685 Louvois began the Pont-Royal, the first stone-arch bridge to cross the Seine, which linked the Faubourg Saint-Honoré on the Right Bank with Faubourg Saint-Germain on the Left.

# The Theatre

Paris theatre came into its own in the seventeenth century. The Comédie Française and the Opéra, where Louis's favourite court composer Jean-Baptiste Lully was the moving force, were two of four companies that performed in such places as the Hôtel de Bourgogne, the Salle du Petit-Bourbon in the Louvre, the Théâtre du Marais, and various *jeux de paume* (tennis courts). Theatres mainly played on the Right Bank until companies realized that their wealthiest clientèle lived across the river. Molière's company moved to Rue Guénégaud, near the Pont-Neuf, in 1674.

## THE PLAYWRIGHTS

The fare included slapstick and farce, and tragedy and satiric comedy. Pierre Corneille, Jean Racine and Molière were among the great playwrights. Their work was reviewed, and not always kindly, in the pages of the Paris literary journal, *Le Mercure galant*. Corneille (1606–84) came from Rouen with a successful comedy, *Mélite*, to his credit. He was mainly a tragedian, however, best remembered for *Le Cid*, a tragic love story based upon a Spanish play about a Spanish legend. It 'took Paris by storm', save for the Académie Française, only four years old but already stuffy, which criticized the play for not adhering strictly to classical rules of construction. Corneille thereafter played by the rules, but at the expense of his genius. His classical tragedies were written with dignity and grandeur, and exalted will at the expense of emotion. The later examples were monotonously declamatory.

Jean Racine (1639–99) replaced Corneille in popularity. His plays exemplified French classicism: simple diction, psychologically realistic characters and skilful dramatic construction. He was a favourite of both Louis and his mistress and later wife (but never queen), Madame de Maintenon. Racine's work included a satire, *Les Plaideurs*, and such tragedies as *Britannicus*, *Bérénice* (based upon an early romance between Louis XIV and Marie Mancini), *Andromaque*, *Phèdre*, and *Iphigénie en Aulide*. In the 1780s he gave up the theatre, married, and joined Nicolas Boileau-Despréaux as a royal historiographer. In 1678 they donned swords, mounted horses, and rode to war with the king, causing, it is said, much amusement among the soldiery.

Jean Baptiste Poquelin, known as Molière (1622–73), is best remembered for satiric comedy. A Paris bourgeois, he took the name Molière when he joined the Béjart travelling theatre troupe. By 1658 he had his own company. His patron was the king's brother, known as 'Monsieur'. Molière's satires and comedies excelled in delineation of character and comic situations which together ridiculed a vice or type of excess. The best examples include: *Le Tartuffe*, on religious hypocrisy, *Le Misanthrope*, on antisocial behaviour, *Le Bourgeois Gentilhomme*, on social climbing, *Les Femmes savantes*, on intellectual pretentiousness among aristocratic women, and *Le Malade imaginaire*, on hypochondria. Ironically, Molière was on stage playing the hypochondriac when he died.

## THE AUDIENCE

Paris theatre-goers ranged from royalty to street rowdies. None of them were well behaved, as indicated by city ordinances forbidding disruptive behaviour in front of theatres, carrying arms into theatres, or creating riots once inside. Rowdyism was endemic among 'footsore, macaroon-munching, wine-imbibing' liveried servants, lackeys and soldiers, who stood in the *parterre* (pit) and stomped, whistled, and treated other spectators, and sometimes the actors, with 'unparalleled brutality'. The king's Musketeers were reputedly among the most notorious, but they were not alone. A young marquis, seated on stage as was customary for the well-heeled, slapped an actor for mocking him, and former Queen Christina of Sweden's posture while watching a performance shocked one theatre-goer into commenting that it was 'so indecent that ... one glimpsed what even the least modest woman should keep hidden'.

## THE CENSOR

Censorship was plentiful, but was applied mainly to the vulgarities of Italian comedy, the main fare of Paris theatre at the turn of the century; it was said then that no respectable woman would go near the theatre. The tradition, which included the famous Scaramouche, continued until the increasingly strait-laced Louis XIV took steps to suppress it. *Double entendre* plays were banned in 1688, along with depicting Châtelet officials as dishonest. In 1696 the Châtelet warned the actors not to indulge in 'indecent postures ... equivocal words ... and anything contrary to modesty', and undercover police agents began attending all Italian performances. The next year *La Fausse Prude* opened, a play in which the lead character was clearly a send-up of

Madame de Maintenon. Châtelet police immediately closed the theatre, sealed the entrance and gave the Italians one month to leave France.

Vulgar such comedy might have been, but it is likely that the real objection was the negative social commentary that lay beneath the surface.

## *The Ancien Régime*

Louis XIV spent thirty-five years of his reign at war, at a cost of tens of millions of livres, and died in 1715, unlamented. Sometimes it seems that his successors merely presided over a system sliding inevitably towards revolution. That is the gift of hindsight; yet such a view is not entirely wrong. Corruption was commonplace, and if Paris flourished during the period known as the *ancien régime*, becoming a commercial centre and capital of the Enlightenment, the fact remained that the rich became richer and the poor poorer and more numerous. The breaking point was 1789.

### LOUIS XV, 'THE WELL-BELOVED,' 1715–1774

Like his great-grandfather, Louis XV ascended the throne as a minor. The regent, Philip of Orléans, was a lazy libertine who frequented the theatre and gambling dens of Paris, often in the company of the Scottish banker, John Law. He backed Law in a joint-stock scheme involving Louisiana and other French overseas territories. Investors were sought and found; speculation grew feverish, stock prices spiralled and a 'bubble' formed (meaning more shares were sold than there was value in the stock). This became known, panic set in and the bubble burst. Confidence in royal government never fully recovered, especially in Paris where most of the investors lived, especially since government corruption and inefficiency, along with war-related taxes and indebtedness, only increased after Louis XV came of age.

Louis pleased no one. He lost most of France's colonial possessions, his marriage to Marie Leszczynska of Poland was considered a *mésal-liance*, and his mistresses, Madame de Pompadour, who meddled in foreign policy, and her successor, Madame du Barry, an 'empty-headed, vulgar beauty', a former shopgirl and possibly prostitute, were no improvement. They were resented by aristocracy and bourgeois alike. Once called Louis *le Bien-Aimé* (Well-Beloved), the king became the most detested in French history. When he died his body was taken at night to Saint-Denis for burial, for fear that the cortège and coffin might be attacked by riotous Parisians.

## LOUIS AND THE *PARLEMENT* OF PARIS

Louis's one action of which Parisians approved was to abolish the *Parlement* of Paris, whose members, now wealthy and ennobled, worked mainly in the interests of privilege. In 1753 the archbishop of Paris banned the fundamentalist and anti-establishment Catholic Jansenists from confession. Louis approved it but the *Parlement* condemned the ban. The king ordered the arrest and exile of *parlementaires* and certain city officials – they returned a few months later, a reconciliation in honour of the birth of Louis's heir. There was co-operation of a sort until 1771, when after another clash Louis abolished the *Parlement* altogether. Louis XVI revived it in 1774, which was a mistake: the *parlementaires* rejected every government effort at resolving pressing social and economic problems, thus contributing signally to the coming of revolution.

## THE URBAN ENVIRONMENT

Visitors responded to *ancien régime* Paris with its half-million plus population in radically different language. To the Abbé Expilly Paris 'passes, and with reason, for one of the most beautiful, the richest, the most populated, the most flourishing, and one of the biggest cities of Europe'. To philosopher Jean-Jacques Rousseau, it was a city of 'small, dirty and stinking streets, ugly black houses, an air of filth, poverty, beggars, carters, sewing women, women hawking tisanes [barley water] and old hats'. Depending on the quarters visited, both descriptions were true.

## THE ENLIGHTENMENT

The Rococo, 'elegant, light and airy,' with decorative swirls and curves in art, architecture and music, replaced the symmetry characteristic of seventeenth-century classicism. Rococo was well represented in Paris

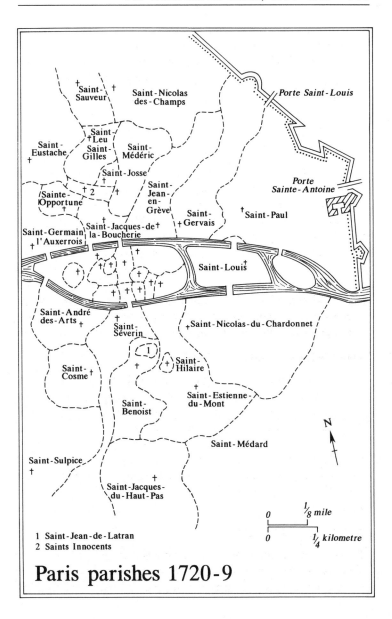

Porte Saint-Louis

Saint-Sauveur

Saint-Nicolas des-Champs

Saint-Leu

Saint-Eustache

Saint-Gilles

Saint-Médéric

Saint-Josse

Porte Sainte-Antoine

Sainte-Opportune

2

Saint-Jean-en-Grève

Saint-Gervais

Saint-Paul

Saint-Germain l'Auxerrois

Saint-Jacques-de-la-Boucherie

Saint-Louis

Saint-André des-Arts

Saint-Séverin

Saint-Nicolas-du-Chardonnet

1

Saint-Cosme

Saint-Hilaire

Saint-Benoist

Saint-Estienne-du-Mont

N

Saint-Médard

Saint-Sulpice

Saint-Jacques-du-Haut-Pas

0   1/8 mile

0   1/4 kilometre

1  Saint-Jean-de-Latran
2  Saints Innocents

# Paris parishes 1720-9

(Robert le Lorrain's bas-relief horse on the Hôtel de Rohan stables, for example), where it complemented the Paris-centred Enlightenment, that 'attempt to free the human mind from long centuries of enslavement to authority of all kinds'. Intellectuals of the Enlightenment went beyond the systems of their rationalist predecessors and demanded specific solutions to specific problems. In the first half of the century they were at risk: sacrilege was punishable by burning, speaking impiously of religion warranted a life sentence in the galleys, and printing establishments were regularly suppressed. However, censorship relaxed after 1740, at least to the extent that it was honoured in the breach as much as in the observance, and the Enlightenment took off.

## THE *SALONS* AND THE PHILOSOPHES

In Paris, intellectuals, called *philosophes*, frequented each other's company, usually in the *salons* of such aristocratic or *haute* bourgeois women as Ninon de Lenclos, Madame du Deffand, Madame d'Épinay, Madame Necker and Julie de l'Espinasse, among many others, who provided a venue for the intellectuals and contributed to the flow of ideas and wit. The *salons* may have encouraged the decline of censorship after 1740; it was one thing to quash a publisher in the Latin Quarter, it was quite another to interfere with doings in a Marais or Faubourg Saint-Germain *hôtel*. *Philosophes* were not uniformly tolerated, however. In 1726, the Chevalier de Rohan had Voltaire beaten up for writing witticisms at his expense, and Jean-Jacques Rousseau's *Émile* was condemned and burned at Paris.

Voltaire, the son of a Paris bourgeois, and Rousseau are the names most nearly synonymous with the Enlightenment. Other important *philosophes* included Diderot, a principal founder of the *Encyclopédie*, Condillac, Condorcet, Helvétius, D'Alembert and La Mettrie, among others. They were much influenced by such English philosophers and thinkers as John Locke and Isaac Newton, and in turn greatly influenced the likes of King Frederick II of Prussia – and the makers of the Revolution of 1789.

## NEW BUILDING

Private *hôtel* building continued in the *ancien régime*, the aristocracy in

Faubourg Saint-Germain and the merely rich in Faubourg Saint-Honoré, north of the Champs-Elysées in Le Roule. Hôtel du Maréchal Tallard, Hôtel Biron, Hôtel de Choiseul-Praslin, and Hôtel d'Evreux and Hôtel de Matignon (respectively residences for French presidents and premiers) were notable early examples. So, too, was the Palais Bourbon, built for one of Louis XIV's illegitimate daughters and now, much expanded and altered, the home of the Assemblée Nationale. Later examples include Madame de Staël's Hôtel de Salm, which became headquarters of the Legion of Honour, and Hôtel d'Hallwyl and Hôtel de Masseran which Marshall Dill described as examples of conspicuous consumption on the eve of revolution.

Public building also continued. Jacques-Ange Gabriel designed Place Louis XV (now Place de la Concorde) in 1748, capped off by a huge statue of the king to which disgruntled Parisians immediately attached placards describing the king's indifference to the plight of the poor, his cowardice and his vices. Gabriel also designed the building east of the square which houses the French navy department, Hôtel Crillon to the west where the US delegation to the 1919 Peace Conference was based, and Hôtel de la Vrillière, now part of the US Embassy. A new church for Sainte-Geneviève was started by Jacques-Germain Soufflot in 1758, on Mont Sainte-Geneviève, and a number of churches were completed in the 1760s. Pont-Louis XV (Pont de la Concorde), the École Militaire on the Champ-de-Mars, and the École de Médecine near Boulevard Saint-Michel were finished in the 1780s. Meanwhile the Palais de Justice and the Collège de France were renovated, *hôpitals* were constructed in Faubourg Saint-Antoine and Faubourg Saint-Honoré, and a new mint, the Hôtel des Monnaies, was built on the Quai Conti. The sixteen-mile (25 km) wall, the infamous Enceinte des Fermiers Généraux for tax collection, was finished in 1789, just in time for the revolution which was directed in part against the purpose for which it was raised.

## *The People of Paris in the Ancien Régime*

As always there were rich and poor in Paris; however, under the *ancien régime* the division between rich and poor was wider than ever.

## WORKERS AND IDLERS

Both the working and idle poor were worse off than in their grand-parents' time, and there was more moralizing about them. Physician Philippe Hecquet described the idle poor *(les misérables)* as debauched, immoral and deserving only of prison or workhouse. They 'only exist to the shame of humanity,' he wrote, 'while the [workers] ... are part of the order of political economy.' That meant workers quite properly could 'sweat all day for a loaf of bread', but it was improper that they be tempted by need to steal it.

Workers divided generally between skilled and unskilled, the former usually guild-associated, the latter free labourers who did whatever menial task came to hand. They were forbidden to strike, but did so anyway and occasionally were successful – a sign of the times perhaps.

An itinerant wood-seller

The gauze workers won a wage increase in 1757, the journeymen book binders a two-hour work-day reduction (from sixteen to fourteen) in 1776, and in 1785 masons, stone cutters and their labourer assistants forced the *Parlement* to revoke a pay cut set by the Chambre Royale des Bâtiments.

Meanwhile, strikes notwithstanding, workers were poorly paid, worked long hours, lived in appalling tenements, and ate what they could afford, which rarely included meat. Mutton and lamb at 7–9 sous per pound, and ham and bacon at 12–14, were well beyond their means. They also suffered a high death-rate from such diseases as smallpox, which spread easily in their crowded districts and for which medical treatment was almost non-existent. In 1758 Arnault de Nobleville described bleeding and purging as almost the only medical remedies that were practised among the poor. An exception was this bizarre treatment for pleurisy: 'Take a live pigeon, cut it down the back lengthwise: place it still warm on the aching side ... and leave it there for 18 or 20 hours until the bad odour forces you to remove it.' Given such conditions, it was mainly immigration from the countryside that kept Paris from actually losing population in the eighteenth century.

## EATING HABITS OF THE RICH AND FAMOUS

The Paris rich, aristocrats or *haut* bourgeois, lived at least as well as their grandparents. This is clear from their dining habits. A typical *haut*-bourgeois menu included: first course, two soups, roast beef, two hors d'oeuvres; second course, veal roast with truffles, lamb chops with basil, duck, poulard; third course, two roasts, three sweets, two salads; and fourth course, fresh fruit, compôte of apple, compôte of pears, biscuits, chestnuts, gooseberry jam and apricot marmalade. No wonder the image emerged of 'greedy, gluttonous, gout-ridden and corrupt rich', or that the criminals who stole from them should become folk heroes.

The working poor were increasingly contemptuous of laws that favoured the privileged, and public executions – 108 in 1775–6 alone – simply made heroes of those executed, or else turned those who watched into a mob. A coachman who had stolen an item of 30 sous value from his master was being whipped in front of the master's house, but in the opinion of the mistress not hard enough. The 4,000 spec-

tators turned on her, forced entry into the house, broke windows, set
fire to the master's carriages and dragged them burning down the street.
This occurrence was merely typical.

## CARTOUCHE

Louis-Dominique Cartouche was the greatest criminal hero of
eighteenth-century Paris, the subject of poems, portraits and even a
play. A cooper's son, he grew up in the Foire Saint-Laurent area,
travelled for five years with a band of gypsies, learned stealing to
provide for an indigent lover, was imprisoned by his father as an object
lesson and then escaped, worked for a time in an army press gang,
served in the army himself, and finally returned to terrorize Paris with a
gang of 200 hoodlums, recruited mainly from among the labouring
poor. They mostly stole from the rich, which gained a sort of Robin
Hood image for their leader. Cartouche was audacious, essentially non-
violent, gallant to women, loyal to his equals, contemptuous of his
betters, and was brave under torture; on the whole an attractive
character whom poor Parisians saw as their champion against the
injustices of privilege and wealth. A large crowd attended his execution.

## POPULAR ENTERTAINMENT

Paris fairs, wrote historian Robert Isherwood, generated a 'marketplace
culture ... built on humorous mockery of the ranks, restraints and
privileges of the official world'. In a variety of plays, dances, acrobatic
entertainments and the like, much of it in the *commedia dell'arte* mode,
audiences were treated to erotic posturing, grotesque grimacing,
insulting language, and activities representing eating and defecating.
Much of it was close to pornography. In the play *Le Marchand de merde*,
for example, a rascal, Gilles, defecates each day on the doorstep of
Léandre. Arlequin enters the scene to persuade Gilles that his excre-
ment is actually a saleable commodity, and that he should become a
*marchand de merde*, at ten écus the barrel. No doubt audiences were
delighted when Gilles offers his product to an apothecary, saying: '*Qui
veut de ma merde? ... C'est de la fraiche*' (Who wants my shit? It's fresh),
and the apothecary flails him with a stick in response.

All of this was a send-up of bourgeois convention conflated with the duplicity commonplace in the Paris commercial world. The fairs were attended by a cross-section of Paris society. The better elements apparently found enjoyment in such irreverent entertainment, even though much of it was at their expense. Of course, many of these elements were to laugh out of the other side of their faces after the summer of 1789.

# CHAPTER FIVE

# Revolution and Empire, 1789–1815

'When Paris sneezes, France catches cold,' the saying goes. In the summer of 1789, 88 per cent of a Parisian worker's income went to buy bread. Paris sneezed.

## The Palais-Royal: Birthplace of a Revolution

This palace and grounds sported cafés, wine shops, restaurants, gambling dens, brothels, a fashionable theatre, and political agitators whose antics both astounded and alarmed English traveller Arthur Young. In his words:

> The coffee-houses in the Palais-Royal ... are not only crowded within, but other expectant crowds are at the doors and windows, listening *à gorge déployée* [open-mouthed] to certain orators, who from chairs or tables harangue each his little audience.... I am all amazement at the ministry permitting such nests and hot-beds of sedition and revolt....

In a very real sense, the Palais Royal was the birthplace of the French Revolution. Such pamphlets as Abbé Siéyès' *What is the Third Estate?*, and newspapers like Jean-Paul Marat's *L'Ami du Peuple* and Jacques-René Hébert's *Le Père Duchesne*, circulated freely and in abundance. They were perhaps the first channels of mass propaganda, combining with the impassioned public oratory of the agitators to inflame discontented Parisians on the eve of revolution.

POLITICAL CLUBS

Political activists formed political clubs, named for their meeting places:

the Feuillants at the Feuillant monastery (pulled down later by Napoleon) on the corner of the Rue de Rivoli and the Rue de Castiglione; the Cordeliers in the former Franciscan monastery on the Left Bank; and the Jacobins in the old Dominican convent house half-way between Place Vendôme and the Church of Saint-Roch, north of the Rue Saint-Honoré. Ironically, these religious houses gave their names to clubs whose members were deists, revolutionary anti-clerics and/or atheists.

## Louis XVI and Marie-Antoinette, 1774–1793

This unfortunate pair had been welcomed to the throne by thousands of cheering Parisians; vast crowds of common people lined the streets as they progressed through the capital. Marie-Antoinette wrote to her mother that, though 'crushed by taxation', the people 'were greatly pleased' to see them. 'How fortunate to be in a position in which one can gain widespread affection at so little cost,' she added. Little cost to the new queen, perhaps, but much to the working poor whose taxes paid for the extravaganza.

Marie-Antoinette was not good at public relations. She looked silly 'disporting herself as a dairy maid among well-scrubbed cows' in the farmhouse constructed for her in the grounds at Versailles. Worse, she alienated those around her, who then spread such outlandish rumours as that she slept with both regiments of guardsmen and lesbian lovers. By 1789 she was known simply as 'l'Autrichienne', the Austrian woman, and while she probably never said that the Parisian poor could eat cake if they had no bread, she was believed to have said it and that was what mattered.

Her husband, meanwhile, was ill-equipped either by temperament or intellect to deal with the massive debts, food shortages and riots, the uncooperative *Parlement* of Paris, and rising unemployment. Moreover, he got bad advice from his brother, the reactionary count of Artois (later Charles X), and his cousin, the conspiratorial and ambitious duke of Orléans, who owned the Palais-Royal. Between 1787 and 1789, the king was let down equally by an Assembly of Notables, the *Parlement* (which approved taxes only on the lower classes), and the weather. A

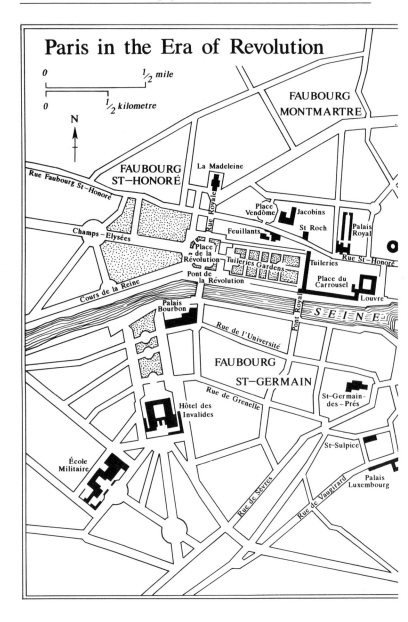

# Paris in the Era of Revolution

0        ½ mile

0        ½ kilometre

N

FAUBOURG MONTMARTRE

Rue Faubourg St-Honoré

FAUBOURG ST-HONORÉ

La Madeleine

Rue Royale

Place Vendôme

Jacobins

Champs-Elysées

Feuillants

St Roch

Palais Royal

Place de la Révolution

Tuileries Gardens

Tuileries

Rue St-Honoré

Pont de la Révolution

Place du Carrousel

Cours de la Reine

Palais Bourbon

Pont Royal

Louvre

SEINE

Rue de l'Université

FAUBOURG ST-GERMAIN

Rue de Grenelle

St-Germain-des-Prés

Hôtel des Invalides

St-Sulpice

École Militaire

Rue de Sèvres

Rue de Vaugirard

Palais Luxembourg

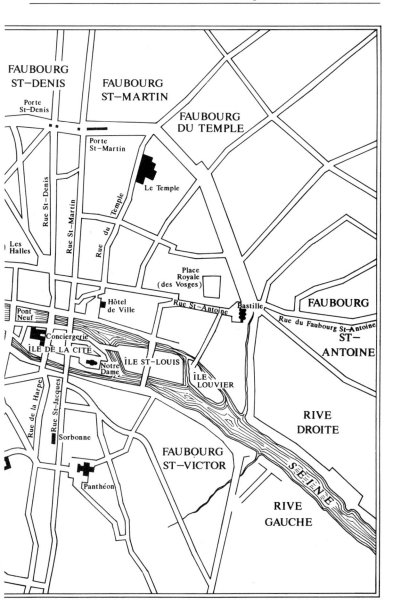

FAUBOURG
ST–DENIS

FAUBOURG
ST–MARTIN

FAUBOURG
DU TEMPLE

Porte
St–Denis

Porte
St–Martin

Le Temple

Rue St–Denis

Rue St–Martin

Rue du Temple

Les
Halles

Place
Royale
(des Vosges)

Hôtel
de Ville

Rue St–Antoine

Bastille

FAUBOURG

Pont
Neuf

Rue du Faubourg St–Antoine

ST–
ANTOINE

Conciergerie

ÎLE DE LA CITÉ

ÎLE ST–LOUIS

Notre
Dame

ÎLE
LOUVIER

Rue de la Harpe

Rue St–Jacques

RIVE
DROITE

Sorbonne

FAUBOURG
ST–VICTOR

S E I N E

Panthéon

RIVE
GAUCHE

cold winter was followed by bad harvests and bread riots. Paris was on the edge of revolt. As a last resort Louis summoned the États-Généraux (Estates General).

## Liberté, Fraternité, Égalité

The Estates General represented the clergy, nobility and commons. So far as anyone knew (the Estates had last met in 1614), each of these three Estates voted as a block.

### THE TENNIS COURT OATH

They assembled at Versailles on 5 May 1789. From the start block voting was not acceptable to the Third Estate, the commons, who represented 96 per cent of the population. They demanded a National Assembly with one vote per member, and were backed by such defectors from the first two Estates as the Abbé Siéyès and the count of Mirabeau. The nobility rejected the change, the clergy temporized over it, and the government did nothing at all. Finally Louis agreed to a royal session with all three Estates, where he would pronounce on the question.

However, on the morning of 20 June the Salle des Menu Plaisirs, where the Third Estate met, was closed to prepare for the royal session. No one informed Jean-Sylvain Bailly, its president, and when the deputies arrived they found the door locked and 200 soldiers on guard. Outraged, they went to a nearby tennis court and took an oath, as Bailly recalled it, 'never to break up and to meet wherever circumstances dictate, until the constitution of the kingdom is established and consolidated on firm foundations. . . .'

On 23 June Louis spoke to the Estates, and his words virtually repudiated the Third Estate and sustained privilege. Moreover he demanded that the Assembly rubber-stamp policies advanced by his ministers, and warned: 'If you abandon me in such a worthy enterprise, I alone will achieve the welfare of my people.' Perceiving this as a threat to dissolve the Estates General, someone – perhaps Mirabeau – shouted '*A bas, Louis!*' Eventually the king gave in, and the Estates General became the National Assembly, and finally the Constituent Assembly.

But first there were those Parisians whose interests were more practical than theoretical.

## THE *SANS-CULOTTES*

The *sans-culottes* (literally, those who wore long trousers as opposed to knee breeches) wanted an end to hunger, poverty and oppression. '[If] we don't rise up against the rich, we should all be done for,' they cried, as they roamed the streets calling for Parisians to support the Third Estate. Rumours spread that the Estates General would be shut down, that speculators would exploit famine to raise the price of bread, that foreign troops would shell Paris from the heights of Montmartre, and much more. In fact Louis had surrounded the city with 20,000 soldiers, and on 11 July dismissed Baron Necker, his principal minister, whom the Parisians regarded as their last, best hope. Two days later, the Paris electorate threw royal city government out of the Hôtel de Ville and elected a Permanent Committee. It immediately created a Milice Parisienne (citizens' militia), which three days later became the Garde Nationale (National Guard) under the marquis of Lafayette, former aide to General George Washington at Valley Forge.

Meanwhile mobs rampaged through the city, opened debtors' prisons and sparked riots among the criminals of the Châtelet. On 14 July agitators in the Palais-Royal urged the citizens 'to arms!'

## THE BASTILLE

The citizens responded by attacking Les Invalides, from which they looted 32,000 muskets and 10,000 pounds of gunpowder, and then crossed the river to besiege the Bastille. That fortress prison contained an arsenal and, it was thought, large crowds of political prisoners. Four different delegations from the Permanent Committee appealed to Governor Launay to surrender, but to no avail. In the afternoon the militia breached the outer defences and trained cannons on the drawbridge to the inner courtyards. The garrison, wrote militiaman Jean-Baptiste Humbert, 'began to attack with musket fire', and in return the militia fired their cannons, about six shots each, Humbert recalled. Meanwhile Launay threatened to blow up the powder magazines, which would have demolished the fortress and much of the

The Bastille

surrounding neighbourhood. His troops grew mutinous and demanded that he surrender instead. He agreed, once he had been promised that the garrison would not be harmed.

The promise was not kept. Six of the soldiers were later killed, as was Launay. Edward Rigby, an English physician making his way along the Rue Saint-Honoré, perceived that the faces around him were agitated and even alarmed. '[As] we pressed more to the centre of the crowd we ... perceived two bloody heads raised on pikes, which were said to be the heads of the Marquis de Launay, governor of the Bastille, and of Monsieur Flesselles, *Prévôt des Marchands*. It was a chilling and horrid sight!'

The Bastille had 'fallen' and its prisoners were released. They were only seven in number, including four cheque forgers and what Alfred Cobban described as 'a desiccated aristocrat'. All the same, the French Revolution had now truly begun, and propagandists soon exaggerated the numbers of Bastille inmates into the hundreds and celebrated the heroic action of the revolutionaries who had released them. July 14 would henceforth be the day when the revolution began. A year later the Bastille was razed to the ground, a symbolic blow against the old regime. It may be noted that the murder of Prévôt Flesselles marked the passing of his ancient office, and on 17 July Jean-Sylvain Bailly became the first *maire* (mayor) of Paris.

## *Women of the Revolution*

Théroigne de Méricourt was in the thick of Palais-Royal agitation, and became the unofficial 'leader' of those *sans-culottes* who crowded the galleries of the Manège, the riding school next to the Tuileries where the Constituent Assembly met after it moved to Paris. 'People were speaking against the aristocrats,' she wrote. 'I joined in too, and that in no uncertain terms.' Likewise Marie-Jeanne Roland, a leading light of the Girondins, and Olympe de Gouges, a Parisian playwright and author of *The Rights of Women* which echoed the revolutionary *Declaration of the Rights of Man*. Both were later guillotined. Madame de Staël, daughter of Baron Necker, emerged a decade later as a principal critic of Napoléon's authoritarian and anti-feminist policies. Meanwhile, 'mixed' political clubs formed, such as the Société Fraternelle des Patriotes des Deux Sexes, and others that were for women only, like Pauline Léon's Société des Républicaines-Révolutionnaires. The revolution did not achieve gender equality, but the participation of women guaranteed that rights for women could never again be completely ignored.

### OCTOBER DAYS

No single action involving Parisian women was more significant than the march to Versailles of 5–6 October. It began as a bread riot in the Place de Grève 'in the hope of hanging a baker accused of false weights', said one source. National Guardsmen rescued the baker, but church bells rang alarms, more women appeared, and the mood of the crowd turned ugly as it descended upon the Hôtel de Ville. Stanislaus Maillard, a 'hero' of the Bastille siege, arrived to find the building taken over by 'a multitude of women who wanted no men amongst them and kept on saying that the Ville was made up of aristocrats'. He persuaded them not to burn the building, but rather to march to Versailles with a petition for the king and the Assembly. Grudgingly they agreed, and 'elected' Maillard their leader. The women crossed to the Cité, then back over the Pont-Neuf to the Right Bank, marched past the Louvre and through the Tuileries gardens, into the Champs-Elysées, and finally out of the city towards Versailles.

More women, and a few men, joined them. In Maillard's description:

> I saw arriving from all directions detachments of women armed with broomsticks, cudgels, pitchforks, swords, pistols, and muskets.... All the houses were closed up, in fear, no doubt, of pilfering. The women in spite of that, went and knocked on every door and when someone refused to open, they wanted to break it down.

At Versailles the crowd mingled with the Assembly while Maillard presented their petition. A deputation was selected to wait on the king, and the rest, ill-fed because the palace was not prepared for so many guests and uncomfortable because it was raining, bedded down in a courtyard.

In the morning the women broke into the palace, where things immediately got out of hand. A newspaper, *Révolutions de Paris*, described it in this language:

> The people scattered out in the streets; they saw one of the bodyguard at a window ... of the château, they provoked him, they taunted him; the madman loads his musket, fires, and kills the son of a Parisian saddler, soldier of the National Guard; immediately the people burst into the château, search for the culprit.... One of the bodyguard is dragged to the foot of the staircase in the marble courtyard; his head is cut off....

More deaths followed on both sides, until the royal family appeared on a balcony with Lafayette. The women shouted, 'To Paris!' The king donned a revolutionary red, white and blue cockade, and agreed to accompany them to 'my good city of Paris'. The procession set off.

Along the way, some of the crowd were in good spirits and cried out '*Vive la reine*'; others made indecent gestures (a drawing from the period shows *sans-culottes* women 'mooning' the monarchy, but that was perhaps some other occasion). One man fired his gun over Marie-Antoinette's head. Finally they arrived in Paris and the royals were installed in the Tuileries, never again to see Versailles.

Marshall Dill found the October days to be among the most 'fearsome episodes' of the revolution, precisely because of the nature of the *sans-culottes* women. '[There] is something particularly frightening about a Parisian virago,' he wrote. 'If you don't believe that, take a look at some of the steely-faced females who invariably preside over the cash registers in almost every bar, tobacco shop, or small restaurant in Paris.' Be that as it may, Parisians now understood the force of insurrectionary politics, and got the idea that Paris had a special role to play in the revolution.

# *A King in Paris*

On 14 July 1790 Louis and Marie-Antoinette were among the 200,000 who gathered on the Champ-de-Mars for the first Bastille Day celebration, the Fête de la Fédération. Prince Talleyrand, bishop of Autun as well as a member of the Assembly, celebrated mass at the massive Altar of the Fatherland. Louis pledged to maintain constitutional rule in France.

### FLIGHT TO VARENNES

However, Louis only appeared reconciled to his new and diminished role. In truth he hated it, and maintained contact with anti-revolutionary exiles such as the count of Artois, and foreign anti-revolutionary rulers such as his brother-in-law, Leopold II of Austria. His hope, encouraged by the queen, was to leave France and organize a restoration of the 'ancient rights and dignities of the house of Bourbon'. Meanwhile the Assembly was divided between constitutional monarchists behind Mirabeau and Lafayette, and republicans led by Georges

Danton and Maximilien Robespierre. Then Mirabeau died in 1791 and Louis lost his strongest supporter among the early revolutionaries. He now became determined to leave the country.

The plan was to slip away at night, in disguise, in a coach to Varennes and on to safety in Brussels. Unfortunately, Marie-Antoinette did not fully grasp the need for bóth anonymity and organization. The royal family travelled in an outsized coach pulled by eight horses, with coachmen, outriders and others, all wearing royal livery. A second coach followed with two ladies-in-waiting, trunks filled with ball gowns, a silver service for dining en route, and a wine cellar. Needless to say, progress was slow. Moreover, on the day of departure, 20 June 1791, they were hours late getting started. In one of those ironic twists upon which events often hang, the royalist cavalry who waited to meet and protect them finally gave up and went home, only an hour before the royals appeared.

A revolutionary at Sainte-Menehould recognized the king and raised the alarm. When the family arrived at Varennes, they were detained until Louis admitted his identity. Then they were returned to Paris. Along the way the country population insulted and scorned them; when they entered the city there was only silence, by order of the Assembly which had put it about that the family had been kidnapped. Louis was restored to his duties, on the promise that he would be loyal and faithful to the new constitution.

## MASSACRE OF THE CHAMP-DE-MARS

It was not enough. Republican sentiment was spreading. On 22 June the Cordeliers took an 'oath of tyrannicide' aimed at the king, and Danton publicly called constitutional monarchists in the Assembly traitors. *Révolutions de Paris* added its voice: 'It is time, it is more than time, to strike a great blow. Let the head of Louis fall . . . let the throne and all the high and mighty baubles of royalty be consigned to the flames!' On 20 July a Cordelier petition to end the monarchy was escorted by 50,000 republicans from the Porte Saint-Antoine to the Champ-de-Mars, where it was placed on the Altar of the Fatherland. Unfortunately two louts were discovered under the altar, where they had crawled in order to have a look up women's dresses. The crowd

killed them in the belief that they were royalist agents. The National
Guard then fired on the crowd, killing fifty and wounding many more.
In the aftermath the government cracked down on both the radical left
and the royalist right, but the damage was done. Republican sentiment
spread still further.

## THE NATION AT WAR

In April 1792 Louis's in-laws organized a coalition of states to rescue
him from the revolution. He was compelled to read a declaration of
war against them. The cry '*aux armes, Citoyens*' went out, and the
people responded. As they marched off to war, some of them sang a
song, penned by Rouget de Lisle, which came to be known as 'La
Marseillaise', and in due course as the French national anthem.

Louis was understandably half-hearted in prosecuting the war, and
on 20 June dismissed the Girondins (the first revolutionary party to
dominate the Assembly) in the war ministry for being overly enthusiastic. Immediately, 8,000 Parisians stormed the Assembly and petitioned for their reinstatement. They then invaded the Tuileries and
forced the king to stand on a bench while the same petition was read to
him. When the crowd shouted '*Vive la Nation!*' he replied, 'Yes, *vive la
Nation*. The nation has no better friend than me.' Louis was required to
prove this by putting on a red cap of liberty and toasting the nation
from a wine bottle someone thrust into his hand: 'People of Paris, I
drink to your health and to that of the French nation.'

## ATTACK ON THE TUILERIES

It was still not enough. On 3 July the duke of Brunswick's manifesto
warning that the allied coalition would destroy Paris if any harm came
to Louis or his family was published in the city. The next day the
Assembly was handed a petition demanding the king be deposed, and
on the day after the *sans-culottes* threatened to attack the Tuileries if the
king was not deposed by midnight on 9 August. He was not, and an
armed, angry mob appeared before the palace. When they advanced
the Swiss guards fired; the mob fired back. In the ensuing battle 300
*sans-culottes* were killed, along with 600 guards whose bodies were

mutilated by the attackers. The mob then plundered the palace, and not for the last time.

The king was with the Assembly, where he thought he was safe. Not quite. Having finished with the Tuileries, the *sans-culottes* crowded into the Manège, hurling insults and roughing up anyone who got in their way. The Assembly got around the crisis by placing the royal family in the hands of the Commune, the new revolutionary city government recently installed in the Hôtel de Ville, which imprisoned them in the Temple, that former fortress of the Knights Templar. With that the monarchy was effectively finished, though it remained for both king and queen to be tried and executed.

## THE SEPTEMBER MASSACRE

On 2 September allied forces laid siege to Verdun, which was close enough to Paris to cause alarm, if not panic. The idea circulated that a conspiracy was afoot, generated from within the city's prisons, to 'betray the revolution' to its enemies. The *sans-culottes* went on a rampage of killing, which the Commune sanctioned largely because it could not prevent it. The Conciergerie, the Abbaye prison adjacent to Saint-Germain-des-Prés, La Force in the Marais, La Salpêtrière in the Faubourg Saint-Antoine, and the Châtelet were attacked with the express purpose of killing the inmates. Over twenty-four hours 1,200 inmates were dragged from their cells into prison courtyards, where they were bludgeoned, shot, knifed, strangled, burned alive, or killed in any way the mob chose. Others, curiously and for no apparent reason, were spared and actually escorted home by people smeared with the blood of those less fortunate.

Those killed included nobles, clergy, wealthy merchants, and criminals major and minor, including a woman incarcerated for having murdered her lover, who was killed with special brutality. So, too, was the Princess Lamballe, friend of Marie-Antoinette, who was stripped, raped, decapitated and mutilated, and her remains paraded beneath the queen's window in the Temple. The horror of the massacres was well expressed by the brother-in-law of one M. d'Espréménil, who recalled that 'as he came out of the Châtelet . . . he plunged up to his knees in a stream of blood'. The British ambassador's comment: 'What a people!'

## THE FIRST REPUBLIC

After the massacre, this mob became part of the citizen army that marched to Valmy, where it faced and defeated the seasoned, disciplined professionals of the allied coalition. Meanwhile, at the urging of the Commune the Constituent Assembly was replaced by an elected National Convention, which formally abolished the monarchy on 22 September and declared that day the beginning of Year I of the French Republic. The Convention was dominated by the extremist Jacobins, led by Danton and Robespierre. It set up a Revolutionary Tribunal 'to try enemies of the new order', and a Committee of Public Safety charged with taking all measures necessary to preserve the revolution.

## THE TRIAL AND EXECUTION OF LOUIS CAPET

But first there was the matter of the king. He was tried by the Convention in December 1792 as 'Louis Capet', so-called because all kings since Hugh Capet were declared to have ruled illegally. The Convention voted unanimously that the king was guilty of crimes against the people of France; his real crime simply was that he was the king. The subsequent vote to execute him was passed by only 387 to 334, with the moderate Girondins leading the opposition. It was sufficient, and on 21 January 1793 'Louis Capet' was guillotined in the Place de la Révolution (as the Place Louis XV had been renamed; now Place de la Concorde). Ironically, prior to its adoption by the Constituent Assembly on 25 April 1792, Louis had approved this instrument, named for Dr Joseph Guillotine of the medical faculty of the University, as a more 'humane' means of execution.

## A NEW CONSTITUTION – BUT NOT YET

On 10 August 1793 the new constitution was presented in a great ceremony at the Altar of the Fatherland in the Champ-de-Mars. There was a caution: the constitution would be put into effect only when the war was over. In fact, it never was put into effect.

The Guillotine – ironically approved by Louis XVI as a more
'humane' form of execution

## The Terror

In September 1793 *sans-culottes* forced their way into the Convention,
demanding both bread and that 'the enemy at home' be suppressed.
Having no better control over the disastrous economic situation than
had its predecessor, the Convention could only act with respect to the
latter. This was the beginning of the Terror, during which perhaps
20,000 people were guillotined in Paris alone.

## THE COMMITTEE OF PUBLIC SAFETY

A committee of twelve men, including Robespierre, the 'sea-green incorruptible', and Saint-Just, known as the 'Angel of Death', organized the Terror. They issued their proclamations and orders from the Hôtel de Ville, including directives to the Revolutionary Tribunal which was enlarged to handle the increased case-load. The Tribunal sat in an upper chamber of the Conciergerie, which still functions as a courtroom, and dispensed that justice which sent its recipients in wooden tumbrils along a route running from the Conciergerie through Les Halles, along the length of Rue Saint-Honoré to Sainte-Marie Madeleine, and then to the Place de la Révolution and the guillotine. It was not easy for anyone. 'I cannot personally be everywhere at once,' complained Citizen Sanson, Executor of Criminal Judgements in Paris. 'I need dependable people. For the public still wants to see us do a decent job. I have to pay for that.'

Why the Terror? The Committee of Public Safety was a wartime government, hard-pressed by the enemy coalition, and it was a revolutionary government which needed to destroy all its enemies – the privileged, profiteers and counter-revolutionaries. In the end, the Committee proceeded from a single-minded ideological world-view to which it maintained a ruthless commitment. Paris in 1793 was much like Geneva under Jean Calvin or Moscow under Joseph Stalin.

## DEATH IN REVOLUTIONARY PARIS

A wide variety of victims followed Louis to the guillotine. Marie-Antoinette went with dignity and a calm demeanour. The twenty-one leading Girondins were next, including Madame Roland who, upon seeing the wooden statue of liberty near the scaffold, exclaimed, 'Oh Liberty, what crimes are committed in thy name!' The duke of Orléans, now Philippe Égalité, had voted in the Convention for the king's death; now he joined him, dying with a bemused smile on his lips. Even Louis XV's last mistress, Madame du Barry, made the journey, but hardly with dignity; she had to be dragged kicking and screaming up the steps to the scaffold. There were also revolutionaries who had fallen out with Robespierre, the extreme anti-religious Hébertists,

Danton and Camille Desmoulins, for example, and poets and scientists – André Chénier and Lavoisier, among others – who had been declared enemies of the nation. Charlotte Corday was an unusual victim, in that she had actually committed a crime by murdering Jean-Paul Marat, the Jacobin propagandist, in his bathtub.

The most enduring vision that remains of this grim procession is perhaps that from Charles Dickens' *A Tale of Two Cities*, in which the notorious *tricoteuse*, Madame Defarge, the very type of the *sans-culottes* women of the October days, sits beneath the scaffold knitting red caps of liberty.

## THE TERROR FADES

Nothing lasts for ever, and when Robespierre himself made the final journey the Terror was over. Sickened by all of the blood-letting, Parisians supported a conspiracy hatched by Robespierre's enemies, Paul-François Barras, Jean-Lambert Tallien and Joseph Fouché. In July 1794 the conspirators got the Convention to arrest Robespierre. When an attempt by the Commune to raise a mob to save him failed to materialize, the Jacobin leader tried to kill himself, but only managed to blow away part of his jaw. That night he, Saint-Just, Georges Couthon and other members of the Committee of Public Safety were guillotined. Ironically, these were the only executions that Robespierre ever witnessed.

That Parisians were glad to see an end to the Terror is attested by a woman of the *sans-culottes* who, as Robespierre's tumbrel approached the Place de la Révolution, grasped the rail, thrust her face into his, and screamed: 'You monster spewed out of hell ... the thought of your execution makes me drunk with joy!' The next day a Paris newspaper proclaimed that 'the tyrant is no more', and described the city celebrating joyously.

# Recasting Paris

The revolution tried to remake Paris and France from the ground up, for the best of ideological reasons. The Christian calendar was outlawed; the names of months now reflected seasons. March was Ventôse (wind), May Floréal (flowers), July Thermidor (heat), and so on. All titles were abolished – even *monsieur* and *madame* became *citoyen* and *citoyenne* – and buildings and sites were renamed. The Tuileries became the National Palace, the Hôtel de Ville the House of the Commune, the Palais-Royal the Palace and Garden of Equality, the Champ-de-Mars the Field of Reunion, and the Place du Trône, where Louis XIV and his bride had been welcomed to Paris, the Place du Trône Renversé (Place of the Overturned Throne). None of this lasted. Nomenclature had returned to its original form by the time Napoléon emerged as leader.

## RELIGIOUS REPRESSION

All churches were to be destroyed, or else converted to some secular purpose. Only fourteen were actually pulled down before 1794, though many suffered damage, often at the hands of *sans-culottes* mobs who committed such acts as burning the relics of Sainte Geneviève on the Place de Grève. Other examples of either vandalism or desanctification included: carved woodwork pillaged from the churches of Saint-Jean and Saint-Gervais; carved bookcases looted from the Celestins convent ending up in the Bibliothèque Nationale; Saint-Paul's Church, where Rabelais was buried, was sold; the church and convent of l'Ave Maria was turned into a barracks, and Sainte-Chapelle into a storehouse for flour; the seminary of Saint-Firmin became a prison in which seventy-seven priests were later murdered; Saint-Germain-des-Prés was used first as a meeting hall for revolutionary sections, and later as a powder factory; and the new Church of Sainte-Geneviève, renamed the Panthéon, was made a mausoleum for French heroes. Meanwhile Notre-Dame Cathedral was converted into a 'Temple of Reason', where the *corps de ballet* of the Opéra performed a 'dance of Reason' in front of the high altar, 'their skirts fairly brushing against an overturned statue of the Virgin'.

## COLLEGES

Colleges of the University of Paris suffered also. Beauvais, Grassins, Reims and Tréguier were closed and sold. Montaigu was used as a hospital and barracks, until it was torn down to make way for the

Bibliothèque Sainte-Geneviève. The Sorbonne housed a factory, and Louis le Grand college was 'de-Jesuitized' and made the headquarters of the University. Écossais college served briefly as a prison.

That more damage was not done was owing to Alexandre Lenoir, art critic and antiquarian, who persuaded the Committee of Public Safety to authorize him to rescue whatever art work and decoration he could from rampaging mobs.

### JACQUES-LOUIS DAVID

This artist played a central role in revolutionary and imperial Paris and survived by taking whatever side was on top. For example, he designed the Festival of Reason in Notre-Dame Cathedral, sponsored by Pierre Chaumette and Jacques Hébert, both atheists. Then, after Chaumette and Hébert went to the guillotine, David designed the Festival of the Supreme Being in the Tuileries gardens for Robespierre, who was a deist. The first festival featured a temple dedicated to philosophy and a dance to honour it; the second displayed statues entitled Atheism, Ambition, Egotism, False Simplicity and Discord. Robespierre delivered a homily, then set fire to Atheism, revealing underneath a non-flammable statue of Wisdom. Though somewhat scorched, Wisdom seemed to produce a good effect.

David also sketched the likes of Marie-Antoinette and Danton on their way to the guillotine, and produced such paintings as *The Oath at the Tennis Court*, *The Death of Marat*, various portraits of Napoléon, and his coronation as emperor in Notre-Dame Cathedral. Jacques-Louis David truly was the artist of his times.

## *Transition*

With the Terror over, the Revolutionary Tribunal was abolished and the Committee of Public Safety lost much of its power. The Commune and the Jacobins were outlawed, and Paris prisons released hundreds of inmates. Parisian *jeunesse dorée* (gilded youth) set the tone for outrageously elaborate new fashions – referred to at the time as '*merveilleuses et incroyables*' – and for conspicuous consumption. They also formed counter-revolutionary gangs which, armed with truncheons, beat up *sans-culottes* and others who dared raise their voices in favour of a return to revolutionary policies.

The *jeunesse dorée* were well off; the *sans-culottes* were not. Inflation soared and bread was in short supply. In October 1795 they attempted to overthrow the Convention in protest against worsening conditions. The *sans-culottes* assembled in the Rue Saint-Honoré in front of Saint-Roch church, where Bishop Bossuet, the philosopher of Absolutism, was buried. However, the Convention was protected by soldiers. The insurrection ended when their young commander ordered his artillery to fire into the crowd. This was the famous 'whiff of grapeshot' that saved the Convention and launched Napoléon Bonaparte on his career.

## THE DIRECTORY

The Convention passed the Constitution of the Year III in 1795. It then disbanded in favour of a bicameral legislature consisting of the Council of Five Hundred and Council of Ancients. These set up the Directory, a committee of five men elected for short terms to exercise executive power. They included Paul Barras, Louis-Marie Lépeaux, Jean-François Reubell, Étienne Letourneur and Lazare Carnot. The Abbé Siéyès replaced Reubell in 1799.

The Directory worked out of the Palais du Luxembourg while the Councils were in the Tuileries. This government solved no major problems, and made no contribution to changing the capital, save for destroying churches and monastic buildings on an even greater scale. In the words of Marshall Dill: 'There is no spot to which one can point and say, "Paris owes this to the Directory." '

# *Bonaparte*

'It appears that France must soon be governed by a single despot ... a dictator produced by the revolution,' wrote Gouverneur Morris, the American ambassador. That dictator was Napoléon Bonaparte, brought to power by a *coup d'état* staged on 18th Brumaire (9 November) 1799.

## 18TH BRUMAIRE

Napoléon Bonaparte had distinguished himself as a general in Italy,

Austria and North Africa, where he won battles, made treaties, gained the devotion of his soldiers, looted, and generally made the inept Directory nervous. The Councils were nervous too, fearful of both royalist and Jacobin plots. They were not reassured by crowds outside the chamber chanting: 'Down with the thieves, the *chouans* [insurgents] and the traitors!', on an occasion when the Five Hundred refused the demand of Jacobin deputies to declare *la patrie en danger*. In October 1799 Napoléon returned from Egypt and was approached by his brothers, Lucien and Joseph, Abbé Siéyès, Paul Barras and others, to aid in a plan to strengthen the constitutional role of the executive. On 9 November, the Ancients put him in command of the Paris military district, and, under threat of a Jacobin plot to overthrow the government, transferred both councils to Saint-Cloud. Meanwhile the Directory – some of them reluctantly – resigned. Posters appeared proclaiming that 'Citizens, Bonaparte must be in Paris if we are to have peace!', words which in the context of Napoléon's campaigns could have had more than one meaning.

At Saint-Cloud it was discovered that the Jacobin plot was a hoax. The Five Hundred voted to uphold the constitution as written, while the Ancients wavered. Napoléon addressed both councils. However, he was no public speaker and his words were delivered in his rough Corsican accent. The Five Hundred shouted him down, jostled him, and he beat a retreat after appearing almost to faint.

Lucien saved the day, though Napoléon later claimed that he had saved Lucien. He told the council that an attempt had been made on Napoléon's life inside. They chased the deputies out, many departing through the windows with cries of 'Long live the Republic!' That night, a rump of both councils established a triumvirate of Siéyès, Roger Ducos and Napoléon to govern France.

Siéyès, author of radical pamphlets, member of the first National Assembly, the Directory, and now the triumvirate, was once asked what he did during the revolution. He responded: *'J'ai vécu'* (I survived).

## *The First Consul*

The councils were replaced by small commissions, and Napoléon took the post of First Consul, elected by popular vote. In February 1800, when he passed through the Carrousel en route to taking up residence in the Tuileries, he could see the liberty-trees and bullet-scarred walls which recalled the 'whiff of grapeshot'. The walls then also bore placards reading: 'Royalty has been abolished in France never to return.' Though not a Parisian, Napoléon was part of the city, having been trained at the École Militaire. He understood the importance of Paris to both the revolution and to France, and he would develop grandiose plans for remaking the city as an imperial centre. His 'whiff of grapeshot' was fired on behalf of the revolutionary government, and while he was no Jacobin, he was like the *sans-culottes* in that he, too, was rough around the edges and had little use for the old aristocracy, save as tools for his ambition.

When Napoléon came to Paris from his native Corsica, he brought his family with him – mother, brothers and sisters. Except when certain of them were off being kings in Spain or Holland, or the wives of princes in Germany, Italy and elsewhere, the Bonapartes lived in the Tuileries Palace. Despite occasional outbursts that inclined toward the peasant (or at least the Corsican, as some returned *émigrés* sniffed), they established a court of some elegance and refinement. Leo Gershoy described Paris style under the Bonapartes in this fashion:

> Madame de Campan, who had once been a lady-in-waiting to Marie-Antoinette, impressed the ways of good society upon the young ladies of the day, and the beautiful Madame de Récamier set the tone of refined *salon* life in Paris. Slowly Paris reasserted its pristine supremacy in politeness, in elegance of dress, and in the culinary arts.

## JOSEPHINE DE BEAUHARNAIS

Josephine, Viscountess Beauharnais, a Creole from Martinique, was among prisoners freed when the Terror ended. Her unhappy marriage to the Viscount Beauharnais produced two children, one of whom, Hortense, was the mother of Louis-Napoléon, the future Napoléon III. The marriage ended when the viscount joined his Girondin colleagues at the guillotine.

Josephine was Paul Barras' mistress, and friends with such leading revolutionary women as Madame Tallien. She met Napoléon in 1795, 'a lank, gangling little man, with piercing eyes, . . . [and] almost devoid of social grace'. He fell passionately in love with her, a love she did not return until she had taken stock of her increasingly difficult financial situation, and Barras had convinced her that the diminutive Corsican would be the greatest man in France. They were married in a civil ceremony near her house in the Rue Chantereine (now Rue de la Victoire). For the next several years the couple were the toast of Paris, and it was upon Josephine's head that Napoléon placed the crown of Empress of France in 1804.

BONAPARTE'S RULES

As consul and then emperor, Napoléon's foreign policy centred on conquest, annexation or domination, his domestic policy on pacification, organization and modernization. He ended civil strife, founded the Bank of France, encouraged commerce, raised the economy to heights it had not enjoyed since the middle years of Louis XIV's reign, created a national educational system, regularized relations with the Vatican, codified civil law (the famous Code Napoléon), and put Paris under the control of the Prefect of the Seine, which office had been created in 1790. He also organized the Prefecture of Police, responsible for public order. The two prefects performed the functions which had once belonged to the mayor. Napoléon's system was costly and authoritarian, and by the end of his reign he had reversed many advances in individual liberty made by the revolution, notably in terms of female liberation.

# Napoléon I

Napoléon's coronation took place on 2 December 1804 in Notre-Dame Cathedral. The day before, he was remarried, so to speak, to Josephine in a secret religious ceremony in the Tuileries chapel. This was done out of deference to Pope Pius VII, who was hesitating to attend the coronation out of loyalty to the Bourbons. In the end, he allowed ecclesiastical legitimization of the marriage to persuade him. Also Josephine, childless with Napoléon, feared that he might divorce her if there were no religious impedimenta. He did just that a few years later, for reasons of state. She was fortunate to be out of it.

The ceremony at Notre-Dame was elaborate, even gaudy, with a classical theme. New gowns for the ladies, flamboyant ceremonial uniforms for the gentlemen of the court, a train of inordinate length for Josephine (carried reluctantly by the jealous Bonaparte sisters, who agreed to do so only after a sharp reprimand from their imperial brother), and an ermine-trimmed velvet cloak and white-plumed black cap for Napoléon. The couple progressed from the Tuileries to Notre-Dame, where a mass was said. Napoléon then took the crown of laurel leaves, turned away from the pope and placed it on his own head. There was to be no question who ruled whom in this empire. After that Josephine knelt on a *prie-dieu* in a symbolically worshipful attitude at the emperor's feet (or so David recorded it), and Napoléon placed a crown on her head.

Napoléon's mother was absent, having made a point of delaying her arrival in Paris until after the ceremony was over. She neither trusted nor believed in all the imperial folderol her son was promoting. When people referred to his fame and glory she invariably replied: 'Provided it lasts.'

## PLOTS AND COUNTERPLOTS

Despite his popularity, Napoléon was never entirely secure. However, he was able to turn plots against his life to advantage. Conspirators ranged from Jacobins to royalists, and drew support from disgruntled veterans, Italian patriots and romantic artists. The plots never succeeded, either due to interior minister Fouché's army of informers, or to the ineptitude of the plotters. One plan was to stab Napoléon during a performance at the Opéra; another was to blow him up in the street; still another was to kidnap him en route to his château at Malmaison. None of these made it beyond the plotting stage. One which did was a bomb in the Rue Nicaise which exploded near Napoléon's carriage. It did him no harm but blew away more than forty houses, and killed or badly hurt more than seventy bystanders. He used the occasion as an excuse to tighten his grip on power.

The most notorious (for Napoléon's handling of it) conspiracy against him involved the duke of Enghien, Prince Condé's grandson and an outspoken royalist. He may or may not have been connected to a plan to kidnap Napoléon from Paris, and English agents may or may not have been involved. In any case Napoléon and Fouché decided that both allegations were true, and the duke, in exile in Baden, Germany, was kidnapped, brought to Paris and summarily shot. So much for the due-process aspects of the Napoléonic civil code. The coronation took place shortly afterward.

Both Fouché and foreign minister Talleyrand conspired with the English against Napoléon after 1806, but nothing came of it save that both were deprived of office and sent away. Both resurfaced during the Bourbon restoration when Napoléon had fallen.

## Napoléon's Paris

Napoléon spent his 'retirement' writing his memoirs on the island of St Helena, after his defeat at Waterloo. Of his contribution to Paris, he noted:

> ... the rebuilding of most of the churches pulled down during the Revolution, the building of new ones; the construction of many industrial establishments for putting an end to pauperism. The construction of the Louvre, of the public granaries, of the Bank, of the canal of the Ourcq; the water system of the city of Paris, the numerous sewers, the quays, the embellishments and monuments of that great city.

Not without exaggeration, but generally accurate. The Ourcq Canal supplied the bulk of Paris water until the 1850s (when Napoléon's nephew took a hand in further improvements), and was typical of Napoléon's practical mindedness.

Public building sometimes connected in Napoléon's mind with social problems. In 1803 he ordered: 'The winter will be ... severe. ... There must be plenty of employment in Paris. Push on with construction of the Ourcq canal, start work on the quays Desaix and d'Orsay. Pave the new streets, and find other work for the populace.' It may be said that both the common people and the bourgeoisie responded to Napoléon's energy from the start. Parisians voted 32,000 to 14 in favour of his constitution, while Paris bankers loaned him 12 million francs at the outset of his régime to get things rolling. After his victory at Marengo in 1800, Napoléon found his strongest support among the poorer – and most revolutionary – sections of the city.

BUILDINGS

At the Tuileries he rebuilt the chapel, theatre and council chamber where the Convention had sat, and added to the north gallery which was intended eventually to connect to the Louvre. He also raised the Arc de Triomphe du Carrousel (copied from the Arch of Septimus Severus in Rome). The architects Fontaine and Percier oversaw this work, which included tearing down old *hôtels* between the Tuileries and the Louvre, and renovating the Louvre itself. Meanwhile Napoléon filled the Louvre museum with paintings, decorative arts, books, manuscripts, jewellery, statuary and anything else he could steal in the course of his wars, including the famous bronze horses, taken from Saint Mark's basilica in Venice, with which he topped the Arc de Triomphe du Carrousel. The Venetians complained, of course, for their ancestors had gone to much trouble to steal the horses from Constantinople centuries before.

Napoléon had classical tastes, and the effect was to be seen in the façade he commissioned for the Palais Bourbon on the Left Bank, and in the buildings which house the stock exchange (Bourse) and the Banque de France near the Palais-Royal. In 1805 he installed the Institut de France in Mazarin's old Palais des Quatre Nations (where it remains), and in 1806 he sent orders from Poland that the Church of the Madeleine, just north of the present Place de la Concorde, should be completed as a 'temple of glory for the army'. It was still unfinished when he abdicated. He was going to build a palace for his heir, the King of Rome, born in 1811 to Marie-Louise of Austria (whom he married after divorcing Josephine). It was to have been a sort of House of Gold on a Palatine Hill, across from the Champ-de-Mars where now stands the Palais de Chaillot. The palace never got beyond the drawing board, which Marshall Dill believed was just as well. Napoléon was more than a little egocentric. He began the Pont d'Iéna connecting the Champ-de-Mars to the Right Bank, to commemorate his most famous victory over the Prussians.

## STREETS

Napoléon built new streets. The most important was the Rue de Rivoli, which stretched from Place de la Concorde to the west end of the Louvre. Both the Feuillants convent and the Manège were destroyed in the process, ending, as it were, a chapter in revolutionary history. In his time, Napoléon III extended this street to the Place de la Bastille. Next was the Rue de Castiglione, running north from the Rue de Rivoli to the Place Vendôme, and the Rue de la Paix (called Rue Napoléon until the emperor abdicated), running north also from Place Vendôme to the Place de l'Opéra. Napoléon directed that houses on his new streets be numbered even on one side, odd on the other, an innovation which apparently had not occurred to anyone before.

## MONUMENTS

In 1803 Napoléon ordered that 'there shall be erected in Paris, in the centre of the Place Vendôme, a column [like that] erected at Rome in

The Place Vendôme

honour of Trajan. The column shall be surrounded by a pedestal adorned with an olive wreath on which there shall be a statue of Charlemagne.' Not so. The column was raised, but with Napoléon on top. After that a most lively history: the Bourbons replaced Napoléon with a fleur-de-lis; Louis-Philippe replaced the fleur-de-lis with a different, lesser Napoléon; Napoléon III replaced this statue with a better one, which the Commune pulled down along with the column in 1871; the Third Republic found the pieces and put it all back, where it remains today, undisturbed even by the underground parking garage beneath it.

At the west end of the Champs-Elysées, the emperor began the Arc de Triomphe de l'Étoile which, like so much else, remained unfinished when he left France. Louis-Philippe finished it along with the Church of the Madeleine in the 1830s, and in 1923 a tomb of the French Unknown Soldier with an eternal flame was placed underneath. As one writer commented, this flame added an 'odour of sanctity' that since has been diluted by the odour of gasoline from what has become 'one of the most feverish and frightening traffic hazards in the world'.

Napoléon also started the Père Lachaise cemetery, named for the Jesuit priest who was Louis XIV's confessor.

# *The Fall of Bonaparte*

In 1812 Napoléon invaded Russia, hoping to make an end to what he considered Tsar Alexander I's betrayal of the Treaty of Tilsit. The invasion was a disaster. Out of 600,000 soldiers in the *Grande Armée* which attacked Russia, only 90,000 returned. Over the next two years the emperor was rarely in Paris, and the Parisians were fed a stream of propaganda in which such losses as the battle of Leipzig were made to sound otherwise.

PARIS INVADED

It was only a matter of time. The coalition of Russia, Prussia, Austria and Great Britain were closing in, the first three from the north and east, the British from the south-west. On 29 March 1814 the Prussians reached Paris. There was fighting in Montmartre on the 30th, in which citizens took part along with soldiers. The city surrendered on 31 March and the Prussian king entered Paris, greeted largely by silence 'except for a sprinkling of royalist applause'. Napoléon was then at Fontainebleau trying to save his régime. That was impossible. He abdicated the throne, and on 20 April was escorted to the south coast, to a ship and to the island of Elba, off the coast of Italy. Meanwhile Tsar Alexander arrived in Paris, where he was the house guest of Talleyrand in the Rue Saint-Florentin adjacent to the Place de la Concorde. The Senate formally deposed Napoléon Bonaparte as emperor of the French.

## LIBERATION AND RESTORATION

The allies came to Paris as liberators, they claimed, and certainly they initially treated the French with lenience. For this the war-weary Parisians were grateful. The allies insisted upon restoring the Bourbons, however, which was not so well received. Even so, a Russian Orthodox service of Thanksgiving was held on Easter Sunday on the Place de la Concorde, and two weeks after that Louis XVIII, corpulent, gouty, fearful of the future and prepared to accept the limitations of a constitutional monarch, entered the Tuileries. However, the family he brought with him were quarrelsome and anxious to re-establish their ancient privileges, which did not bode well for the future.

In February 1815 Napoléon escaped from Elba, and Europe held its breath. He arrived in France on 1 March; a Paris newspaper trumpeted the news: 'The Monster has Escaped!' A few days later the Bourbons climbed back into their carriages and trundled out of the city, following news that former Napoléonic Marshal Ney, who had promised to bring Napoléon to Paris 'in a cage', had gone over to him. (Ney was executed for his pains, in the Avenue l'Observatoire, where Bonapartists raised a statue in his memory.) On 20 March the Bourbon white and gold disappeared from the Hôtel de Ville, the Vendôme Column, the Tuileries, the post office and other government buildings, each of which were peacefully taken over by Bonapartists. On the day Napoléon entered Paris, the same newspaper that had described him as a monster announced: 'The Conquering Hero has Returned!'

On 1 June there was a *Champ de Mai* (Mayfield) on the Champ-de-

Mars, whereupon Napoléon reclaimed his throne, submitted his constitution for the acceptance of a newly elected Assembly, and generally let it be known who was in charge. There was an altar and a grandstand, and gun salutes, drum rolls, parading soldiers, speeches, oaths taken, and an open-air Mass.

A few weeks later Napoléon faced the British and Prussians at Waterloo. On 21 June he was back in Paris, defeated and at the mercy of enemies unlikely to show mercy. Again he abdicated, remaining for several days at the Hôtel d'Élysées thinking of escape, and appreciating the occasional contingent of soldiers who passed his window and shouted *'Vive l'Empéreur'*, but knowing that there really was no escape. Finally he gave himself up to the British, who made sure this time by taking him to St Helena in the South Atlantic. There he languished, writing his memoirs and convincing himself that all his failures were the fault of others.

Once again a gouty, obese and still uncomfortable Louis XVIII trundled into Paris. He dismounted from his carriage in front of the Tuileries with great difficulty, no doubt wondering as he did how long it would last this time.

## THE NAPOLÉONIC LEGACY

Napoléon returned to Paris in the 1840s to be interred at Les Invalides. His impact on the city was not laid to rest with him, however. The Paris landscape has the Arc de Triomphe de l'Étoile, the imperial 'N' which still adorns some buildings within the Louvre complex, and the Avenue de la Grande Armée, stretching from the Arc de Triomphe de l'Étoile to the Place de la Porte Maillot. Both revolution and Bona-partism would play a role in Paris from then to the present – in 1830, 1848 and 1871, and in the appearance of Louis-Napoléon, General Boulanger, and even Charles de Gaulle. Part of that role would have a decidedly romantic quality.

# CHAPTER SIX

# The Romantic City,
## 1815–1871

Romanticism was a philosophy that in Paris, as elsewhere, embraced emotion and experience rather than reason. Its adherents were passionate and rarely tranquil. Romantic Paris featured an intense intellectual, artistic and social life. For these reasons, according to Girault de Saint-Fargeau, the city was a 'capital of civilization' compared with London, which he termed merely a 'capital of industry'.

## The Restoration

'The spectacle of a gouty old gentleman,' wrote Frederick Artz, 'arriving in his capital "in the baggage of the Allies" . . . savoured of the ridiculous.' This was Louis XVIII, a product of the *ancien régime* who, as king, had to put up with Russian soldiers camping in the Tuileries gardens, Prussian Field Marshal Blücher wanting to blow up the Pont-d'Iéna (he was persuaded not to by both Louis and the king of Prussia), and a virtual war of riots and assassinations between the absolutist and clericalist Ultras and the Republican Left. Ridiculous, yes; it was a ridiculous epoch. All the same, Louis XVIII was the only French monarch after Louis XV to die in office of natural causes.

### THE URBAN ENVIRONMENT

By 1817 715,000 people, including resident foreigners, were rammed into a Paris of narrow, ill-paved and filthy streets. The old aristocracy still lived in the Faubourg Saint-Germain, bohemians in the Latin Quarter (artists, youth, and social rebels whose life-style mocked the bourgeois values of the rising industrial age), Napoleonic nobility and *haute* bourgeoisie in the Faubourg Saint-Honoré and the Chaussée d'Antin, the *petite* bourgeoisie in the Marais, and the working poor in the Faubourg Saint-Antoine and around the Butte de Montmartre.

Louis XVIII added and changed little. The Rue d'Arcole became the Rue de Beaujolais, and Rue Napoléon was renamed the Rue de la Paix. He built the Pavillon de Rohan in the Tuileries–Louvre complex, expiatory chapels for the late king and queen in her cell in the Conciergerie and in the cemetery near Boulevard Malesherbes where they were buried, rebuilt the Institution des Sourds-Muets, and began the churches of Notre-Dame-de-Lorette at the Opéra end of the Rue Lafitte, Saint-Vincent-de-Paul near the Gare du Nord, and Saint-Denys-du-Saint-Sacrement in Rue de Turenne, by the Place des Vosges.

Meanwhile, the regime started the École des Beaux-Arts between the Quai Malaquais and the Rue Pot-de-Fer (Rue Bonaparte), completed the Bourse in the Rue du Louvre, raised a bronze equestrian statue of Henry IV on the Pont-Neuf – cast by a Bonapartist who supposedly filled the horse with anti-Bourbon pamphlets – and restored Bourbon statues in the Place des Vosges and Place des Victoires that had been pulled down by revolutionaries.

Building during the Restoration was mostly private. Between 1815 and 1830 developers built 21,000 apartment houses and sixty-five streets, introduced gas-lighting in the Place Vendôme in 1825 (there were 10,000 outlets and 1500 subscribers by 1828), and in 1826 opened a public bus line along the grand boulevards from Place de la Bastille to the Madeleine, which had expanded to fifteen lines by 1829. Meanwhile, a fascinated crowd watched the first pavement laid along the Rue de l'Odéon, and Parisians began riding in a new type of carriage, the *fiacre*, a name which the English soon perverted into 'hackney' and the Americans into 'hack'.

## THE LIFE OF THE PEOPLE

Not yet transformed by industrialization, Restoration Paris was elegant, relatively quiet and reasonably prosperous. For most Parisians life was at least comfortable. They strolled or sat in the boulevards and gardens, shopped, lunched, dined, gambled, or frequented brothels in the Palais-

Royal, or paid a small fee to dine, dance and watch puppet shows in private amusement parks. Dining out first became an important feature of Paris life during the Restoration. Chez les Frères Provençaux and Chez Vézour in the Palais-Royal, and the Maison d'Or in the Boulevard Saint-Germain, were then among the finest restaurants in Europe.

Parisians also worked. Carts driven by 'heavy, overclothed, moustached peasants, their wives fast asleep on top of the greens', arrived at Les Halles before daybreak, laden with produce. By nine in the morning, housemaids and housewives were out buying the day's food. Retail stores generally opened after six or seven, and labourers were out and about by six, stopping for breakfast at nine and for dinner at two in the afternoon. The building trades called it a day at six and the factories at nine. Schools ran from eight until two, and professional people, bankers and financiers were in their offices from eight or nine until four.

Restoration Parisians had a high opinion of themselves; to the rest of France, they were merely arrogant and ignorant. Stendhal told of a Parisian visiting Mâcon who, when told that the local river was the Saône, replied: 'In Paris we call it the Seine!'

THEATRE

Theatre returned to its pre-revolutionary state during the restoration, and much of it was again government-supported. The leading 'public' theatres included the Opéra, the Comédie-Française which featured Talma and Mlle Mars, the Théatre des Italiens where Mesdemoiselles Sontag and Malibran sang, the Odéon, now the Odéon Théâtre National, and the Société des Concerts orchestra, founded in 1828 by Cherubini and Habeneck and housed in Le Conservatoire. Franz Lizst and Frédéric Chopin were in the audience for its premier concert which featured an all-Beethoven programme. There were a number of private theatres, mainly in the boulevards, and they were more popular: Franconi's, the Folies-Dramatiques, the Variétés-Amusantes, the Vaudeville, the Cirque Olympique, the Port Saint-Martin, the Ambigu-Comique, and the Théatre du Gymnase.

All theatres performed comedy, farce and melodrama which ridiculed in turn the National Guard, bohemians, porters, peasants, the *nouveaux riches*, the old aristocracy, and Ultras and Leftists, who regularly came to blows as one group approved a performance which lampooned the other. One such clash, in 1817 in the Comédie-Française, injured a number of prominent citizens. Thereafter management collected canes, umbrellas and other weapons at the door, and the modern-day theatre cloakroom was born. Satiric content was censored only if it was too Bonapartist or too anti-clerical. The popular playwright Eugène Scribe attacked fraud, family tyranny and social prejudice aimed at illegitimate children, labourers and prostitutes, and poked fun at Romanticism. For example, he described a happy marriage as having less to do with love than with a good dowry, steady emotions and equality of social position. Naturally such Romantics as Alexándre Dumas *père* and Théophile Gautier regarded him as hopelessly bourgeois.

## FASHION

Paris was as fashion conscious as ever under the Restoration. Valerie Steele described 'hourglass, with a padded chest, cinched waist, and flared hips' as the 'fashionable silhouette' for both sexes. Fashion indicated power and status, or as Honoré de Balzac phrased it in 1830, *'la toilette est l'expression de la société'* (society is expressed through dress). The 'hero' of Balzac's novel *Traité de la vie élégante* is Lucien Chardon, a provincial who dresses like a Paris dandy in order to find acceptance in the best circles. However, being a provincial he is behind the times, and what he thought was fashion for the élite had by then become fashion for working men. Chardon therefore is denied entry to the Opéra. Working women, meanwhile, dressed as fashionably as they could. As Steele explained it: 'Her clothing, though "humble", indeed "cheap", was nevertheless "pretty" and "smart".... The industries of fashion were so ubiquitous and had reached such a high degree of quality that even Parisian ribbons were prettier than those elsewhere.'

Paris fashion was becoming associated with 'names'. The Parisienne was 'dressed by Palmyre', and 'orders her hats from Herbeaux', for example. Other names included Madame Vignon and Madame Victorine, Monsieur Staub and Monsieur Buisson.

THE PRESS

Newspapers proliferated in Paris, profiting from Louis XVIII's determination not simply to re-create the past. All had a political point of
view. *Le Moniteur* was the government-supporting and therefore
royalist paper; its purpose was to lead public opinion. *La Quotidienne, Le
Drapeau Blanc, Le Conservateur* and *Le Journal des Débats* were also
royalist, though the *Journal* moved to the Left after 1824. Liberal papers
included *La Minerve Française, L'Indépendent* (later *Le Constitutionnel*), *Le
Courrier Français* and *Le National*, founded in 1830 by Adolphe Thiers.
Youthful and radical ideas were served by *Jeune France, Le Producteur* and
*Le Globe*, which had a European readership and promoted Romanticism as the path to liberation from old rules and values. There was also
an English-language newspaper, *The Messenger*. These papers enjoyed
great freedom until Leftists assassinated the duke of Berry in 1820.
Thereafter censorship increased, symptomatic of what was to come
when Berry's father came to the throne as Charles X in 1824.

# The July Monarchy

Charles X was a thoroughgoing reactionary. His coronation at Reims
Cathedral, including touching for scrofula, was 'the most elaborate
medieval mummery'. As king he gave indemnities to those who lost
property to the revolution, made sacrilege a crime punishable by death,
dissolved the National Guard, symbol of the Paris bourgeoisie, and in
1829 appointed as first minister the absolutist Prince Polignac, who
reputedly 'carried proudly the burden of his family's great unpopu-
larity'. Charles soon outlived his welcome, despite being given a giraffe
by Mehemet Ali, Pasha of Egypt, which was enormously popular in
Paris.

THE REVOLUTION OF 1830

On 25 July 1830 Polignac ordered an end to the free press, dissolved
the Chamber and altered the election laws, all in violation of the
Charter of Liberties granted in 1814 by Louis XVIII. At the same time,
Marshal Marmont, a duke, was put in command of the Paris garrison,
which offended the bourgeois. On 26 July 5,000 printers and other

press workers were in the streets shouting, '*A bas les ministres! Vive la Charte!*' (Down with the ministers! Long Live the Charter!) Polignac remarked sarcastically that he found illiterates rioting in defence of a free press was a bit odd. Charles hunted at Saint-Cloud and paid little attention. Then *Le Globe*, *Le National* and *Le Temps* defied the press ban and published. The police tried to seize the issues, and disorder spread to include artisans and small shopkeepers.

From that moment the revolution of 1830 was a working-class uprising, though the bourgeois profited the most from it. The free press issue soon lost out to work and wages. As Vincent Beach put it, 'Chronic unemployment, low wages, and rising prices left tens of thousands of men and women in Paris ... dissatisfied with a regime dominated by great landowners and the upper-middle-class business-men. ...' On 28 July barricades went up, the disbanded National Guard appeared in arms, Republicans organized insurrection committees, and whole regiments of the Paris garrison defected. By nightfall a full-scale battle raged across the city between rebels and those of Marmont's forces who were still loyal. At Saint-Cloud King Charles played whist.

## THE HÔTEL DE VILLE

Meanwhile a provisional government formed, and ordered the tri-colour raised at the Hôtel de Ville, Nôtre-Dame Cathedral, and var-ious bridges. Three days of fighting followed, until Marmont admitted he could not subdue the capital and Charles was persuaded to abdicate in favour of his heir. However, no Bourbon was accep-table in France, and king and dauphin went into exile. The ageing marquis of Lafayette, a republican at heart but no Jacobin, appeared at the Hôtel de Ville on 30 July, where he proposed that Louis-Phi-lippe, duke of Orléans and son of Philippe-Égalité, become king. This suggestion generated little enthusiasm until the next day, when Louis-Philippe presented himself on a balcony of the Hôtel draped in the tricolour. This gesture recalled that he had fought at Jemappes in 1792 as a soldier of the Revolution. Lafayette appeared beside him and they embraced. This '*coup de théâtre*' sent the crowd wild. The Republicans were upstaged and France was again a monarchy. Louis-Philippe at once guaranteed the constitution, dropped all pretence of

Hôtel de Ville

ruling by divine right, and promised to work with the Chamber in introducing legislation.

Hector Berlioz's *Symphonie fantastique* was first performed in Paris on 5 December 1830. The fourth movement, 'March to the Scaffold', ended with a graphic re-creation in sound of the guillotine falling. The effect upon the audience, many of whom remembered the Terror and all of whom had just survived a revolution, was electric, and perfectly consistent with the archetypical Romantic form and style that characterized the composition.

## LOUIS-PHILIPPE

The new king, wrote Alexis de Tocqueville, 'had no flaming passions, no ruinous weaknesses, no striking vices.... He hardly appreciated literature or art, but he passionately loved industry.' He was a banker by trade, and he received businessmen, bankers and industrialists at his court in the Tuileries, and ignored the old aristocracy. Louis-Philippe frequently strolled in the Tuileries gardens in frock coat and top hat, carrying a green umbrella, very much the bourgeois gentleman. The philosophy of his reign was summed up in first minister François Guizot's words to Paris businessmen: '*Enrichissez-vous* [get rich] – and leave politics to me.'

## INDUSTRIALIZATION

Paris industrialized slowly. By 1848 the city had 65,000 industrial enterprises, many dealing with textiles, but only 7,000 of them employed more than ten workers. Meanwhile the population expanded steadily, mostly by immigration from the countryside, increasing by 25 per cent between 1830 and 1848 and reaching one million in 1844. This far outstripped the ability of nascent industry to provide adequate employment. Public health and sanitation deteriorated also, contributing to the cholera epidemics in 1832 and 1849 which claimed 60,000 lives, including Auguste Casimir-Perier, a minister of state. Other problems included low pay, poor working conditions and lack of education for the poor. Lower-class anger and frustration looked like becoming endemic.

On the other hand, Paris was becoming an international centre for banking and investment, a fact that was at odds with the curious attitude of many Parisians regarding railways, which elsewhere were becoming synonymous with economic growth. Adolphe Thiers, for example, remarked that a railway line from Paris to Saint-Germain would have value only as an amusement. In 1848 France had only a third as much railway line as Great Britain, and just over half that of Prussia. Parisian bankers invested mainly in urban development. Building up the area between the Champs-Élysées and the Seine began in 1820, financed by Jacques Laffitte and James de Rothschild, two of the richest bankers in the city.

## SOCIAL UNREST

Most Parisians rioted for political and ideological, rather than economic, reasons. In 1831 a riot outside the church of Saint-Germain-de-l'Auxerrois, where a memorial mass was being said for the duke of Berry, was anti-clerical and anti-monarchist. The mob made an ugly scene, then proceeded to the palace of the archbishop of Paris next to Notre-Dame and destroyed it. Bonapartists and Republicans inspired a virtual insurrection in 1832, raising barricades in the Faubourg Saint-Antoine and other poor districts; shots were fired, leaving 800 dead or wounded. In 1834 Republican barricades went up in Rue Transnonain in the Marais, which led to a massacre by the National Guard. The next year, on the anniversary of the July Revolution, several onlookers were killed when a bomb was thrown at Louis-Philippe. The king took that personally and cracked down on the press, took direct control of the government, and surrounded himself with the likes of François Guizot, ministers who would do as they were told. After all, as the king pointed out, *'C'est moi qui mène le fiacre'* (I drive the carriage).

All the same, industrialization was bringing a new level of consciousness among Paris workers. Trades unions were illegal, but that did not prevent demands for social and economic improvement. Strikes and acts of industrial violence were frequent, and the first workers' newspaper, *L'Artisan, journal de la classe ouvrière*, appeared in Paris in September 1830. It argued a republican and socialist line: 'The condition of the worker . . . is to be exploited by a master. . . . [C]ompelled to earn a minimal sum each day, the worker doubles and triples the fortune of his employer,' proclaimed the inaugural issue. Industrial socialism would ever after play a role in Paris life and politics.

## THE ROMANTIC IMAGINATION

Cultural and intellectual life during the July monarchy was flamboyantly Romantic, even if Louis-Philippe was not, and Romantics frequently addressed social and political themes. Eugène Delacroix's paintings honoured insurrectionists and revolutionaries. Novelist George Sand (Aurore Dupin) was a feminist, though with a small 'f'; her lovers included Romantic poet Alfred de Musset and Romantic composer Frédéric Chopin. Henri Saint-Simon, socialist and ardent revolutionary, envisioned religion directing society towards amelioration of the plight of the poorest classes. Victor Hugo decried the plight of the urban poor in his Paris-based novels, *Les Misérables* and *Notre-Dame de Paris*, while Alexandre Dumas *père*, who was at the barricades in July 1830, defied tyranny in *Les Trois Mousquetaires*, and exacted retribution from dishonourable men in *Le Comte de Monte-Cristo*.

## HONORÉ DAUMIER

Satiric journals, no new phenomenon in Paris, led by *Le Charivari* joined in the political battles of the day. *Le Charivari* featured Honoré Daumier, the most brilliant cartoonist of his day. The portly Louis-Philippe, with his pear-shaped head covered with long curly hair, and his regime of corrupt bankers and generals were grist for Daumier's mill. He summed up the whole regime in his drawings of Robert Macaire, an amoral adventurer portrayed on stage by the actor Frédérick Lemaître. Daumier depicted him as a scruffy ruffian; Macaire both irked Parisians and made them laugh. Daumier also drew the massacre of insurrectionists in the Rue Transnonain, which made no one laugh. The censor occasionally caught up with the *Charivari* editor, and with Daumier himself who occasionally went to prison for libel.

## BONAPARTISM

Many of the generation which grew up after 1830 were in love with the Bonaparte legend. It included Bonaparte's nephew, Louis-Napoléon. Twice, in 1836 and 1840, he tried to inspire a Bonapartist coup; both failed, but the writing was on the wall. After the second attempt, Louis-Napoléon was sent to prison at Ham, from where he escaped in 1846 and made his way to London. There he stayed until 1848, and served as a truncheon-wielding special constable during the episodes of Chartist unrest in 1838-9.

The Chamber of Deputies

Louis-Philippe did not openly oppose Bonapartism, so long as it remained nostalgic and historical. He put a statue of the emperor atop the column in Place Vendôme, finished Napoléon's Church of the Madeleine and the Arc de Triomphe, and brought the emperor's remains home from St Helena for reburial in Les Invalides. This arrangement was announced in the Chamber of Deputies by Charles de Rémusat in language that cannot altogether have pleased the king: 'The mortal remains of Napoléon will be placed in the Invalides. . . . He was the legitimate sovereign of our country, and as such has the right to be interred in Saint-Denis; but Napoléon must not have the ordinary burial of a king. . . .'

In December 1840 the prince of Joinville, Louis-Philippe's son, brought the remains from St Helena to Paris, via Cherbourg, Le Havre and the Seine by barge, stopping at Rouen for a memorial service. The barge was decorated with a golden eagle figurehead and a Greek temple featuring fourteen Doric columns. Napoléon's remains were within this temple, surrounded by cloth of gold and velvet hangings. (The barge ended ignominiously: it was moored on the river near Les Invalides, and eventually turned into a public swimming pool.)

On 15 December 1840, a bitterly cold day, Napoléon's remains were taken with great ceremony to Les Invalides. The coffin was placed in the 'imperial car' which carried it to the Étoile, then down the Champs-Élysées to the Place de la Concorde and across the river. The route was decorated with wooden statues of goddesses painted to appear marble, funereal urns burning incense, and white columns bearing bronze bucklers with the names of Napoléon's victories. The procession included the Seine gendarmerie with trumpets, the Municipal Guard on horseback, two squadrons of lancers, the commandant of Paris, a battalion of infantry with a band, more soldiers followed by a horse decorated with Napoléon's own harness, banners from all of the *départements* of France, Joinville himself and the sailors from the ship *Belle Poule* which brought the remains from St Helena, and finally the funeral car with huge wheels and its draperies embroidered with Ns and eagles.

The Invalides chapel was packed with onlookers. The coffin was placed on an elaborate catafalque, next to which stood Louis-Philippe and various dignitaries, including the archbishop of Paris. Joinville approached Louis-Philippe and said, 'Sire, I bring you the body of the Emperor of France.' The king replied, 'I receive it in the name of France.' That was it. Later the sarcophagus of Finnish red granite was installed, a gift of Tsar Nicholas I of Russia ironically. The emperor was now in place in Paris, ready to inspire future Bonapartists.

## 'A TOUCH OF ORLÉANS'

Paris had no Orléanist tradition beyond the Palais-Royal, and that was more bourgeois than royal. Therefore Louis-Philippe sought to create one by building in the neo-Gothic or neo-Byzantine style then popular. His contributions include the small theatre, built by Gabriel in Château Versailles for Louis XV, reconstructed in Byzantine style, and he replaced the royal apartments with the ostentatious Galerie des Batailles, which he filled with huge paintings of French military victories all the way back to Clovis. The idea was to make Versailles the national treasure it has, indeed, become. An Egyptian obelisk (a gift from the same Egyptian pasha who had sent a giraffe to Charles X) was erected in the centre of the Place de la Concorde, and the Colonne de Juillet in the Place de la Bastille celebrated Louis-Philippe's ascent to the throne (it replaced a plaster model of a fountain, shaped like an elephant, put there by Napoléon). When Louis-Philippe's heir was killed in a carriage accident, the king had a Byzantine chapel erected on the spot. The stained-glass window was designed by Ingres, a pupil of Jaques-Louis David.

Louis-Philippe also built a new city wall. Paris had not been a fortified city for many years, and in 1840, after a decade of discussing the implications, the Chamber voted funds to construct a new wall with appropriate fortifications, in places a mile beyond the old tax-farmers' wall. The Hôtel de Cluny in the Boulevard Saint-Michel, built over ancient Roman baths, was next. Alphonse du Sommerard had purchased the building in 1833 for his collection of medieval art; when he died in 1844, the government took it over and turned it into the Musée de Cluny. The same year the Fontaine Louvois, decorated with statues dedicated to French rivers, was raised near the Bibliothèque Nationale, followed at once by the Bibliothèque Sainte-Geneviève in the Place du

Panthéon. This structure used cast iron in ways similar to those used later in the railway stations and exhibition halls. In 1845 the foreign office building was completed on the Quai d'Orsay. One new church, Sainte-Clothilde, a neo-Gothic effort based upon the Church of Saint-Ouen in Rouen, was started in the Rue de Champagny, half-way between the Palais Bourbon and Les Invalides. Also a new street, Rue Rabuteau on the Right Bank, attempted with limited success to alleviate increasing traffic congestion.

These additions represented a somewhat limited Orléans legacy, but that did not matter. Louis-Philippe was the only Orléans ever to sit on the French throne.

## The Revolution of 1848

In February 1848, after years of inflation, corrupt politicians, rising unemployment, opposition to the government voiced loudly by *Le National* and *La Réforme*, Paris exploded. An outdoor banquet – bourgeois radicals eating while the proletarian poor looked on wistfully, and speakers berating the government, especially minister Guizot – was scheduled for 22 February. At the last minute the government forbade the banquet, and an angry crowd, including students from the Left Bank, gathered in front of the Madeleine. Soon the usual barricades went up, riots began, and police, troops and the citizenry fought. The following morning, insurrectionists attacked soldiers loyal to the monarch in the narrow streets of the Faubourg Saint-Antoine and other poor districts. Then the National Guard defected, and royalist troops opened fire on them and other citizens in the Boulevard des Capucines, killing some forty or fifty people. On the morning of the 24th Louis-Philippe dismissed Guizot in hopes of saving the throne. It was too late. Hours later, he abdicated and left Paris in disguise. A mob invaded and looted the Tuileries Palace, played games in the garden with the throne, and then burned it at the foot of the Colonne de Juillet.

### THE REPUBLIC

A frightened Chamber of Deputies endorsed a Provisional Government, which included leading Republicans and Socialists, the latter put forward by demonstrators at the Hôtel de Ville. There was even an actual member of the working class named Albert. However, sabotaged by conservatives and moderates in the Chamber, the government was unable to solve economic and social problems. The city seethed with unrest. On 16 March the bourgeoisie demonstrated at the Hôtel de Ville to protest against opening the National Guard to all comers; on the 17th thousands of radicals demonstrated in support of the change. A month later 40,000 protesters marched from the Champ-de-Mars to the Hôtel de Ville determined to seize the government, and the National Guard staved them off. The government survived these episodes, and to celebrate staged a 'festival of fraternity' at the Arc de Triomphe, wherein government officials handed out colours to the army and National Guard regiments.

May elections returned a conservative Chamber. On 15 May a huge crowd marched from the Place de la Bastille to the Palais Bourbon, where they forced their way into the hall, read petitions, made demands, and thoroughly upset the deputies before heading for the Hôtel de Ville to try to seize power. The National Guard was now clearly on the side of moderation. They confronted the crowd at the Hôtel de Ville, broke it up and arrested many of the leaders. This time the government celebrated victory on the Champ-de-Mars.

## THE JUNE DAYS

The worst violence came in late June. The National Workshop scheme was failing and unemployment in Paris was rising. On 23 June the Assembly dissolved the Workshops, and rioting began. By evening the eastern half of the city was in the hands of insurrectionists, and thousands of troops from the provinces, who had no love for Parisians in any case, were brought in by train to help the National Guard. General Cavaignac was in command. He assembled his forces at the Palais Bourbon, the Place de la Concorde and the Panthéon, and on 24 June began the counter-attack. Using artillery to destroy the barricades, Cavaignac pushed forward street by street until insurgents were isolated in the Faubourg Saint-Antoine. It had lasted six days, over 4,000 were killed and thousands more arrested. Prisoners were crammed into improvised dungeons before being transported to labour camps in Algeria. Gustave Flaubert described one of these dungeons: 'Nine hundred men were there, crowded together in filth pell-mell, black with powder and clotted blood, shivering in fever and shouting in frenzy. Those who died were left to lie with the others.'

## THE MAN OF DECEMBER

Louis-Napoléon, back from London, was elected to the Assembly. In September he announced his candidacy for president of the Republic; few regarded him as much of a threat. His first speech in the Assembly was given haltingly and with a German accent. Oudilon Barrot called him, rather patronizingly, 'our excellent young man'; Adolphe Thiers remarked privately that he was 'a cretin whom we will manage'; and Alexis de Tocqueville described him as an 'enigmatic, sombre, insignificant numskull'. Be that as it may, the presidential returns gave Louis-Napoléon a four-to-one edge over his nearest rival.

## THE COUP OF DECEMBER

The new president intended from the start to resurrect the Napoleonic Empire. His term was up in December 1851, and that the constitution forbad re-election gave him his opportunity. On the night of 1 December placards were put up around the city announcing a plebiscite to approve a presidential *coup d'état* to be carried out the next day. The next morning, 50,000 troops commanded by General Saint-Arnaud occupied the Imprimerie Nationale, the Palais Bourbon, strategic points around the city, newspaper offices and print shops. Resistance was minimal; a few barricades went up accompanied by sporadic shooting, the worst being in the Boulevard Poissonière where soldiers mistook a crowd of onlookers for a mob and opened fire. Later, the president left the Élysée Palace with his generals to proclaim victory. The supreme court judged that he acted illegally and was dismissed. Some deputies protested and were arrested. Most Parisians went to work as usual.

Louis-Napoléon – who had called himself prince-president – took the title of First Consul, as his uncle had done. A year later – again on 2 December – riding the tide of a general economic recovery, he proclaimed the Empire and himself Napoléon III. The decision was submitted to the promised plebiscite, which returned 7,800,000 in favour, 250,000 against.

# *Napoléon III*

Napoléon III was disappointing in most respects. The Crimean War achieved little, the Mexican adventure nothing at all, his Northern Italian policy was a fiasco, and rivalry with Prussia produced a war that ended in national humiliation. The emperor's impact on Paris, however, was a different story.

## YET ANOTHER IMPERIAL CITY

Napoléon occupied the Tuileries Palace with what his critics called a 'tawdry little court', where he looked out over a city that fell well short of his idea of an imperial city. Years before, Louis-Napoléon had written: 'I want to be a second Augustus, because Augustus . . . made Rome a city of marble.' As Napoléon III he moved to act upon this desire. His instrument was Georges, later Baron, Haussmann, to whom he handed his plan in 1853, on the day he named Haussmann prefect of the Seine. The timing was perfect: industry was growing, and state and private revenues were expanding, in part because Paris financiers had finally accepted the railway boom and were investing in it across France and Europe. Above all, the need for urban renewal was evident on every side.

## PARIS IN 1850

The population was well over one million, and lived largely in extremely narrow apartments five plus storeys high, and without courtyards. Over a third of all Parisians occupied an area on the Right Bank less than twice the size of New York City's Central Park. One house in five had running water, and only 150 houses in the entire city had water piped above the ground floor. The Seine, a source of water, was also part of the sewer system, along with the River Bièvre and the ancient stream of Ménilmontant. Parks and open spaces were almost non-existent except on the outskirts. The Île de la Cité was one of the worst areas. 'The mud-coloured houses, broken by a few worm-eaten window frames, almost touched at the eaves, so narrow were the streets,' wrote Eugène Sue. 'Black, filthy alleys led to steps even blacker and more filthy and so steep that one could climb them only with the help of a rope attached to the damp wall by iron brackets.' Among the 14,000 people living in the Cité, Sue noted many 'released convicts, thieves, murderers'. The death-rate there was exceeded only in the Rue Saint-Denis area.

Paris streets were narrow, crowded and twisting, little changed from the middle ages. Every attempt at a thoroughfare over the centuries had ended at some barrier: the Rue de Tournon and the Rue de Seine, for example, began at the entrance to the Luxembourg Palace, 'started purposely toward the Seine and ended ignominiously behind the Institute [de France], one hundred yards short of the river'. On the whole, Eugène Sue concluded, the city was 'fearfully inconvenient and squalid', and dangerous as well.

## BARON HAUSSMANN

An Alsatian Protestant educated at the Collège Henri IV, the Collège Bourbon and the School of Law, the prefect knew Paris. As a student he lived in the Chaussée d'Antin quarter on the Right Bank, and walked to the Latin Quarter on the Left. Squalid streets, squalid houses and even more squalid citizens were no mystery to him. When Napoléon handed him his plan for Paris in 1853, Haussmann not only approved it, he made it his mission to extend it. Napoléon III was the architect of modern Paris but Baron Haussmann was the engineer. When all was done, the bill was, in today's terms, more than £55,000,000,000.

# *The Modern City Emerges*

## STREETS

Streets came first. In 1850 Boulevard des Capucines carried 9,000 horses daily; by 1868 that number was 23,000, and traffic was nearly at a standstill.

To make wider streets, old buildings had to be razed. Parisians

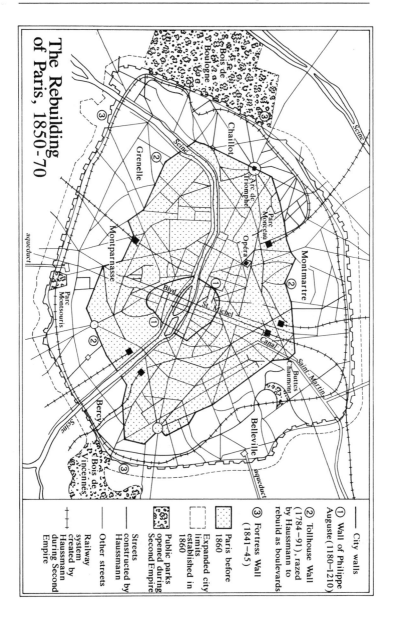

The Rebuilding of Paris, 1850-70

Bois de Boulogne

Seine

Chaillot

Grenelle

Arc de Triomphe

Parc Monceau

Opéra

Montmartre

Montparnasse

Blvd

St. Michel

Canal

Saint-Martin

Buttes Chaumont

aqueduct

Parc Montsouris

Bercy

Seine

Bois de Vincennes

Belleville

aqueduct

— City walls

① Wall of Philippe Auguste (1180–1210)

② Tollhouse Wall (1784–91), razed by Haussmann to rebuild as boulevards

③ Fortress Wall (1841–45)

Paris before 1860

Expanded city limits established in 1860

Public parks opened during Second Empire

Other streets

Streets constructed by Haussmann

Railway system created by Haussmann during Second Empire

endured years of 'flying dust, noise, and falling plaster and beams'. When finished, new boulevards opened thoroughfares across long stretches of the city, as for instance from the Gare de l'Est south and across the river to the Avenue l'Observatoire. New street networks improved access to places such as Les Halles and the Hôtel de Ville. Boulevards Pereire, Beaujon (Avenue Friedland), Malesherbes, Haussmann, Ornano, Magenta, Strasbourg, Sébastopol, Richard Lenoir, Mazas and Prince Eugène were opened north of the Seine between Porte Maillot in the west and Porte de Vincennes in the east. South of the river, boulevards Saint-Germain, Saint-Michel, Port Royal, Arago and Saint-Marcel were laid out. The medieval jumble of the Île de la Cité was cleared, and the Boulevard du Palais was built in order to facilitate the north–south connection. Thereafter the line from the Gare de l'Est to l'Observatoire was as straight as it would ever be.

Haussmann wanted twelve grand avenues with Bonapartist connections to emanate outward from the Arc de Triomphe in the Place de l'Étoile (Place Charles de Gaulle) like spokes from the hub of a wheel. Some were in place already. The prefect added l'Impératrice (Avenue Foch), Carnot, MacMahon, Wagram, Marceau, d'Iéna, and Kléber. Other Haussmann avenues on the Right Bank included Villiers, l'Empéreur (Avenue Georges Mandel and Avenue du Président Wilson), Napoléon (Avenue de l'Opéra), Victoria, in honour of the English queen, and Daumesnil. Meanwhile Avenue des Gobelins was completed on the Left Bank, bisecting Boulevard Arago.

Dozens of lesser streets were added, at the cost of many ancient dwellings but to the advantage of traffic and light. The major ones were rues Lafayette, the last 1,000 yards of Rivoli, Saint-Antoine and Faubourg Saint-Antoine on the Right Bank, and rues de Rennes, Gay-Lassac, Claude Bernarde, des Écoles and Monge on the Left Bank.

Surfacing was a major problem. Sandstone crumbled, macadam produced dust when dry and smelly mud when wet, and asphalt was slippery. Asphalt was better than the others, however, especially when small stones were mixed with it. Haussmann made asphalt the surface of choice for Paris streets. Paving began in earnest in 1867.

BUILDINGS

In 1859, the city annexed the area between the tax-farmers' wall and
that of 1840. The following year, this expanded city was divided into
twenty *arrondissements*, each of which was represented on the city
council. The emperor and Prefect Haussmann built seventy schools
in the annexed areas, and fifteen churches and synagogues, nine barracks, seven markets and two major hospitals elsewhere. Nothing
escaped the prefect's eye. Private building, especially apartments –
Paris was becoming a city of apartments, it was said – had to con-
form to strict rules governing height of buildings, width of pavements, styles of façades and so forth. Meanwhile new or modernized
bridges were built, such as Pont d'Alma, Pont-au-Change and Pont-
Saint-Michel.

A new Central Market was constructed on the site of Les Halles. The
first effort of stone, for which then President Napoléon laid the cornerstone in 1851, resembled a fortress more than a market, and was an
instant laughing-stock. 'Iron! Iron! Nothing but iron!' Haussmann
shouted, and another attempt was made, resulting in a series of very
modern structures of iron and glass, inspired in part by the design of the
new Gare de l'Est.

Glass and iron dominated the new architecture. The Salle du Travail
(reading room) of the Bibliothèque Nationale, and the Palais de
l'Industrie, raised between the Champs-Élysées and the Cours la Reine
for the Great Exposition of 1855, were iron and glass construction. The
latter, in Marshall Dill's view, was 'one of the ugliest structures of all
time'. Perhaps, but it was state of the art then, as was the exposition it
housed. Five million visitors saw 20,000 exhibitors – 12,000 of them
foreign – emphasizing science and technology. A second Exposition in
1867 featured an even larger glass and iron hall erected on the Champ-
de-Mars. More international in spirit, there were even more visitors,
including royalty, who came to see the exhibits but also the wonders
that Haussmann and Napoléon III had brought to Paris itself, including
hydraulic lifts.

The new wonders included a new wing extending to the Tuileries
on the Seine side of the Louvre, and on the other side the Jeu de Paume

(a 'real', meaning royal, tennis court) and the Orangerie. The Louvre additions were meant to approximate the Renaissance style of adjacent portions: the new wing completed the quadrangle that had been under construction on and off since the reign of Francis I. Ironically, fourteen years later the Tuileries were destroyed as a result of the Communard uprising, and never rebuilt.

They did not include the Paris Opéra, completed only after Haussmann's death. This was among his greatest projects, and it was inspired in part by Felice Orsini's attempt on Napoléon's life in the maze of narrow streets around the old Opéra in the Rue Le Peletier. A new Opéra, surrounded by open space and straight, wide streets, seemed in order. The prefect chose the area at the end of the new Avenue Napoléon (Avenue de l'Opéra), which was cleared of old buildings, and access streets were laid out, named for operatic composers: Meyerbeer, Auber, Gluck and Halévy. Charles Garnier was the architect for the project. The finished result was monumental.

New buildings on the Île de la Cité included the Tribunal de Commerce and a new Hôtel-Dieu, not quite on but near the site of the old hospital. At Haussmann's direction, Eugène Viollet-le-Duc carried out renovations to Notre-Dame and much else besides, doing less artistic harm, critics said, than he might have done. Elsewhere, two major new churches were built, Saint-Augustine in the Boulevard Malesherbes, and La Trinité north of the Opéra. Also, the Gare de l'Est and the Gare du Nord, the oldest railway stations in Paris, just inside the ring of the grand boulevards, were opened just before or during the Haussmann period. These stations were the perfect symbols of the Napoléon–Haussmann urban-renewal concept, for they blended the new architecture of iron with traditional designs. Some windows in the Gare de l'Est, for example, were inspired by the Gothic rose windows in Notre-Dame.

Meanwhile, having spent years in London Napoléon III appreciated green space within the city. In 1848 Paris had forty-seven acres of parks; in 1870 there were 4,500, including the Bois de Boulogne west of Paris, the Bois de Vincennes far to the east, the Parc Buttes-Chaumont, the Parc Monceau north-east of l'Étoile, and the Parc Montsouris near the Porte d'Orléans.

WATER AND WASTE

Perhaps Haussmann's most important contribution was to the water supply and sewer system. In 1850 Paris received 27 million gallons of water per day, or an average of 26 gallons per person. However, the delivery system guaranteed that most Parisians got nothing like that much. Haussmann's water system involved a series of aqueducts to bring water from springs and rivers miles from the city, and raised the average to fifty gallons per person; unfortunately, individual Parisians still depended for delivery upon owners of buildings, many of whom decided that running water was 'an unnecessary luxury, since it involved payment of a water rate'.

The new sewer system greatly expanded that which existed under the July monarchy. When completed it provided nearly every street with an underground drain which connected with large mains called Collectors. Sewage no longer ran in the streets, and the Seine, at least in the centre of Paris, was no longer polluted, though the North, Bièvre and Asnières Collectors continued to dump sewage into the river beyond city limits. These Collectors became a wonder of the world. Guidebooks recommended them and tourists visited them. However, clean, spacious and well lighted, they may have disappointed visitors hoping to see the dark, dangerous caverns associated with Victor Hugo's *Les Misérables*.

## *The City of Light*

Tourists flocked to Haussmann's renovated Paris, to see what he had done and because Second Empire Paris was the centre of *haute couture* (the House of Worth, which clothed the Empress Eugénie, dates from this era), an epicure's paradise, and the home of the fluffiest light opera to be found anywhere. Second Empire fashion stressed curls, pinched waists, and yards of highly decorated material for women and dark suits for men. The life-styles of the fashionable were addressed in such journals as *La Vie Parisienne*, which happened to be the title also of a Jacques Offenbach operetta. Accommodation had to be provided, so a spate of new *hôtels* – in the modern sense – were built, the two most famous and opulent being the Hôtel du Louvre in the Rue de Rivoli and the Grand Hôtel near the Opéra, which still exists. Haussmann's Paris had become a 'city of light', and that was only nominally the result of gas lighting.

# The End of the Second Empire

Napoléon's popularity faded after the Mexico fiasco of 1864–7. War with Prussia in 1870 provided his subjects with an opportunity to be rid of him.

## THE FRANCO-PRUSSIAN WAR

At first the war was popular. '*A Berlin!*' cried the crowds thronging the streets around the Palais-Royal when war was declared on 19 July. However, the ill-prepared French army was routed at Sedan, and the emperor and Marshal MacMahon taken prisoner. On 4 September the Chamber of Deputies pronounced the emperor deposed, and created a provisional Government of National Defence. That afternoon the Paris populace demanded a Republic, and a mob occupied the Tuileries gardens. Deciding that discretion was the better part of valour, Empress Eugénie made her way through the new galleries to the Louvre doorway opposite Saint-Germain-l'Auxerrois, where she found a *fiacre* which she directed to the home of a family friend, the American dentist Dr Thomas Evans. He paid the cabman and helped her get out of the country. The Prussians released Napoléon several months later and he joined Eugénie in London. The Second Empire was finished.

## THE PRUSSIANS

Attempts to negotiate a peace after Sedan failed because Bismarck, the Prussian minister-president, made demands the French could not accept. The Prussians advanced, surrounded Paris, and laid siege to it beginning on 25 September. It was now possible to leave only by balloon, which Léon Gambetta did in hopes of raising an army of provincial volunteers. In November General Trochu, military governor of Paris, led an advance out from the city intended to link Paris with the army of the Loire. He failed and the city settled down to endure. Paris was well fortified and armed, and 350,000 men were in the National Guard. However, they lacked discipline and soon deteriorated into a rabble. That little mattered, because the Prussians had no intention of storming the city. They could have it so much more easily through starvation.

Food is vital in withstanding a siege, and despite having let loose 40,000 oxen and 250,000 sheep to graze in the Bois de Boulogne as a food supply even before Sedan, Paris was soon suffering from hunger. During the winter of 1870–1 meat, milk and bread began to run out, and no raw materials for manufacture could enter the city. Trees in the Champs-Élysées were cut for firewood when the weather turned cold. Theatres closed early, or ceased to function at all. The situation was especially harsh for the poor, who found themselves eating bread adulterated with bone meal, much of which came from human remains. A 'ragged army' prowled daily in the area beyond the city fortifications in search of roots and edible plant, and diarist Edmond de Goncourt recorded being approached in the street by a girl who said, '*Monsieur, voulez-vous monter chez moi ... pour un morceau de pain*' (Sir, will you come home with me ... for a piece of bread).

The well-off, on the other hand, were merely inconvenienced; they had hoarded food in expectation of hard times. Also luxury restaurants offered complete menus – except for vegetables and sea food – throughout the siege, to those who could afford to dine out. Admittedly the menus included 'pieces of Pollux', from a slaughtered zoo elephant sold to restaurants at 40 francs a pound, and even rats, in taste 'a cross between pork and partridge'. Interestingly, at no point during the siege was there a shortage of wine.

## BOMBARDMENT

Bismarck grew impatient as resistance continued. He persuaded his generals to introduce terror into the siege by shelling Paris, just as they earlier shelled Strasbourg. For twenty-three successive nights, beginning on 5 January, some 12,000 Prussian shells rained down on the city, resulting in about 400 casualties and extensive physical destruction. However, the effect was the same as at Strasbourg: resistance stiffened.

THE FIRST COMMUNE RISINGS

The idea of the Commune was a patriotic and nationalistic concept, with roots as old as Paris itself. From the moment Napoléon III was overthrown, republicans and communards alike agitated for popular control of government and the conduct of the war. Paris was called upon, in the impassioned language of Louise Michel, the 'red virgin', to rise 'in remembrance of its proud and heroic tradition'. Parisians listened because in addition to deprivation, the siege produced tedium and tension, which together encouraged rumour and criticism of whoever was in charge.

The first rising occurred on 31 October 1870, when news spread that the Prussians had captured Metz, and that Adolphe Thiers was negotiating an armistice. A protest rally began at the Place de la Concorde and proceeded to the Hôtel de Ville, where radicals called for a Commune to govern the city. Disaffected National Guardsmen joined in, and several ministers of the provisional government, including General Trochu, were arrested. Much speechifying with little practical content followed, and other guardsmen, disgusted with the Commune radicals, released the ministers, who in turn ordered the military to arrest the insurgent leaders. At day's end those still at liberty went home, 'rather ashamed of their incompetence'.

A second rising occurred on 22 January 1871, following a failed attempt by the National Guard under General Trochu's command to break through the German defences around Saint-Cloud, Malmaison and Buzenval. Crowds of angry Parisians released the extremists arrested after the October rising (including Louise Michel), who then led mutinous National Guard units to the Hôtel de Ville and demanded control of the city. General Vinoy ordered his troops, who were still loyal to the provisional government, to open fire. Casualties were few and the crowd quickly melted away. However, it was a portent of events to come.

The government went forward with the negotiations for an armistice and peace treaty. National Assembly elections on 8 February returned an overwhelmingly conservative majority, including 400 monarchists; a French Republic would be a conservative Republic, or it would not be at all. On 21 February France signed the Treaty of Frankfurt with the new German Imperial government, which had been proclaimed in the Galerie des Glaces of Versailles palace, the first of many humiliations. Those included in the treaty were payment of a large indemnity; cession of Alsace and Lorraine to Germany; occupation of Paris by 30,000 German soldiers; and German soldiers marching in review down the Champs-Élysées. After the parade Parisians 'purified' the surface of the Place de l'Étoile with fire.

Wealthy Parisians, having the most to lose from its continuation, were simply relieved to have the war over. Those who had starved, frozen, and offered their lives to defend the city, saw this peace as a betrayal perpetrated by a reactionary government that had gone out of its way to insult Paris. Meanwhile the new Assembly revoked the wartime moratorium on debts and rents and the National Guard daily dole, all of which added further economic privations to the overburdened populace. The final insult was that the Assembly made its quarters not in Paris but at Versailles, from where, the Parisians had not the slightest doubt, the government intended to make war against them.

## THE COMMUNE OF MARCH 1871

On 18 March, a detachment of soldiers came to Montmartre to take custody of 200 cannons, paid for by popular subscription, that had been used to defend Paris. A crowd drove the soldiers away and killed the two generals with them. Adolphe Thiers immediately ordered all government officials and regular army to leave Paris for Versailles. Many wealthy Parisians came with them, leaving the city in the hands of the poor and the radical Left, who elected a Commune to govern. The Germans, meanwhile, repatriated Marshal MacMahon and thousands of prisoners of war, who would assist the Thiers government in what became the second siege of the city.

The next ten weeks were as bloody as any period in the history of Paris. The Commune was extremist by its very nature. Marxist trades unionists, old Jacobins, Hébertists, anti-clericals and Republican National Guard elements shared the governing powers in an uneasy partnership. The Commune represented, on the whole, a most 'un-

Marxist' insurrection, despite what Karl Marx himself tried to make of it when he wrote *The Civil War in France*. So far as there was a coherent programme, it included abolishing night work in bakeries, turning abandoned bourgeois enterprises into workers' co-operatives, extending the moratorium on debts and rents but without abolishing either one, and leaving property alone. Incredibly, wrote Paul Gagnon, 'many bourgeois Parisians remained quietly in the west end, and the Bank of France calmly financed both the Commune and the Versailles governments'.

There was violence, however. A Commune sortie towards Versailles failed, and all of the Communards captured by the Versaillais were shot out of hand. The Commune retaliated by arresting members of the Paris clergy, including the archbishop, and later shooting them. Artillery barrages were aimed against the city in mid-May. On 21 May anti-Communards opened the Porte de Saint-Cloud and the Versaillais came through. They were able to occupy the west end because barricades did not work well in Baron Haussmann's open Paris. A systematic street-by-street conquest followed, with no quarter given. Louise Michel loved it: 'Barbarian that I am, I love cannon, the smell of powder, machine-gun bullets in the air.' Numerous atrocities were committed by both sides, but probably more by the Versaillais. Then on 24 May the Communards tried to burn the centre of the city. The Louvre, the Palais de Justice and the Palais-Royal were damaged but survived; much else did not, including whole streets of private dwellings. Most notably, the Hôtel de Ville, headquarters of the Commune government, was burned, taking with it some 600 Communards. Notre-Dame and Sainte-Chapelle were meant to be fired but those in charge could not bring themselves to do it.

The Versaillais took the Saint-Germain-des-Prés and Boulevard Saint-Michel areas first, and then pushed through the city to the Faubourg Saint-Antoine, the traditional seedbed of Paris insurrections, which held out until 26 May. There the Versaillais did 'horrible justice' and the legend of Marquis Gallifet, the 'butcher of the Commune', was born. This Versaillais general, 'his mistress on his arm, twirling his moustachios, pointed out who should die, who should live, making caustic jests as he did so'. The Communards' last stand was in the Père

Lachaise cemetery, where they were cornered, taken, and executed against the Wall of the Federalists. It is so marked to the present day.

THE COST

In the following weeks, over 40,000 people were arrested, 30,000 prosecuted, and 13,000 incarcerated or transported to such colonial hell-holes as Devil's Island. Thiers was determined to 'wipe out his opposition root and branch', once and for all. The death toll was around 20,000, and the rift left between the ordinary people of Paris and the government of France lasted well into the epoch of the Third Republic.

# CHAPTER SEVEN

# The Republican City,
## 1871–1939

Writers, artists, war and political crisis, and scandal put the Third Republic among the liveliest, and in a way most brilliant, epochs in Paris history.

## The New Republic

Parisians were not to be trusted. The president was installed in the Palais de l'Élysée, but the government remained at Versailles until 1879, when the Chamber moved to the Palais Bourbon and the Senate to the Palais du Luxembourg.

### CONTENTIOUS PARIS

Between 1872 and 1913 the population grew from 1.8 million to over 2.8 million, which brought increased urban problems and a contentious citizenry. Auguste Blanqui's funeral in 1881 inspired a Communard demonstration, rioters saw a German flag among the national banners displayed on the Hôtel Continental on Bastille day in 1884 and smashed windows in protest, and in 1886 '*Vive l'anarchie*' was shouted from a balcony at the Bourse, a bottle of vile-smelling liquid thrown on those below, and shots fired. No one was hit, but many a Bourse member took an extra cognac with lunch that day. With all of this, Paris was granted universal male suffrage for electing city councillors, which was likely to make the Hôtel de Ville more radical than ever. Parisians also endured one of the coldest winters on record (1878–9), which was followed by an outbreak of typhus that killed thousands.

REPAIRING THE DAMAGE OF THE TERRIBLE YEAR

Not to miss a commercial opportunity, Thomas Cook, the British tour company, organized trips to see ruined Paris. The city ignored them and got on with rebuilding, beginning with the Hôtel de Ville, which was finished in 1882. The new Place Vendôme column, and the Rue de Rivoli wing of the Louvre, which thereafter housed the finance ministry, were finished in 1875. The Cour des Comptes waited until the 1890s to be reconstructed as the Gare d'Orsay (now the Musée d'Orsay), the railway terminus for the Orléans line. Meanwhile the rebuilt – on a smaller scale – Palais-Royal became home to the Conseil d'État, Ministre de la Culture and the Conseil Constitutionnel. The Comédie-Française is part of this complex – and it should be remembered that Comédie Française refers to theatre, not to the bureaucracy.

Preservationists wanted the Tuileries rebuilt for historic reasons if for no other. Others associated the building with monarchism and wanted it destroyed. They prevailed. In 1882 the Marsan and Flore pavilions were restored, and the rest was pulled down. Ironically, the stones were bought by Count Jérôme Pozzo di Borgo, descended from Napoléon I's bitter enemy Count Carlo Pozzo di Borgo of Corsica. He used them to build a château which replicated the central Tuileries pavilion. The palace that had housed both Napoléons was now home to one of Europe's leading anti-Bonapartist families.

Private reconstruction proceeded as well, much of it directed by former Haussmann officials. Not everything was completed by 1878, but enough was so that visitors to the Exposition could agree with Italian writer Edmondo de Amicis, that Paris was again a 'vast gilded net, into which one is drawn again and again'. The only completely new edifice linked to the Terrible Year was the Basilique du Sacré-Coeur atop the hill of Montmartre, started in the 1870s as an act of expiation for the events of 1870–1, but not completed until well into the next century.

THE EXPOSITION OF 1878

This Exposition was said to exhibit a 'Republican face'. That is, it was meant to show the world that Paris had recovered from the Terrible Year, and that the Republic was responsible for this. Political conflicts were set aside and both the Chamber and the radical city council of Paris voted subsidies for the fair. A 'festival of the people' was arranged for 30 June (not 14 July, be it noted) at which La Marseillaise was played. The exposition was held in buildings on the Champ-de-Mars and in the new Palais du Trocadéro, where the Palais de Chaillot now stands. Designed by G.J.A. Davioud, the palace featured a huge rotunda topped by twin minarets 230 feet high, and flanked by twin semi-circular galleries. The effect was vaguely Moorish, and not uniformly popular. Some were reminded of a donkey's hat, others of a Mississippi steamboat. Edmondo de Amicis dismissed the palace as an 'enormous architectural braggart ... that crowns the horizon and crushes all the surrounding heights'. All the same, the Trocadéro was the centrepiece, and thousands of tourists, including Queen Victoria's eldest son, came to see it and the café near the Champ-de-Mars which displayed an electric light. Paris in this epoch was a haunt of British visitors of every degree, both long- and short-term.

## Seeing Haussmann Through

Paris was 2,500 million francs (£100 million) in debt in 1871. However, there was much to recommend completing what remained of Baron Haussmann's great project. His critics had been historians, artists and the literati who wished to preserve the past; engineers. bureaucrats and architects were enthusiastically for the project, however. Above all, many Haussmann officials were still in public works offices. It was no real surprise when the new radical city council took over Haussmann's plan in 1874 as if they had invented it.

### THE STREETS

The Avenue de l'Opéra and the Boulevard Henri IV were first, beginning in 1876. Both were completed in time for the 1878 Exposition. The Avenue would be a prestigious street linking the thriving commerce of the Rue de Rivoli with that of the Boulevard des Capucines. Funding was solved by floating a huge loan that would cover the Avenue, the proposed 1878 Exposition, and the completion of other Haussmann projects. Owners had to be compensated for property razed along the route, which, when the dust had settled, cost an average of 225,000 francs (£9,000) per owner. The Avenue was made perfectly level by cutting through the Butte de Moulin; side streets were widened and new buildings constructed, largely by private builders who had purchased lots from the city. They had to follow Haussmann's building regulations to the letter. The Avenue de l'Opéra cost the city 45 million francs (£1.8 million) and was an immediate commercial success. Most of the Boulevard Saint-Germain was finished by 1870, but its continuation on the Right Bank, the Boulevard Henry IV, had just begun. Now the work resumed and posed relatively few difficulties, in part because the boulevard ran through the poor Arsenal district, where property compensation was roughly half that along the Avenue de l'Opéra.

Between 1885 and 1914 the council also completed and extended a number of street projects that were part of Haussmann's scheme for slum clearance, and improved sanitation and access. They began by widening the Rue des Filles-Dieu, which was expensive but urgent, claimed the council, owing to the 'taint of prostitution' associated with the old street. Other such street work included the Rue de Franche-Comté, connecting the Temple market to the Boulevard du Temple, the Rue du Louvre, which improved sanitation and access to Les Halles, widening the Rue Jean-Jacques Rousseau and clearing access to the central post office, and the Rue Réaumur, 'a great, rectilinear thoroughfare' running from the Bourse to the Rue du Temple. The construction cleared away old and crowded buildings, reducing the fire danger to the Conservatoire des Arts et Métiers and opening the way for a later *Métro* (underground) line.

## THE BUILDINGS

Decorative building also resumed or was completed following the Terrible Year: the church of Saint-Pierre-de-Montrouge, an imitation medieval basilica, in 1872; the Fontaine de l'Observatoire between the Luxembourg Gardens and the Observatory, and the Opéra in 1875; the war ministry on the Quai d'Orsay in 1877; and the Théâtre de l'Odéon in its present form in 1879. Meanwhile, thousands of *maisons de rapport* were constructed (that is buildings for lease, either as apartments or offices and shops). These buildings provide the image most characteristic of contemporary Paris.

## *The Arts in Interesting Times*

Despite all of the rebuilding, Paris after 1871 is more popularly associated with art, theatre, literature and music.

### ART

The astonishing variety of artistic expression in Paris represented a clear break with the Romantic and Classical past and uncertainty regarding the future. After the Salon des Refusés in 1863, an independent show of work rejected by the arbiters of artistic respectability in the Salon des Beaux-Arts, new and controversial styles set the tone. Impressionists created soft, yielding shapes and figures, while Neo-impressionists painted in broad, heavy strokes or experimented with light and shape. Abstractionists dissected the human form or distorted it with unconventional use of colour. Whether they worked, studied or only visited Paris, it was spiritual home to Claude Monet, Edgar Degas, Pierre Renoir, Georges Seurat, Vincent van Gogh, Paul Cézanne, Pablo Picasso, Henri Matisse, and many others from across France, Europe and the Americas.

### WRITERS

Paris writers also sought new forms of expression. Émile Zola was the Naturalist, filling his novels of Paris life with lust, murder, prostitution, drunkenness and brutality amongst the poverty-stricken working class, 'a sort of clinical realism that makes his works very strong medicine'. Joris Karl Huysmans was 'the protesting aesthete attempting to transform an abhorred materialism into a spiritualism full of strange thrills'. Stéphane Mallarmé's *L'Après-midi d'un faune* depicted one mythical creature dreaming of other mythical creatures, suggesting a reality with no clear boundaries. This Impressionist concept was not lost on composer Claude Debussy.

## MUSIC AND OPERA

Camille Saint-Saëns 'could write pieces in imitation of other composers with remarkable accuracy', for which reason his operatic masterpiece, *Samson et Dalila*, was rejected as being 'too Wagnerian in idiom'. It was performed finally in 1890, just three years after protesters demonstrated against Wagner's *Lohengrin* at l'Opéra. However, other composers were led by Impressionists and Naturalists: in the first instance, Debussy's *Pelléas et Mélisande* (based on Maurice Maeterlinck's drama and first performed amid protest in 1902) and his orchestral compositions *La Mer* and *Prélude à l'après-midi d'un faune* (inspired by Mallarmé's poem), and Maurice Ravel's *Daphnis et Chloé*. They did in music what Monet's *Water Lilies* did in painting; and in the second, Georges Bizet's opera *Carmen*, first performed in 1875 at L'Opéra Comique. They were, in music, what Monet was in painting and Zola in literature.

## THEATRE

Theatrical censorship largely ended after 1871, and box office receipts reflected the fact. The principal theatres – the Comédie-Française, l'Odéon, Palais-Royal and l'Opéra, for example – brought in nearly 20 million francs (£800,000) in 1877, and more than 54 million francs (£2.7 million) in 1913. The fare ranged from Henri Becque's Naturalist *La Parisienne*, through Edmond Rostand's historical romance *Cyrano de Bergerac*, to Georges Feydeau's farce *La Dame de chez Maxim's*. Stage personalities were sometimes more famous than the scripts they followed. Among those whose fame has lasted well beyond their lives were Sarah Bernhardt, who played Napoléon II (Bonaparte's son, the Prince of Rome) in Rostand's *L'Aiglon* in 1900, Isadora Duncan, the stylish if not necessarily brilliant dancer, and the brilliant actor Constant Coquelin, whose involvement in a lawsuit when he tried to cancel his contract with the Comédie-Française gained him international notoriety.

## RIOTOUS PERFORMANCE

As always, Parisians confronted change with mixed emotions. On 29 May 1913 Igor Stravinsky's *Le Sacre du printemps* premièred at the

Théâtre de Champs-Élysées. The composer described it as a ballet suite based upon 'a solemn pagan rite: sage elders, seated in a circle, watched a young girl dance herself to death ... to propitiate the god of spring.' To many critics it was a 'blasphemous attempt to destroy music as an art'.

The production, staged by impresario Serge Diaghilev with sets by Picasso and danced by Vaslav Nijinsky, turned into a riot. Part of the audience whistled, shouted and made 'audible suggestions as to how the performance should proceed' which drowned out the orchestra, while another part praised the brilliance of both music and choreography. Camille Saint-Saëns left the theatre in indignation; music critic André Capu shouted that the 'music was a colossal fraud'; the Austrian ambassador laughed derisively; and the Princesse de Purtalès left her box claiming: 'I am sixty years old, but this is the first time that anyone dared to make a fool of me!' On the other hand, one woman slapped a man who hissed, and her escort arranged a duel with him; a society lady spat in the face of a protester; Maurice Ravel shouted 'genius' repeatedly; Roland-Manuel had his collar torn off for defending the music; Debussy pleaded with those around him to be quiet; and backstage, Stravinsky had to restrain Nijinsky from going out and physically attacking members of the audience. This was all in the finest Paris tradition.

## Vieux Paris or Paris Nouveau?

Conflict between those who favoured and those who opposed change was not limited to the arts. The deepest divisions were between those who preferred the pre-Haussmann *vieux Paris*, such as Victor Hugo and Charles Baudelaire, and the *Paris nouveau* modernists who pointed out that '[t]he streets of Old Paris may be interesting to visit, but it is no pleasure to live in them!' Preservation societies – the Society of the History of Paris and the Île-de-France, and the Old Paris Committee, for example – argued, among other things, that as tourists (300,000 in 1913) came to see old Paris, money was to be made by conserving rather than by replacing. The *vieux Paris–Paris nouveau* argument played out on many levels, with some interesting results over several decades.

## COMMERCIALIZING THE BOULEVARDS

'Business invaded the boulevards of *fin-de-siècle* Paris as surely as the Prussians had invaded France in 1870,' wrote Philip Nord. He described luxury shops, tailors and couturiers who favoured English styles of dress and shop design, all of which Paris traditionalists considered 'vulgar'. Even worse, in their eyes, were the *grands magasins* (department stores) that were changing the character of such boulevards as de la Madeleine, des Capucines, des Italiens and Saint-Germain. These stores developed out of *magasins de nouveautés* (novelty stores), which carried a variety of 'fancy goods' at fixed, clearly marked prices. The largest *magasin de nouveautés* was the Ville de Paris, with sales of 12 million francs (£480,000) in 1844. However, Au Bon Marché soon surpassed that, and in 1876 opened the first *grand magasin* in the Rue de

Frontage of the Samaritaine department store

Bac near Boulevard Raspail. The building, designed by Louis-Charles
Boileau and Gustav Eiffel, was a series of multi-storeyed galleries, each
with a glass roof, and the separate floors were connected by a grand
staircase that rivalled the one in l'Opéra. The diversity of goods and
prices in the forty-seven departments appealed to a socially mixed
clientèle who came from across Paris, often by omnibus. There were
also tea shops, children's rooms, and modelling rooms where husbands
were not permitted (salesmen, called *garçons de magasin*, were, however). Mannequins of almost flesh-and-blood realism modelled clothing in the windows. The store advertised in illustrated magazines and

The grand interior of the Galeries Lafayette

newspapers. Émile Zola modelled the department store in his *Au Bonheur des Dames* after Au Bon Marché. Sales of 67 million francs (£2.8 million) in 1877 had risen to 150 million (£6 million) in 1893. It was a profitable enterprise.

By the 1880s, one could choose among department stores: the Grands Magasins du Louvre, Au Gagne-Petit, Au Printemps, La Belle Jardinière (unusual because it was in the working-class XVIII$^e$ *arrondissement*), Crespin-Dufayel, the Grande Maison de Blanc, A La Ville de Londres, Galeries Lafayette, Aux Classes Laborieuses, and A La Ville de Strasbourg. Department stores 'democratized' the boulevards; shoppers from Montmartre, La Villette and Belleville rubbed shoulders with others from the Marais, Faubourg Saint-Honoré, and perhaps even Faubourg Saint-Germain, which delighted Jules Vallès, an old revolutionary: '...[T]he crowd has erupted on to the scene, and... everyone has a place in public life.... Legitimists, bourgeois, aristocrats, merchants, workers, how many find themselves side by side on the pavement.'

'PLUS ÇA CHANGE...'

The more shoppers, and the hustlers and kiosk-vendors they attracted, mobbed the boulevards, creating traffic jams and other discomforts, the more the boulevards resembled the *vieux Paris* Preservationists claimed to long for. An Englishman, Arthur Savile-Grant, invented the kiosk, and made a nice fortune selling it in Paris. A Paris journalist in 1891 described

> kiosks, square kiosks, round kiosks, oval kiosks – like hatboxes – kiosks for all purposes, kiosks abandoned for lack of renters, kiosks of florists spilling out over the pavement, kiosks for bars, kiosks for the pleasure of being kiosks since they have been closed since birth....

He also complained that

> the oyster peddler tosses shells at our legs, the distributor of broadsheets bars the passage, the perambulating salesman draws a crowd ideal for pickpockets; deprived of the pavement, we must hop quickly into the street, where the omnibus waits to run over us, if we have, happily, escaped the carriage.

## 'C'EST L'IMMORALITÉ'

Was the *grand magasin* a social menace? Gustave Macé, *chef de service* of the Sûreté, thought so. He estimated 600 shoplifts per store per day, and worse, claimed that in the crowded atmosphere people became depraved or hysterical, sexually promiscuous, and were easily victimized by 'fetishists, mashers, and sexual deviants'. The stores were 'an abyss, a Babel, a spider web,' where '[w]ith her little bird's head, the daughter of Eve enters into this inferno of coquetry like a mouse into a mousetrap'. What was the *grand magasin*, he posed? '*C'est l'immoralité*' was the answer. Georges Montorgueil and Guy de Maupassant blamed these dens of iniquity on 'money-grubbing Jews'. In fact, only three of the *grands magasins* were run by Jews.

'*C'est l'immoralité*' apparently also applied to the 1890s fad of women on bicycles, because in order to ride them women had to wear trousers, which violated social convention. Paris fashion designers created a bicycle costume: hip-length waistcoats over puff-sleeved blouses, full knickerbockers (a cross between men's trousers and women's bloomers), long stockings, and a man's hat or cap. Women cyclists loved it, but others accepted it only so long as she was on a bicycle. In 1895 certain women were observed 'promenading on the boulevards' in trousers, and the Prefect of Police intervened, forbidding these 'pseudo-bicyclists' to appear in trousers unless they were on bicycles.

## LE MÉTRO

*Vieux Parisiens* also objected to the *Métropolitain*, the underground rail system favoured from the 1880s on by those who recognized the extent to which the expanding population was creating transportation problems. Preservationists argued it would destroy the *vieux Paris* landscape; small shopkeepers complained that it would carry shoppers away from the centre of Paris and to the boulevard stores; and the Fédération des groupes républicains socialistes denounced it as a capitalist plot. In the end *Paris nouveau* won out, and construction on the *Métro* began in the 1890s.

## LA LIGUE SYNDICALE

This league of small shopkeepers included the most enthusiastic *vieux Parisiens*. Louis Boeuf, a candidate for city council in 1890, was a member, a *ligueur*: 'Son of Paris, having always lived in this great city, my speech bears no trace of an exotic origin. Raised in the class of the ... labouring people, I know and share the aspirations of the Parisian democracy.' Boeuf felt threatened by a Paris of 'power and luxury, swarming with parasites, money-grubbers and a mass of unemployed'. He and other *ligueurs* resented the Eiffel Tower, built, it was said, with Italian rather than French labour for the Exposition of 1889; hated department stores against which they could not compete; resisted the urban centralization inherent in development of the *Métro* system, the start of which they delayed for two decades; and railed against a 'Jewish Feudality' plotting to take over the city and country. Populist, republican, democratic and even socialist in their views, these traditional Paris shopkeepers were also reactionary, xenophobic and racist. They had much in common with Paris Fascists a generation later.

## MONTMARTRE

*Ligueur* 'sentimental patriotism tinged with xenophobia and anti-semitism' joined up with populist radicalism and socialism in Montmartre, when that old working-class quarter became a centre for populist cabaret entertainment in the 1880s. Montmartre residents included Georges Clemenceau (mayor 1871), playwright and Boulangist Paul Déroulède, who frequented the Cabaret de l'Enfer with Alexandre Dumas *fils*, Henri Rochefort, a radical journalist who deteriorated into a 'prince of the gutter press', and painter Adolphe Willette, *artiste révolté*, who lived at 79 Rue Rochechouart and proclaimed Montmartre the last bastion of French patriotism. Montmartre's bohemian appearance was borrowed from the Latin Quarter, but the political language was all its own. Aristide Bruant's brutal cabaret songs were aimed at the 'snobs and nabobs' and the Jews who directed them, who were ruining Paris.

Elements of the political cabaret survives in at least one café, just off the Boulevard de Clichy, where an entertainer in cap, denim and red neckcloth goes from table to table singing populist and socialist songs.

## LE CHAT NOIR

The quintessential Montmartre cabaret was the Chat Noir in Boulevard de Rochechouart, opened in 1881 by the painter Rodolphe Salis. The style was irreverence and independence, and a sentimental regard for a romantic past. Waiters wore the green palms of the Académie Française, and the rooms were decorated with pseudo-Renaissance accoutrements. Adolphe Willette was a regular, claiming that the Chat Noir was 'a last-ditch resistance against the invasion of foreign influences'; his mural '*Parce Domine*' (Be lenient, Lord) covered one wall. Entertainment included songs, comic patter and, after 1885, silhouettes made of cardboard or metal projected on to a screen with musical accompaniment. One such show, 'Épopée,' depicted a Napoleonic military triumph.

Joseph Oller and Charles Zidler opened the Moulin Rouge in 1889, in Place Blanche on the Boulevard de Clichy. Unlike the Chat Noir, this club was entertainment rather than political statement, despite the off-beat artists and others who were its *habitués*; for tourists, at any rate, it came to symbolize 'gay nineties' naughtiness. Meanwhile, at the Rat Mort in Place Pigalle, women clad in men's clothing danced with each other.

## BOULANGISM: 'LA PATRIE EN DANGER!'

General Georges Boulanger – republican, militarist, patriot, Bonapartist and populist – was the perfect object for Montmartrais admiration, even though he preferred the life of the boulevards. He was a useful minister of war, but could not resist adulation, whether of society women who seemed eager to add to his notoriety as a womanizer, or of the Paris mob. The general allowed his name to appear on the ballot for an Assembly seat in various constituencies with some success, though it cost him his military office.

The crucial year was 1889. The département du Nord elected Boulanger with a huge majority; so too did the boulevards and Montmartre. Georges Clemenceau only briefly favoured the general, but Paul Déroulède, Henri Rochefort, Adolphe Willette (who stood for the Chamber in 1889 as an anti-Semite) and Rodolphe Salis supported him without reservation. On the night of 27 January the Cabinet met in the Palais de l'Élysée, while Boulangists gathered around the general at Durand's Restaurant (now the Paris headquarters of Thomas Cook) in the Rue Royale. Crowds thronged the streets outside, singing La Marseillaise, Boulangist songs, and chanting:

> *C'est Boulange, lange, lange,*
> *C'est Boulanger qu'il nous faut,*
> *Oh! Oh! Oh!*

Occasionally they also shouted '*A l'Élysée!*' A *coup* seemed to be inevitable.

Nothing happened. Boulanger left Durand's, it was thought to spend the night with his mistress, and was driven off amidst wild cheers. The next day, hearing that he was to be arrested for 'placing the Republic in danger', the general decamped for Belgium. There he remained until 1891 when, distraught over the death of his mistress, he lay down across her grave and shot himself. Little wonder that this episode came to be known as *La Comédie boulangiste*, or that Georges Clemenceau proposed as his epitaph: 'Here lies General Boulanger, who died as he lived – like a second lieutenant.'

## *The Dreyfus Affair*

Captain Alfred Dreyfus, a Jewish member of the French general staff, was accused of spying for Germany. He was arrested, convicted under questionable circumstances, and sentenced to life imprisonment on Devil's Island. The Dreyfus family pressed to reopen the case and persuaded Émile Zola to help. He published *J'Accuse*, questioning the conviction, in Georges Clemenceau's newspaper, *L'Aurore*. Then Paris got into the act: crowds demonstrated for and against Dreyfus, such literary luminaries as Anatole France, André Gide and Marcel Proust signed the *Manifesto of the Intellectuals* denouncing the conviction, and the Leftist and Rightist press postulated and denounced. *L'Aurore* and Jean Jaurès' socialist *L'Humanité* were pro-Dreyfus, while Édouard

Drumont's *La Libre Parole* and Charles Maurras' *L'Action Française* led the anti-Dreyfus attack.

In due course the captain was retried, exonerated, restored to rank and awarded the Légion d'Honneur. The affair was not about him, however; rather, it was a dress rehearsal for Paris politics in the 1930s.

## More Fairs

Neither Boulanger nor Dreyfus could dissuade Paris from one of its favourite occupations, putting on Expositions.

### 1889

The sites were the Palais de l'Industrie and the grounds of the Palais de Trocadéro. The French colonial empire was the central theme, ironic in that the Exposition was held on the centennial of a revolution meant to liberate people. Wild West showman Buffalo Bill put in an appearance, and exhibits featured the latest in new technology including electricity, by which the fair complex was illuminated. The Galerie des Machines, a magnificent building 420 by 115 metres and 43 metres high, housed heavy machinery exhibits; architect Frantz Jourdain called it 'a work of art as beautiful, as pure, as original, as elevated as a Greek temple or a cathedral'. The famous Eiffel Tower, built for this fair across the river from the Trocadéro, was a great hit with visitors, but *vieux Parisiens* called it 'metal asparagus'. They also sniffed at the crass commercialism of the Exposition, complaining that its 'vulgar cosmopolitan products' compared poorly to the 'works of pure Parisian taste' that could be found in the arcades of the Palais-Royal.

### 1900

The site began on the Champ-de-Mars and extended along the river to include the approach to Les Invalides. More new construction came with this fair than any of its predecessors. The Avenue Nicholas II and the Pont Alexandre III (a bridge reminiscent of London's Westminster Bridge for its use of gas lights and wrought iron) were built to connect Les Invalides and the Champs-Élysées. The Grand Palais and Petit Palais along Avenue Nicholas II, featuring metal skeletons, concrete

The Pont Alexandre III, which used gas lights and wrought iron as embellishment

exteriors and skylights, were constructed to house exhibits. A colonial exhibit in the Palais de Trocadéro included 'Hindu temples, savage huts, pagodas, souks, Algerian alleys, Chinese, Japanese, Sudanese, Senegalese, Siamese, Cambodian quarters.... The universe in a garden!' Electricity was again featured, along with Paris fashions, the latter aspect stressed by a fifteen-foot sculpture of 'La Parisienne' atop the main entrance, wearing a Madame Paquin dress.

More than any other, the 1900 Exposition reflected a mass consumerism, because it was put together through 'the conjunction of banking and dreaming, of sales pitch and seduction, of publicity and pleasure....' Perhaps so; 50 million visitors from around the world came to see it.

## INDUSTRIAL PARIS

Mass consumerism was a phenomenon of modern industrialization. More and more after 1870 Paris and its suburbs were industrialized. Factories in Saint-Denis, Ivry-sur-Seine and Alfortville, among others, produced bicycles, carriages, household goods and, in due course, cars. They also exploited workers, which resulted in industrial action and the formation of trades union organizations, such as the Confédération Général du Travail (CGT). The CGT was linked to the socialist Section Français de l'Internationale Ouvrière (SFIO), founded and led by Jules Guesde, Édouard Vaillant and Jean Jaurès. There were many unions and socialist factions but these were the most influential. All were national in scope but all were centred in Paris.

Early on, industrial action was often violent. In 1887 pay reduction at a Saint-Denis chemical plant resulted in the shooting of a foreman; in 1888 pay reductions at the Forges of Alfortville led to a workers' riot. Later, organized strikes replaced random violence. In 1906 tens of thousands of construction, jewellery, cabinet and other workers joined car workers striking for the eight-hour day, for example.

## HUBERTINE AUCLERT

The suffragist movement paralleled trades unionism, though with far less success. The leader prior to 1914 was Hubertine Auclert, the French equal of Emily Pankhurst in Britain and Elisabeth Cady Stanton in the United States. Auclert came to Paris from Allier in 1873, and set to work. She led marches, founded two feminist organizations, Droit des femmes and Suffrage des femmes, edited *La Citoyenne*, the first French suffragist newspaper, and was brought to trial for disrupting a polling place during Chamber elections in 1908. Steven Hause described what happened.

> [A] stout woman dressed in widow's black marched forcefully past the doorman at a Parisian polling place. Her strong eyes and determined features persuaded voters to withdraw from her path.... [O]fficials sat motionless at

the sight of a woman in the sanctum sanctorum of masculine politics.... They watched as she seized the ballot box ... and then hurled it to the floor. As the contents of that 'urn of lies' spread at her feet, Auclert denounced the 'unisexual suffrage' of the French republic, then stamped on the evidence of it. The police arrested her a few moments later.

Hubertine Auclert enjoyed no lasting success, nor was she honoured in retrospect. All the same, she stirred the pot of female discontent and encouraged others to keep the pressure on.

## *Paris in the Great War: la bavure*

The coming of war in 1914 is best summed up in the phrase *'la bavure'* (cock-up). No European nation wanted it; but after Austria invaded Serbia in retaliation for the assassination of Archduke Franz-Ferdinand by a Serb nationalist, Russia, fearing the consequences of the Austrian action, began to mobilize. The Germans mobilized because the Russians mobilized, the French mobilized because the Germans mobilized – and on and on, until on 3 August German cavalry units crossed the border into Belgium, inevitably drawing Britain into the conflict. The Great War, later to be known as the First World War, was under way.

FRANCE RESPONDS

It was feared that mobilization would signal a general strike. Labour unrest had increased after 1910 (was it because Lenin was in Paris that year?) and strikes became larger – for example, the Renault car-works strike in 1913. Should the government arrest those named on 'Carnet B', a list of 2,501 potential revolutionaries, trade-union leaders, anarchists and others? The chief of the Sûreté scoffed, 'They will follow the regimental bands.' He was right, at least for a while, until life in the trenches drove several regiments, comprised largely of working-class men and peasants, to mutiny. Some of them were court-martialled and shot in retaliation. Then strikes resumed, encouraged by the Communist Party, and such Radical journals as *Le Bonnet Rouge* (formerly subsidized by the government) called for peace and even revolution. Of course, an equal number of fanatics wrote in favour of the war in such journals as *La France Libre*.

## PATRIOTS IN PARIS

Official anti–German propaganda was supplemented by anti–German sentiment expressed voluntarily by the Parisian literati. André Gide wrote of 'brutish Germans', Romain Rolland of 'ugly Germans', and Marcel Prévost of 'devious Germans'. In a travel book Octave Mirbeau sensationalized some Berlin gossip about homosexuals at the Kaiser's court, and both Saint-Saëns and Debussy argued that German culture was barbaric and corrupting – which was a shot at Richard Wagner, if nothing else. Meanwhile Marie Curie bought war bonds with her Nobel Prize money, Georges Braque went to the front as a soldier, and music patron Misia Edwards formed an ambulance unit in which playwright Jean Cocteau was a driver.

## THE MARNE

For Paris, the worst moment was in September 1914 when it appeared that the Germans might attack the city. General von Kluck out-manoeuvred General Maunoury at the Ourcq and reached the Marne. His troops seized the racing stables at Chantilly, and cavalry units came within sight of the Eiffel Tower. Parisians panicked; it was 1870 all over again. However, the Germans made mistakes, the French fought with determination, and on 6 September General Gallieni transported several thousand troops of the Paris garrison in taxis to reinforce the French attack on the German flank. This was the 'miracle of the Marne', which turned the tide of the German advance.

## PARIS AT WAR

The Louvre and other museums packed away art treasures for safety, and Parisians learned to live with 'tedium and inconvenience', aerial bombardment (zeppelins dropped 222 bombs altogether, which did minimal damage), rationing, an increase in tuberculosis, the presence of rumbustious Americans after 1917, and a moment of panic when it appeared that the German spring offensive in 1918, supported by Big Bertha, a German railway gun which fired shells called 'blockbusters' from eighty miles away, might succeed. Big Bertha dropped 286 shells on Paris, killed 205 and wounded 563. One shell hit the church of

Saint-Gervais and Saint-Protais during mass, collapsing the roof and killing or wounding 175 worshippers. That was the worst that the Germans did to Paris, and was as close as they came to reaching the city. An armistice was signed on 11 November 1918.

PEACE

Paris was the venue for the peace conferences. United States President Wilson, the 'Galahad from the west whose army, uttering the felicitous words, "Lafayette, we are here," had arrived in time to clinch the victory,' was cheered as he drove down the Champs-Élysées with French President Poincaré. The Americans stayed in the Hôtel Crillon, and the British in the Hôtel Majestic on Avenue Kléber. Meetings of the Council of Ten and associates took place throughout the city. The treaty with Germany, which returned Alsace and Lorraine to France among other things, was signed on 28 June 1919 in the Galerie des Glaces at Château Versailles. On Bastille Day Parisians paraded in the Champs-Élysées, and a year later entombed the body of an 'unknown soldier' beneath the Arc de Triomphe. The commemorative flame for French war dead was lighted in 1923.

# After the Great War

It is often said that the war 'liberated' Paris from pre-war conventions in almost every sphere. Certainly there was a different feel about the city. Cars appeared in great numbers, led by Renault and Citroën. Lamented one Parisian: 'It's finished, the tranquillity of our streets, and the charm of promenading either on foot or in a carriage … Paris belongs to the machines.' Fashionable women smoked cigarettes in public, shortened their skirts, 'crossed their legs at any angle', played sports, and gave the impression of being independent and liberated. Sometimes they lived openly with their lovers. They did not, at the same time, gain political rights as did American, British and German women. Frenchmen showed little interest in seeing the status of women change.

BUILDING BOOM

There was much going on all the same. The last wall of fortifications, long obsolete, was pulled down and the *Métro* extended into the suburbs. Parisians moved with it, and the population declined in the centre of the city to just over 2.7 million in 1939; Greater Paris grew to about 4.5 million. Apartment building boomed. Auguste Perret, Henri Sauvage and Pierre Charreau designed such modern structures as Charreau's Maison de Verre in Rue Saint-Guillaume, built entirely of steel and glass. Le Corbusier designed the grandest dwelling house of the period, the Swiss House in the Cité Universitaire near the Parc Montsouris, for University of Paris students.

## TOURISTS FROM ACROSS THE SEA

Americans came to Paris in droves, but many more than in the past were of limited means. However, Parisians profited most from the wealthy few who typically spent their Paris day in this manner: the wives shopped for Paris clothes while their husbands kept track of the

The Moulin Rouge

stock market; together they 'did' the Louvre and Napoléon's tomb in the afternoon, dined at Maxim's or an equivalent restaurant in the evening, enjoyed an apéritif at Fouquet's, and finished the evening watching Josephine Baker at the Folies Bergères, or Mistinguett and Maurice Chevalier at the Moulin Rouge. Then it was back to such opulent hotels as the Ritz, Crillon, Meurice or George V, to retire in 'almost identical bedrooms with french windows, gilded mirrors, and Louis XV type of furniture upholstered in gray or rose satin'.

These tourists rarely saw the real Paris of ordinary people. Elliot Paul did. His two decades of neighbourhood life in the Rue de la Huchette area on the Left Bank was chronicled in *The Last Time I Saw Paris.*

## *The Avant-garde and their Fellow-Travellers*

The arts in post-war Paris were avant-garde, which is to say new, different and irreverent. The Dadaists espoused 'the permanent revolt of the individual against art, against morality, against society,' which does not leave much. The Surrealists strove for a 'pure psychic automatism by means of which it is proposed to express in either spoken or written language, or by any other means whatever, the real functioning of thought'. There was also the frivolous, imitative, but also imaginative art-deco style which emerged from the Exposition des Arts Décoratifs in Paris in 1925. An entire generation was influenced by art deco well beyond Paris.

### THE BOHEMIAN FRINGE

For the avant-garde and their imitators, the 'bohemian fringe', Paris was a life-style. They could be found at the Deux Magots, the Café de Flore and the Brasserie Lipp in the Boulevard Saint-Germain, at the Café de la Rotonde and Le Boeuf sur le Toit next-door in Montparnasse, and at the Chat Noir and Rat Mort in Montmartre. A typical bohemian was Max Jacob, as degenerate an artist as could be wished for until he converted to Catholicism, became a monastic lay brother and denounced Montparnasse as sinful. Armand Lanoux wrote that he was one of only two Montparnassais who ever 'laid eyes upon the Virgin. The fact that it was in the subway that Max saw her is beside the point.'

There was also Man Ray, the American Surrealist, who photographed the nude back of Kiki (Alice Prin) as a violin. Kiki was known as 'the queen of Montparnasse', a singer and model who 'was not ashamed of her breasts'. She was one of many women in Montparnasse and Montmartre who lived with artists and writers – of both sexes – in a bohemian *demi-monde* where bourgeois conventions were scorned or, worse, simply ignored.

Artists, writers and composers were less orthodox, more discontented and more on the fringe than at any time in Paris history. Marcel Proust penned *A la recherche du temps perdu*, a testament to a failed pre-war society; Paul Valéry wrote narcissistically, including this play on René Descartes: '*L'Homme pense, donc je suis, dit l'Univers*' (Man thinks, therefore I am, says the universe); Jules Romain, Georges Duhamel, Marcel Achard, Jacques Deval, Henri Bernstein, Marcel Pagnol, Luigi Pirandello and Jean Cocteau (who also made films) were leading playwrights, while François Carco told the story of the bohemians of both Montparnasse and Montmartre in poetry and the novel. André Malraux based his writing on his own experience as a Communist in the 1920s and an anti-Fascist in the 1930s.

Pablo Picasso evolved beyond his Blue and Cubist periods in his Montmartre studio in Rue de Bateau-Lavoir, while Amedeo Modigliani strove for a new emotional effect through distortions of classic forms. In music, Igor Stravinsky remained dominant; Erik Satie, a bohemian at least in appearance, was more notable as an influence on others than for what he composed; and Francis Poulenc, also a bohemian, achieved a reputation for his ballet *Les Biches*, which premièred in 1924. Gabriel Fauré and Paul Dukas, best known for *Requiem* and *L'apprenti sorcier* respectively, were as respectable as the others were bohemian. Dukas, who set teaching policy at the Paris conservatory, was elected to the Académie des Beaux-Arts in 1934.

## EXPATRIATES

Paris knew many expatriates. Gertrude Stein and Alice B. Toklas, who lived at 27 Rue de Fleurus, Ernest Hemingway, F. Scott Fitzgerald, Ezra Pound, Ford Madox Ford and James Joyce, among others, socialized on the Boulevard Saint-Germain and in the cafés of Montparnasse.

Hemingway's *A Moveable Feast* evokes the unique experience of these literati. Josephine Baker from Saint Louis, Missouri, opened at the Folies Bergères in 1925, 'clad only in a tutu made of rhinestone-studded bananas and three bracelets'. Baker introduced the Charleston to Parisians while fellow American Duke Ellington popularized American jazz. She worked for the *Résistance* during the Second World War, for which she was awarded both the Croix de Guerre and the Légion d'Honneur. There were exiles from the Russian Revolution also; it was not unusual to encounter a Russian prince driving a Paris cab.

## CINEMA

To painting and writing was added a new art form, the cinema. This appealed from the start to a mass audience. For a few centimes one could see Pola Negri, Catherine Hessling (later to marry the film-maker Jean Renoir), or Charlie Chaplin, known in Paris as 'Charlot', in any of 184 cinemas in Paris. Most French films were less popular though of better quality than American films, two exceptions being *La Roue* and *Napoléon* by Abel Gance, which were both popular and superior. On the other side, Chaplin's films, made in Hollywood, were also an exception among American films. They were extolled in Paris as works of art and genius. Jean Cocteau admitted that words were inadequate to describe Chaplin's contribution as a film-maker.

## SCIENCE AND EDUCATION

Scientific research and the University of Paris began to regain lost prominence when, in the 1880s and 1890s, bacteriologist Louis Pasteur, Sorbonne professor and first director of the institute which bears his name, created the process of pasteurization, and developed vaccines against anthrax. Pierre and Marie Curie followed, winning the Nobel prize for physics jointly with Antoine Becquerel in 1903 for their work on radiation. After Pierre's death, Marie Curie assumed his chair at the Sorbonne and won the Nobel prize for chemistry in 1911. Thereafter she headed the Institut Curie, created in her husband's name by the University of Paris and the Institut Pasteur. In his field Urbain Leverrier had discovered the planet Neptune in 1846, and revised existing planetary theories.

After the war, University of Paris scientists excelled in the new area of nuclear physics. Nobel laureates included Jean Perrin in 1926 for work on molecular structure, Louis de Broglie in 1929 in quantum mechanics, and Frédéric and Irène Joliot-Curie (she was Pierre and Marie Curie's daughter) in 1935 for radioactivity. In 1946 Frédéric Joliot-Curie was appointed chairman of the French Atomic Energy Commission.

Higher education in Paris recovered from decades of stagnation when such luminaries as Émile Durkheim and Gabriel Monod emerged. By 1914 46 per cent of all university students in France studied in Paris, whether at the University of Paris or the École Normale Supérieure and the École Polytechnique. There were fewer science students in Paris, owing to improving provincial universities, but more women, commonly in teacher training but after 1900 in medicine as well.

## *Politics Before the Second World War*

The Great Depression began with the New York stock market crash of 1929 and reached Paris in 1931. It lasted until 1938, giving encouragement to those wanting a Communist revolution, and to others leaning toward a Fascist revolution. George Valois claimed that France, not Italy, was the birth place of Fascism, which he described as 'a fusion of socialism and nationalism, of Barrès and Sorel'.

THE LEFT

During the Great Depression bankruptcies increased as production fell. Unemployment rose, 260,000 nationwide in 1932 and 426,000 in 1935, and strikes were more numerous: one million came out on a single day in Paris in 1934. Desperate workers flocked to the Communist Party (PCF) in such 'red' suburbs as Ivry, Saint-Denis, where Communists gained control of the municipal government in 1924, and Belleville. However, the party slipped after Moscow-trained Stalinist Maurice Thorez became leader, a post he would retain until 1964. As a solution, in 1934 at a PFC conference in Ivry Thorez advocated forming a front with the Socialists and Radicals, focusing on Fascism as the common enemy. This was the Popular Front that won the Chamber in 1936 under the leadership of Socialist Léon Blum.

## THE RIGHT

Desperate workers also turned Right, though less often. There were many Rightist groups, but with only nominal differences. Lesser ones, at least in number, included Action Française with 7,000 Paris members, which was monarchist with recognizable Fascist traits; so too were the Camelots du Roi. Pierre Taittinger's Jeunesses Patriotes was Bonapartist, while Croix de Feu, once a veterans organization, became openly Fascist under Colonel de la Rocque. It was banned in 1936, but reorganized as Le Parti Social Français, soon to have 800,000 adherents. Solidarité Française was a uniformed Fascist organization funded by François Coty, the *parfumeur*, and commanded by Jean Renaud; the Left referred to the organization as *Sidilarité Française* because they suspected its members were mercenary '*Sidis*' from Algeria. Meanwhile Jacques Doriot, ex-Communist mayor of Saint-Denis, organized Parti Populaire Français, which had 100,000 members by 1937.

On it went. Extremes of Left and Right spread across the country, but their proclivity for violence tended to be let out in Paris, the centre of government.

## THE PRESS

Paris newspapers, long a part of French political life, contributed signally to the political discontent of the 1930s. *L'Action Française* was the Royalist daily; *Écho de Paris* (later *Jour-Écho de Paris*) espoused other elements of right-wing politics; and the weekly tabloid *Gringoire* regularly criticized Britain and extolled Fascist Italy. *L'Aube*, a Catholic daily, supported the Popular Democratic Party and Republicans in the Spanish Civil War; *Le Populaire* advocated Socialist causes; *L'Humanité*, originally Socialist, had become the organ of the Communists; and *Ce Soir* was pro-Communist though unofficially so. These and other Paris newspapers and journals were vigilantly anti-government, manipulative and usually scurrilous, and frequently called for violence. The 'poisonous filth pumped out by the right-wing press', in James Mac-Millan's words, had much to do with the physical assault on Léon Blum outside the Palais Bourbon in February 1936 by an Action Française mob.

## THE STAVISKY SCANDAL

Corruption was commonplace. In 1933 a warrant was issued against one Serge Alexandre Stavisky, a shady financial wheeler-dealer of Jewish origin, concerning a stock fraud scheme. His reputation was well known and he appeared to be immune from prosecution. *L'Action Française* published some letters proving Stavisky was connected with a cabinet minster; there was also a question of campaign funds distributed in the right places in order to protect him. *L'Action Française* urged that he was just the sort that was ruining France.

Early in 1934 Stavisky committed suicide at Chamonix just as he was about to be arrested. The question arose, did the government murder him to keep him from talking? Prime Minister Chautemps pretended that there was no Stavisky case – a denial that reeked of a cover-up because the prime minister's brother-in-law was head of the *parquet*, the bureau responsible for prosecuting financial irregularities. Henri de Kerillis of *Écho de Paris* and editorialists from *L'Action Française* stirred up agitation against the government, and for nearly a month nightly riots in central Paris, with shouts from the Right of 'Down with the thieves', and from the Left of 'Up the Soviets', intruded upon late sessions of the Assembly and the Cabinet. The police were surprisingly gentle in their treatment of rioters, even when the Camelots du Roi threw marbles under the hooves of police horses and short-circuited the tram system.

Chautemps was replaced as premier by Édouard Daladier and the rioting quietened down. But then Daladier moved in all the wrong directions. He transferred Chautemps' brother-in-law from the *parquet* to a high judicial office (the odour of corruption), transferred the head of the Sûreté to be director of the Comédie-Française (in its own way comical), which was interpreted to mean that the theatre was going to be censored, and sacked Prefect of Police Jean Chiappe, who was immensely popular with the Right because he not only harried pimps and prostitutes but Communists even more. Chiappe refused to accept another post and retired, taking with him Édouard Renard, Prefect of the Seine. With that, more problems emerged.

## THE FEBRUARY RIOT

On 6 February 1934 the Chamber of Deputies greeted Daladier with such shouting that he could not be heard. 'The Right howled, the Communists sang the Internationale,' while outside demonstrators of all political persuasions massed on the Place de la Concorde and began forcing their way across the Pont de la Concorde to the Palais Bourbon. Police tried to stop them and the demonstration turned into a riot, and then an uprising. Some rioters produced guns while others made pikes out of the iron railings used to protect trees. Others threw bottles and rocks, and tied razor blades to long sticks to use against mounted police. A bus was set ablaze; a mob broke into the Ministry of Marine and tried to burn it, but was dissuaded by a naval officer in full uniform; police charged the rioters and fired on them, killing some and wounding others; firemen were attacked; and a procession of ex-servicemen singing La Marseillaise was joined by others singing the Internationale. Inside the Palais Bourbon, the government persevered until the Chamber gave it a majority. Then the deputies fled, many being assaulted by rioters in the process.

The disturbance continued through the night, picking up tempo on the morning of 7 February. Now it featured the 'scum of Paris' taking advantage of the situation to loot and pillage. The police were exhausted and unable to prevent mobs from going where and doing what they pleased. There was a brief respite on the 8th, then riots again on the 9th, particularly in such poor working-class quarters as Belleville. Finally, on 12 February the Socialists led more than a million Paris workers into a general strike, and the city was virtually shut down. This spelled the end of the Daladier government, at least for the time being.

The violence did not end, however. Students rioted in 1935 when Professor Gaston Jèze, former counsel to Emperor Haille Selassie, spoke at the University of Paris against the Italian invasion of Ethiopia. Catholics at the university were divided between those who supported Mussolini's policies and those who condemned them as immoral. The latter included Jacques Maritain, Paul Claudel and François Mauriac. This confrontation continued later over the Spanish Civil War.

## BLUM

In 1936 the Left won the Chamber, and Léon Blum formed a Popular Front government with Socialists, Radicals and Communists. He took office against the backdrop of two million workers on 'sit-down' strikes in the Paris region – the workers remained in the factories and were brought food by their families. The Chamber enacted long-needed labour legislation, including introduction of the forty-hour week. Bastille Day 1936 was a happy occasion. It did not last.

## CITY OF DISCONTENT

Blum's government was plagued with violence and unrest. In the last four months of 1936 2,400 strikes occurred, many of them in Greater Paris. In March 1937 the Parti Social Français held a rally at a cinema in Boulevard de Clichy which was attacked by Left-wing counter-demonstrators. The police came in with truncheons flying and guns blazing, leaving seven dead and hundreds injured. A Socialist government had spilled workers' blood was the cry, and two days later Paris was engulfed with strikes, and the CGT was calling for a general strike. The Blum government fell three months later.

Also in 1937, a bomb went off in the Hôtel Astoria near the Étoile, blowing out the side of the building. The Communists claimed it was an attack on them, though this was never proved.

# *Pre-War Modernization and One More Fair*

All of this did not prevent an increase in cars in Greater Paris from 150,000 in 1922 to 500,000 in 1938, state funding to complete the *Métro* system and build more housing for urban workers, widening of parts of Rue des Deux-Ponts and the Quai de l'Hôtel de Ville, improving Les Halles, building a new Pont du Carrousel, or demolishing the last sections of the old city fortifications and erecting 38,750 new dwelling units where they had stood. The result, said a critic who was clearly conscious of the pun, was 'a dense wall of mediocrity encircling the city'. There was also the Exposition in 1937.

## THE EXPOSITION OF 1937

The Exposition provided a respite, however brief, to the upheavals of the decade. The sites were the Champ-de-Mars and the grounds of the Trocadéro. Opening was planned for Bastille Day, but planning and preparation, which included the demolition of the Palais de Trocadéro and the construction of the Palais de Chaillot, was not complete. The joke went that the fair opened on schedule and closed the next day. Only the Soviet and Nazi pavilions, which faced each other across the esplanade leading to the Palais de Chaillot, were ready on time, and that, it was said, was because each kept adding height in competition with the other, until fair officials made them stop. This probably was not true. Albert Speer designed the German building, which was square and topped by an eagle holding a swastika within a wreath.

Even when it was complete, the 1937 Exposition seemed to pale in comparison to earlier ones. There were a few bright spots: the Hungarian pavilion gave out free glasses of Tokay, and the British and Belgian pavilions were large and sumptuous. The United States pavilion was particularly disappointing: dependent entirely upon private funds, the exhibit contained photographs of America, a model of the new Empire State building, a display devoted to the California wine industry, and little else, in what one observer termed a structure that resembled a filling station.

## THE COMING OF WAR

Between 1938 and 1939 Germany annexed Austria, dismembered Czechoslovakia and threatened Poland, all in keeping with a policy of overturning the Versailles Treaty of 1919. On 1 September 1939, after all diplomatic efforts to prevent it had broken down, Germany invaded Poland, and two days later France and Britain declared war on the Third Reich. War came to Paris eight months later, and Parisians entered upon an episode that had few parallels in their history.

# CHAPTER EIGHT

# *War and Peace,*
## 1939–Present

In June 1940 the French government surrendered Paris to the Germans. Was this the end of the city as a great centre of European civilization? Not a bit of it. After the war Paris modernized and became again a centre of western civilization. 'This city', wrote a Paris prefect, 'knows how to rejuvenate and adapt itself resolutely to its time.'

## *The Coming of the Second World War*

The European war of 1939–45 was either inevitable or an accident, depending upon whether one reads Hugh Trevor-Roper or A.J.P. Taylor. What is certain is that, like most other Europeans, Parisians did not want it.

### THE MAGINOT LINE

A line of elaborate fortifications, ordered in the 1920s by war minister André Maginot for whom they were named, stretched from Switzerland to Belgium. Concrete bunkers, underground railways, gun emplacements, tank traps, and 500,000 gallons of red wine in stock, characterized the arrangement. The Maginot Line would save France from the 'boche', if ever the need arose. At least that was what chief of staff General Maurice Gamelin believed. Paul Reynaud and tank officer Colonel Charles de Gaulle did not. De Gaulle had read writings on tank warfare by English General J.F.C. Fuller and German General Heinz Guderian, and tried to acquaint his superiors with the importance of the tactics they described. Only Reynaud listened, but could act only after he became premier in March 1940 and made de Gaulle his war minister. By then it was too late.

## AUGUST 1939

Crisis followed crisis prior to the outbreak of war. Germany remilitarized the Rhineland in 1936; annexed Austria and the Sudetenland in 1938; occupied Prague and threatened Poland in 1939; and on 24 August signed a non-aggression treaty with the Soviet Union, which effectively made Poland defenceless. Parisians feared the worst. The Louvre, for instance, when the Sudeten crisis loomed, had made preparation to send truckloads of art works to Château Chambord in the Loire Valley for safekeeping. Few Parisians were surprised when German forces crossed the Polish frontier on 1 September, nor that France joined its British ally in a declaration of war two days later.

## THE DRÔLE DE GUERRE

The collective feeling in Paris, as elsewhere, was to wonder why 'we must die for Danzig'. Beyond that it was captured in the phrase '*il faut en finir*' (let's get it done with). On 3 September Paris theatres closed. They reopened the next day. 'Paris must remain Paris so that soldiers on leave can find a bit of Parisian charm despite all,' explained Maurice Chevalier. This began the *drôle de guerre* (funny war), so named because nothing happened. Tanks remained parked, guns were silent save for occasional 'symbolic' barrages, and soldiers grew bored. The newly formed Ministère d'Information (propaganda ministry) based in the Hôtel Continental dropped leaflets over German lines. Patrols occasionally ventured beyond the Maginot Line; one of them once captured some German soldiers, who were surprised to learn that France and Germany were at war. German aircraft occasionally flew reconnaissance over Paris and were fired upon by French anti-aircraft batteries. This caused more harm to the city than to the aircraft. On one occasion an anti-aircraft shell fell near the Censier *Métro* station on Rue de Mirbel, killing and wounding a number of people and damaging an elementary school in the Rue Monge.

Parisians went through the motions of war. They carried gas-masks, obeyed air-raid warnings, donated scrap metal, volunteered for war work, and perhaps resented the fact that the 200 truckloads of art from the Louvre were on their way to Chambord and safety while they remained behind. Rationing was planned, which included the anomaly that, while all fancy twist bread would be banned, croissants would not. A newspaper notice warned that when rationing was put into effect, shops selling meat, cold-cuts, alcohol, candy or pastry would be closed at least two days a week. Parisians seemed to think that soldiers were underemployed. The story goes that the wife of a shopkeeper in uniform sent some paperwork to her husband at the front. 'You write to the customer, since you don't have anything to do. I've got my hands full.' For their part soldiers resented the fact that, the threat of rationing notwithstanding, it was business as usual in Paris.

In the spring of 1940, the Germans advanced.

## Blitzkrieg

During the months of the *drôle de guerre*, the Germans had cut access roads through the Ardennes Forest in Belgium, at the edge of which the Maginot Line ended. Panzers used these roads to outflank the French defences. This was '*Blitzkrieg*' (lightning war), the tactic that Colonel de Gaulle had been warning against. It combined tanks with close air support, and General Gamelin's decision to attack the advancing Germans, which drew the French away from their fortifications, made it all the more effective.

MAY 1940

The battle for France began on 9 May, and by the 10th it was already turning into a rout. On that day Paris theatres and cabarets continued to operate, including a *Drôle de Revue* which satirized the 'warless war'. Forty-three films were showing. Parisian *école supérieure* teacher and writer Simone de Beauvoir, whose lover, Jean-Paul Sartre, was at the front, became an avid newspaper reader for the first time in her life. The first manifestations of German propaganda were heard, radio broadcasts in French and ostensibly by French people unhappy with their government.

After 10 May Paris was a montage of seeming contradictions. Parisians were calm, excited, indifferent, romantically patriotic, fearful, joyful and confused. It was also business as usual and sandbags piled against the Notre-Dame façade. Paris called upon Sainte-Geneviève to 'stop the barbarian hordes', as she had done many centuries earlier. A huge crowd assembled before her tomb in Saint-Étienne-du-Mont; her relics were brought out, the crowd chanted and prayed for her intercession, then sang La Marseillaise. To some, an outpouring of religious fervour from Parisians had a hollow ring; Jean Clauvel saw only a gathering of local 'spinsters and housemaids' at Saint-Étienne-du-Mont. A few hundred yards away in the Rue Soufflot, outside cafés were packed with men and women knocking back glasses of beer.

A sense of impending defeat began to permeate the city at every level. Evacuation of Paris children began on 14 May. On the 15th Defence Minister Daladier informed Premier Reynaud that 'the road to Paris is open. There is nothing to prevent the Germans from reaching the capital.' Male enemy nationals were interned earlier; now the women were ordered to report to the Vélodrome d'Hiver near the Quai de Grevelle, dubbed by *Le Matin* 'a vast concentration camp'. A nice irony: some of the women were German Jews, and in 1942 the Vélodrome d'Hiver was again used when Parisian Jews were being rounded up for detention. Meanwhile rumour ran wild: deserters were being shot in Paris streets; generals were being court-martialled and executed; there were Communist uprisings spreading through the city. That at least had verisimilitude because *L'Humanité*, publishing underground in defiance of the censorship, called for workers and soldiers to strike. The officer corps also listened to rumours it would appear, for some officers abandoned their men and went home, convinced that the situation was hopeless. In a case known even to Premier Reynaud, one Parisian returned to his apartment to discover his son, an officer in General Corap's army, relaxing in the bath. 'The war is over,' he told his father.

The gloom spread when, on 16 May, foreign office staff were seen throwing boxes and loose papers into the ministry courtyard, where they were soaked with petrol and set ablaze. This bonfire was clearly visible to the Chamber in the Palais Bourbon, to foreign diplomats, including the still neutral Italians, and to ordinary Parisians. Also on the

16th, Frédéric and Irène Joliot-Curie were told to gather the Collège de France nuclear-research team and leave the city with their research materials on nuclear fission. Many did, though Frédéric stayed on until 10 June. This team contributed to the research that produced nuclear weapons, and some of them witnessed the first atomic tests in New Mexico in 1945. Three decades later the Collège de France received a citation and symbolic payment by the US Atomic Energy Commission, in recognition of their wartime contribution.

On 18 May American journalist Clare Booth (Clare Booth Luce) heard references to 'betrayal' for the first time. The Germans were only seventy miles from Paris. Whether or not Parisians felt betrayed, they held on to their morale – or perhaps it was a sense of being suspended in time. University classes were well attended, restaurants and cafés did as well as rationing permitted, and people flocked to see *Carmen* at the Opéra-Comique and *Madame Sans-Gêne* at the Comédie-Française, and the films *Ninotchka*, *The Hunchback of Notre-Dame*, *Goodbye Mr Chips*, and *Wuthering Heights* – none of which were French-made.

All the same, morale cracked on 17 May when news spread that the Belgian army had surrendered. Some Parisians feared a Communist uprising; after all, were not Hitler and Stalin in league with one another? The city armed the police, though not well, made armoured cars out of dust-carts, and installed some fifty-three concrete barriers and artillery emplacements across main roads into the city and on Seine bridges. These 'fortifications' followed a line connecting the suburbs of Cormeilles, Argenteuil, Saint-Denis, Noisy-le-Sec, Neuilly-sur-Marne and Joinville. Winston Churchill came to Paris at the end of May to encourage resistance and promise that England would fight to the death. He did not deliver the squadrons of Spitfires for which Reynaud had been pleading.

## ROADS FULL OF REFUGEES

Now refugees from Belgium and the north of France flooded the roads leading to Paris. Some were in expensive cars, but most were on foot, bicycles or wooden carts drawn by horses. They were not always welcome, though some Parisians, Montparnasse artist Hélène Azenor for one, did what they could to help. The refugees represented tragedy. In Clare Booth's words:

> With bicycles and bundles and battered suitcases, holding twisted bird-cages, babies, and dogs in stiff arms, or holding one another up, they came and came and came.... The great station echoed with the saga of their suffering and numbed your brain and sometimes almost your heart.

Most of the refugees continued through Paris to. the south. A growing number of Parisians, driven by rising fear and panic, went too, by train and by car; Maurice Chevalier fled in a Fiat. The exodus was terrible to behold, but it had its light moments. In the Gare d'Orsay actor Sacha Guitry found himself at the nether end of a panicky crowd trying to shove its way past the barriers. Guitry roared chastisement for such unseemly and cowardly behaviour, and got them into an orderly formation. Then he moved himself and his baggage to the head of the line. When the crowd protested he replied: 'It's different for me. I *am* afraid.'

The statistics are staggering. The population of Greater Paris in 1936 was 4.96 million; by the end of May 1940 it was 3.5 million, and by 27 June stood at 1,938,832. Departures reached 300,000 a day by mid-June from the central city, and by the month's end it stood at less than one million. Most of the well-off were gone, such as Peggy Guggenheim who, 'with maid and Persian cats, drove off in her Talbot in the direction of Megève'. Who could blame them? All the same, leaving Paris workers and the poor to face the occupiers alone provided wonderful grist for German propaganda minister Joseph Goebbel's mill.

## JUNE

If there was any doubt left as to the fate of Paris, it was overcome in the early days of June. Perhaps the crowds thronging Montmartre on Sunday 2 June for a prayer day at Sacré-Coeur, were a good indication. On the 3rd German aircraft targeted the Renault and Citroën factories, and dropped a thousand bombs on objectives in Billancourt, Maisons-Lafitte and the XV$^e$ and XVI$^e$ *arrondissements*. There were nearly a thousand casualties. Ironically, the only government building hit was the Air Ministry on Boulevard Victor, where US ambassador William

Bullitt was a lunch guest; he was spared when a bomb that came through the ministry roof did not explode. The effect of the raid was to bolster slipping morale. That was not sufficient to turn the tide of defeat, however.

By 8 June Paris had taken on the appearance of a city under siege. Those who remained were preoccupied with their danger, and at least one theatrical performance that evening was compared to 'a low mass served by a distracted priest'. The next day the government departed for Bordeaux, Reynaud leaving interior minister Georges Mandel in Paris to keep things under whatever control remained possible. On 10 June Italy entered the war, a particular blow to France, and Mandel placed the Italian ambassador and his staff under house arrest.

June 10 was pivotal. Most newspapers shut down on that day; the stream of people fleeing the city became a flood; actors and directors of the Comédie-Française made their departure, in a large lorry filled with actors, crew and equipment; and some deputies from the Chamber set up camp-beds in the Hôtel de Ville in preparation to receive the conquerors. Jean Chiappe, former prefect of police who had been fired in 1934 for questionable conduct, was one of them; his son-in-law was editor of the pro-fascist weekly, *Gringoire*.

On 11 June a pall of smoke, origin unknown, covered the city. One Parisienne insisted it signalled the end of the world. Meanwhile the Saint-Denis hospital was close enough to the fighting to have become, in effect, a field hospital, and food shortages were critical because the small farms in the *banlieu* had been abandoned and nothing was entering the city. Stocks were diminished, and distribution of what remained was problematical. It is hardly surprising that Paris was declared an open city, in the hope that its people would be treated with at least a degree of compassion by the conquerors, and that monuments would be spared destruction.

## THE FALL OF PARIS

Resistance ended on 14 June. Units of the German Sixth Army marched along the Champs-Élysées and paraded in the Place de la Concorde. General Henri Dentz, military governor of Paris, watched from the window of his office in Les Invalides as the soldiers crossed the

Pont Alexandre III. At the Hôtel de Ville, Prefect of the Seine Achille Villey received representatives of German General Bogislav von Stutnitz, while outside the tricolour was lowered and the swastika raised. That flag soon hung from every public building and monument, including the Eiffel Tower. Prefect of Police Roger Langeron was pleased to inform General Stutnitz that he could not release political files, because they had been shipped out of the city. Associated Press correspondent Louis Lochner looked around the city and observed, with a sense of awe, that 'boulevards normally teeming with life ... were ghost streets'. As for the Parisians: some cried, a few applauded, and Thierry de Martel, surgeon at the American hospital in Neuilly and son of the novelist 'Gyp', was one of fifteen Parisians to commit suicide. The rest, after at first closing their doors, came out and watched the Germans parade. Le Chabanais, a famous Paris brothel, took the path of least resistance that most Parisians followed, for at least the first year of occupation. The brothel had closed as the Germans came in; however, a note on the door read: 'The establishment will reopen at three o'clock.'

That night General de Gaulle, who had escaped by air from Bordeaux rather than accept defeat, for which the Vichy government condemned him to death *in absentia*, broadcast from London calling upon the French people to resist. It is doubtful that many Parisians heard him.

## *Paris Under German Occupation*

For Parisians, 1940–4 was a particularly ugly version of Moss Hart's *The Man Who Came to Dinner*, which concerns an unwanted, uninvited and annoying guest who shows no inclination to depart. Like him, the Germans arrived uninvited, and stayed and stayed and stayed.

### HITLER COMES TO SEE FOR HIMSELF

Adolf Hitler paid his only visit to Paris on 23 June, with an entourage that included architect Albert Speer. They visited the Opéra ('the most beautiful theatre in the world,' Hitler said), where he was snubbed by a uniformed attendant, then the Madeleine, Place du Trocadéro and the

Eiffel Tower. Hitler stood in silent tribute at Napoléon's tomb in Les Invalides. Then there was a drive-by look at government buildings on the Quai d'Orsay, and a brief stop at the Palais du Luxembourg and the Panthéon. The group crossed the Île de la Cité to the Right Bank for a drive along the Rue de Rivoli, which street Hitler admired. They by-passed the Palais de Justice, Sainte-Chapelle, Notre-Dame and the Louvre, much to Speer's disappointment, on their way to visit Sacré-Coeur. The basilica was an 'appalling' building, Hitler said, as they drove out of the city.

That night Hitler made this observation: 'Wasn't Paris beautiful? But Berlin must be considered far more beautiful. In the past I often considered whether we would not have to destroy Paris. But when we are finished in Berlin, Paris will only be a shadow. So why should we destroy it?' In Marshall Dill's words, 'What a mentality.'

## THE GERMANS IN PARIS

The occupation was administered from the Hôtel Crillon, the Hôtel Meurice (headquarters of the military governors), other luxury hotels and former French government buildings. The Luftwaffe found a home in the Palais du Luxembourg, and the Gestapo at 74 Avenue Foch and 9 Rue des Saussaies. At night, screams coming from those buildings often made sleep difficult for next-door neighbours. Mansions near the Étoile and in Neuilly were requisitioned as well, as living quarters for the higher officials. The Germans established a curfew, censorship, and street lamps with blue paint for black-out purposes. While stuffing himself with caviar and pâté de foie gras at Maxim's, Reichsmarschall Hermann Goering announced the establishment of German economic services to assist Paris businesses. German soldiers went through Paris shops like locusts, buying up silk stockings, perfume, cosmetics, clothing and other items for wives and girl friends back home, for which they scrupulously paid in occupation currency. Signs in German appeared everywhere, including Parc Marceau where people were warned, '*das Gras nicht betreten!*' (keep off the grass!).

Many Parisians who had fled now returned, sometimes in German transport. 'Fashionable Paris' made its peace with the occupiers; Germans joined Parisians at the *salons* of Marie-Laure de Noailles, Marie-

Paris under Occupation: German soldiers browsing among bookstalls on the Left Bank

Louise Bosquet and Florence Gould, among others. Sacha Guitry, back in Paris and apparently no longer afraid, and Jean Cocteau held forth side by side with German writer Ernst Jünger (talented, elegant, and thought to be a genuine opponent of Hitler) and German sculptor Arno Breker. Breker delighted guests with 'colossal Aryans reminiscent of athletes doped with estrogens'.

Clocks were set on German time; the Opéra reopened (half of the seats were reserved for Germans), as did cinemas, theatres, cabarets and music halls. Guitry, Edith Piaf, Yves Montand, Maurice Chevalier, Josephine Baker and others performed for audiences which were at least as much German as Parisian. A few newspapers, such as *Le Matin*, began publishing and featured the menus in German of restaurants like

La Tour d'Argent and La Lorraine. Entertainment resumed, largely because Josef Goebbels ordered it so that the world would understand how much gaiety the New European Order could generate. The propaganda minister also arranged to flood the Paris cinema market with such German propaganda films as *President Krüger*.

Other inconveniences included the banning of private cars. Horse-drawn carriages appeared, along with something called 'vélo-taxis', in which a cart was towed behind a bicycle. There was even an express service in this mode, pulled by four riders, the fastest of which was one pulled by veterans of the Tour de France. The *Métro* was made to work overtime: it had carried 761 million passengers in 1938; that figure was 1,320 million in 1943. The system was stressed nearly to breaking point, as were those Parisians crammed into it. This was all weekday traffic, for the *Métro* was closed at weekends, the Germans apparently wanting the city to themselves. On the bright side, motor traffic no longer polluted the boulevards, which now regained much of their nineteenth-century allure.

The over-riding fact of the occupation was that *feldgrau* (field grey) was everywhere – the Moulin-Rouge, the Moulin de la Galette, the Mimi Pinson, the Auteuil racecourse – and Parisians were expected to remember who had conquered whom. It was not unusual for a man who forgot to step aside for a German to be kicked into the gutter. In December 1940 Jacques Bonsergent, an engineer, was executed for having jostled a German officer in a crowd at the Gare Saint-Lazare.

Whatever their social status, Parisians tried to get back to normal as quickly as they could. By the end of July they had succeeded, to the extent possible. On a Sunday in August American journalist William Shirer walked from Place Vendôme to mass at Nôtre-Dame Cathedral. Along the way he saw children playing in the Tuileries and men fishing in the Seine. At Nôtre-Dame Cardinal Suhard preached on calm, work and prayer. After mass Shirer walked along Boulevard Saint-Michel, where he heard, among other things, proper bourgeois women denouncing younger women for flirting with German soldiers. He ended in Montparnasse for lunch and found the cafés 'as jammed with crackpots as ever'.

Intellectual and artistic life resumed as well. The University reopened, and Jean-Paul Sartre, Simone de Beauvoir, Paul Valéry, Ramon Fernandez, Albert Camus and other writers and philosophers, who did their best to ignore the Germans, could be found again in the Boulevard Saint-Germain, the Deux Magots, Café Flore and Brasserie Lipp. Sartre's *Les Mouches* opened in 1943, and *Huis-Clos* in 1944. Camus published *L'Étranger* in 1942, and de Beauvoir *L'Invitée* a year later. Meanwhile Pablo Picasso and Henri Matisse remained in Paris, kept their mouths shut, and painted.

## SHORTAGES

'Normality' was an illusion, however. Germans ate and lived well; Parisians did not. Bread, sugar and noodles were rationed in August, followed in October by butter, cheese, meat, coffee, pork and eggs. Soon it was chocolate, dried vegetables, fresh fish, potatoes, offal, milk, and even wine. In due course coffee was replaced by a brew made of acorns and chick-peas, called *café national*. The ration card became the Parisians' most important document. Housewives would pay a concierge for permission to spend the night on a porch or in an empty cellar, in order to be first in line when a nearby food shop opened.

Heating fuel was in short supply, and an early winter brought death to many old and poor people trying to survive in unheated garrets. Ironically, the *Métro* was a help here, simply because it was warm. Martial Massioni recalled that '... we dreamed of prolonging our trips to avoid shivering in our offices and homes'. A makeshift cooking stove was invented, made of ten-gallon tins welded together, called the *réchaud '44*. For fuel, newspaper scraps were crumpled into balls and sprinkled with water, which made them burn longer. One department store advertised that 'a six-page paper ... could bring a litre of water to boil in twelve minutes'.

How little Hitler understood the Paris he had so briefly visited is clear from his 'gesture of magnanimity' in December. He ordered the remains of Napoléon's son to be transferred from the Habsburg burial vault in the the Stephansdom in Vienna to Les Invalides, where they may still be found. The ceremony was accomplished by torchlight, and left cold and hungry Parisians both unmoved and uninterested. Returning young Bonaparte was to them like the Germans taking

French coal and giving back ashes. On the other hand, they did not reject the cheese ration that day, which included 40 grams of meat 'as a special treat'.

Malnutrition became chronic, bringing with it epidemic diseases. The occupiers made sure that elegant restaurants were well supplied; for the rest, people made city parks and rooftops into vegetable gardens, kept rabbits in their bathtubs and fed them on blades of grass stolen out of the parks at night, netted pigeons for the cooking pot, and ate cats. A black market for food developed; however, so did inflation, which quickly put black-market food out of reach for vast numbers of the poor, elderly and infirm. In 1943 the average Parisian had 876 francs per month, which was the price of two kilos of black market butter.

COLLABORATORS

By accepting leadership of the Vichy government, Marshal Pétain became the first '*collaborateur*'. Others lost no time in surfacing: there was Pierre Laval, who managed Vichy France in the German interest and with a certain fascist style; those in the Paris police who kept order according to rules laid down by the occupiers; those of the Paris élite who fraternized with German officers and intellectuals; concierges who helped the police and Gestapo round up Jews and *Résistance* members; Parisian women who invited German soldiers into their beds (for which they had their heads shaved after Liberation in 1944); and a number of fascist intellectuals and bully boys.

A case could be made that at least some of these were merely trying to survive. Among the literati, Jean Cocteau's behaviour was questionable, though he did defend Jean Genet which got him into trouble with the Germans, as was novelist Colette's, who received protection for her Jewish husband by writing for *Combat* (not to be confused with a *Résistance* group by the same name), the weekly journal of Milice Français. Then there was the irrepressible Sacha Guitry, who claimed that returning to the Paris stage actually made him part of the *Résistance* because he had 'entertained the French people in those tragic times'.

No such case could be made for the Paris fascist intelligentsia who wrote for such collaborationist newspapers as *Je Suis Partout, Le Petit Parisien* and *Paris-Soir*. They included Robert Brasillach (executed in

1945 as a collaborator), Alain Laubreaux, Louis-Ferdinand Céline, Lucien Rebatet and Henri Bardèche, among others, all of whom welcomed at least the concept of Hitler's 'new order'. They soon held all the important jobs left to Parisians, and, as Herbert Lottman phrased it, 'often went further in their publishing, broadcasting and speech-making propaganda than the Germans asked or expected them to'. They praised and encouraged the work of Joseph Darnand, Marcel Bucard and Marcel Déat, leaders of the Milice Française, whose 'cohorts', to use Giles Perrault's language, marched up and down the Champs-Élysées and used violence and intimidation 'to impose terror and gain power'. At the war's end they all paid a heavy price for their collaboration.

## THE FINAL SOLUTION

Jews suffered more than other Parisians, simply because they had to put up with the shortages *and* with being singled out for special abuse. On 20 August 1940 the Garde Française and Jeune Front, both of which wore a uniform of dark shirt, leather belt and boots, attacked Jewish shops on the Champs-Élysées. Police prefect Langeron described these thugs as 'simple trash'. That did not help. On 29 August Jews were ordered to register with the police; Nobel laureate philosopher Henri Bergson complied in order to show solidarity, even though he had long since converted to Catholicism. On 11 November all Jewish businesses were required to post a yellow sign with the words *Entreprise juive*. Soon after, the wholesale confiscation of Jewish property began.

The first collection of Jews for deportation, mostly foreigners, occurred on 14 May 1941. Then in August Paris police sequestered some 6,000 Jewish men, women and children in the XI$^e$ *arrondissement* for shipment to a concentration camp at Drancy, and from there to Auschwitz. The largest round-up was in July 1942 when 12,000 Jews were herded into the Vélodrome d'Hiver.

The yellow star was introduced in May 1942. In June regulations banned Jews from restaurants, tea-rooms, bars, concerts, cinemas, theatres and music halls, from using public telephones and libraries, markets, fairs, museums, historical sites, beaches, exhibitions, race-courses, sports grounds or camp sites, and most jobs. They were allowed only to ride in the last car on the *Métro*, and were also forced to do their shopping in mid-afternoon when most food shops had long since run out of goods. It became nearly impossible for Jews to survive.

Parisian gentiles responded to persecution of Jews in a variety of ways. Some protested by wearing the yellow star themselves, or by singling out Jews to befriend. Others favoured the persecution: *Je Suis Partout* filled its pages with a steady stream of anti-Semitic abuse, and thousands of Parisians turned out for the 'Jew and France' exhibition at the Palais-Berlitz, and to see the film, *Le Juif Süss*, both of which opened in September 1941. In between were the majority of Parisians, who tried to stay out of it. The precedent for all attitudes may well have been the shooting, on 7 November 1938, by a Polish Jew, Herschel Grynszpan, of German diplomat Ernst vom Rath, in protest against the deportation of Polish Jews from Germany. Two nights later, the infamous *Kristalnacht* of anti-Semitic rioting and looting took place across Germany, all carefully orchestrated by the Gestapo. In Paris *Je Suis Partout* deplored the assassination and made out that the German Jews well deserved what happened to them. Most Parisians ignored both assassination and riots.

All the same, some Parisians tried to make a real difference, as illustrated by this story. A Christian woman who had advance knowledge of the July 1942 round-up went to the Vélodrome d'Hiver intending to protest. She pushed her way to the railing, where a desperate Jewish mother pushed her baby through. The Christian did not know the Jew, but she took the baby and went home to raise it as her own. The child survived, grew up, and as of 1987 was a member of the Orchestre de Paris.

## RÉSISTANCE

General de Gaulle's broadcast from London of 14 June 1940 led to the formation of *résistance* movements across France. Separate at first, they soon united under the Mouvements Unités de la Résistance, directed by Jean Moulin and then by Gaullist Georges Bidault after Moulin was caught in June 1943. Only the Communist *Résistance* remained apart; the rest looked to de Gaulle as leader.

The *Résistance* was slow to get started in Paris, where most people were preoccupied with survival. There was passive resistance, of course: black armbands worn to commemorate the Wehrmacht arrival in Paris; red, white and blue worn on Bastille Day, which got 1,667 people arrested; a blind beggar playing La Marseillaise on a concertina; an old grandmother tripping German soldiers with her cane, and another deliberately walking through the Place de l'Étoile to disrupt a German military review. There were tracts slipped into coat pockets, broadsheets pushed into letter-boxes, and clandestine newspapers such as *Pantagruel*. All called for confrontation. These kinds of activities were carried on by a mere handful, however, and inspired very few Parisians to direct action. Nevertheless, the collaborationist press responded as if the entire population was threatening the very fabric of the New Order.

On 21 August 1941 Pierre Fabien shot at a German officer at the Barbès *Métro* station, and everything changed. The *Résistance* war now became violent. German officers were killed, and reprisals taken, the victims often Parisians caught violating curfew. The German bookshop Rive Gauche, on the Place de la Sorbonne, was blown up and there were more reprisals. Parisians were sickened by the violence, and the Germans blamed everything on the Communists, hundreds of whom were arbitrarily executed at the fort on Mont-Valérien, in hopes of winning the populace to their side. When that failed, sharper curfews were imposed and places of entertainment shut down – as if, sneered Giles Perrault, 'closing restaurants and nightclubs would turn us into traitors overnight'. But that was for ordinary Parisians. *Résistance* members, when caught, faced Gestapo torture chambers in the Avenue Foch, Avenue Henri-Martin, Boulevard Victor and Rue des Saussaies. Asbestos-lined walls with handprints dug into them testify to the suffering endured in those places.

In due course, such intellectuals as Albert Camus, Jean-Paul Sartre (in August 1944 Sartre was writing *Résistance* tracts in a room only a few blocks from the Vieux Colombier theatre where *Huis-Clos* was playing), Robert Desnos and François Mauriac lent their pens to the *Résistance*, and an increasing number of Parisians sympathized with it, even if they did not directly participate. Communists, Royalists, Catholics, Protestants, anti-clericals, youth and maturity all found a common ground in opposing the occupation. Women played prominent roles. One, Marie Hélène Lefaucheux, whose husband commanded the Paris *Résistance* until he was arrested, learned that he was to be sent to Buchenwald. She went there and managed to effect his release. Marie was later a member of the French United Nations delegation. Another, Noor Inayat Khan, an Indian princess born in Paris, was a radio operator for the British Special Operations Executive; she was caught and executed in 1943. There were hundreds of others.

## Liberation, 1944

The Allies landed in Normandy on 6 June 1944. By August they were closing in on Paris, the liberation of which de Gaulle had convinced them to undertake. The future of France was at stake, he told them. So, too, was his own, though he did not necessarily tell them that.

GENERAL CHARLES DE GAULLE: THE LEGEND

The general understood that Paris was the key to everything. He also understood that his principal rivals for power were such Communist *Résistance* leaders in Paris as Henri Tanguy, 'Colonel Rol'. Rol urged the *Résistance* to lead an insurrection to drive the Germans out of Paris before the Allies or the Gaullists arrived. 'Paris is worth 200,000 dead!' he claimed – at least, Communist control of the city was worth that number. Meanwhile de Gaulle persuaded the Allies to give General Jacques-Philippe Leclerc the job of liberating Paris. He also acknowledged that a popular revolt probably could not be avoided, and directed that anti-Communist Gaullists within the city should lead it. His representatives seized the Prefecture of Police on the Île de la Cité on 19 August and the popular rising began. Whether the Gaullists were actually in charge is debatable.

LIBERATING PARIS

The days following were a combination of hell and hallelujah. Both Germans and insurrectionists suffered heavy casualties; schoolboys attacked German tanks with Molotov cocktails and were killed. General von Choltitz, the German commander, considered blowing up the city, or having it bombed, in order to restore order. Raoul Nordling, a Swedish intermediary, persuaded him that nothing was to be gained by destroying Paris. Nordling also arranged a cease-fire for 20 August. However, the next day barricades went up across the city, as if in recollection of 1848 and 1871. *Résistance* newspapers published openly for the first time, calling upon Parisians to fight. Many did, again with heavy casualties. An important change was that the gendarmerie, once collaborators, turned against the Germans and joined the rebels.

Barricades could not resist tanks; on the other hand, there were hundreds of barricades, in the boulevards Saint-Germain, Saint-Michel and de la Chapelle, and the rues de Rivoli, Saint-Jacques, Nation and République, and throughout the poorer faubourgs in the east end. Also there were tens of thousands of Parisians armed with everything from paving stones to machine-guns. The Germans, unsure of themselves for the first time since they came to Paris, set fire to the Grand Palais and then retreated to defensive positions in the Palais du Luxembourg, l'Opéra, l'École Militaire, and various barracks around the city. Rumours spread among Parisians that the Luftwaffe would drop bombs, or that there would be an assault by two SS divisions.

On 24 August three tanks from Leclerc's army (crewed by Spanish Republicans who were FFI volunteers) fought their way through the German defences to the Place de l'Hôtel de Ville. Word spread and church bells began to peal across the city, even though the Germans continued to resist. French and Allied soldiers – including 'General' Ernest Hemingway with a rag-tag unit of Free French irregulars – poured into the city. They were greeted by both German gunfire and Parisians hysterical with relief, who kissed everything in uniform. It was a common sight to see soldiers fighting from street to street with lipstick smeared over their faces. Even General de Gaulle was kissed when he walked down the Champs-Élysées later.

The next day the Place de la Concorde saw heavy fighting, with damage to the Hôtel Continental. The façade of the Hôtel Crillon was destroyed. Mobs began attacking collaborators, shaving the women's heads, forcing both men and women to parade along the streets in their undergarments, and sometimes simply killing them outright. In the Rue du Val-de-Grâce an Indo-Chinese student was thrown to his death from a fourth-floor window, while a crowd chanted 'Death to the Japanese'. General von Choltitz ate an elegant lunch with his staff at the Hôtel Meurice that day, and then went to his office to wait for the liberators. When they arrived, he signed the capitulation on a billiard table.

THE LEGEND GROWS

About five in the afternoon of 25 August, ever after celebrated as Liberation Day, General de Gaulle drove to his old office at the war ministry in Rue Saint-Dominique. This was to symbolize that the past four years had only been a temporary interruption in the normal course of affairs. He then went to the Prefecture of Police and the Hôtel de Ville, where he ignored the Communist representatives, went to a window, and offered himself to the French people. He was a perfect target for snipers, but no one took a shot. The people accepted him with enormous cheers. Later de Gaulle met American represenatives at Les Invalides to sign an assistance agreement. They were surprised to find him both in Paris and in charge. On 27 August General Eisenhower, the supreme Allied commander, came to Paris and agreed to march American forces on their way to the front through the city as a sign of Allied support for de Gaulle. The Communist leadership now had to acknowledge that the general was in charge, at least for the moment.

De Gaulle started down the path to immortality on 26 August with a gesture that easily could have got him killed. The Germans were still fighting in Paris, and Vichyites and Communists, both of whom hated him, were at large. On that day, with Georges Bidault, officers of the FFI and various other Gaullists at his side, the general led a great crowd in a walk from the Étoile, where he placed a wreath on the Tomb of the Unknown Soldier, relit the flame and led in singing La Marseillaise, to Nôtre-Dame, where a Te Deum was sung. Not even a German air raid that night could cast a pall over the moment.

## Post-War Paris

War in Europe ended in May 1945. It was time to heal. Marshall Dill, then a US naval officer, passed through Paris in October 1945 and described the city as 'curiously muted'. The tricolour was much in evidence, but the *Métro* was still the main source of transport, cars not yet having reappeared; taxis were reserved for transporting wounded veterans. He found two rooms open at the Louvre museum filled with the most famous pieces in the collection, 'for the benefit of GIs passing through the city', and a few bookstalls open along the river. The cognac was both plentiful and cheap, however, and French chefs in the Royal Monceau Hotel where he was billeted did wonders with US army rations. Otherwise, save for the absence of Germans in the streets, the city seemed little changed since liberation.

## COMING BACK TO LIFE

Dill's visit was brief and his impression superficial, which he freely admitted. In reality everything was in flux. General de Gaulle was calling upon the French to 'marry their century', meaning, among other things, constitutional change and the liberation of women. He had called for votes for women in 1943, in recognition of their wartime service, and because 'France needs them'. In March 1944 the Committee of National Liberation enacted a law granting women the vote. Then came liberation, and almost immediately hundreds of women from various backgrounds were appointed municipal councillors in Paris, made mayoral aides in two *arrondissements*, and put in control of supply and cost at Les Halles. French women went to the polls for the first time in October 1945.

Meanwhile there were roads, bridges, railways, ports and factories to be rebuilt, in Paris and across France. All of this cost money, and the economy was in shambles. The black market continued to operate, and Parisians found that their francs had lost much of their pre-war value. Moreover, a population that suffered four years of malnutrition did not recover its health overnight.

In 1947 the United States announced the Marshall Plan for economic recovery, which pumped millions of dollars into France. This helped, but did not cure, the economy, however, as the French were committed to keeping a costly occupation force in Germany, and to fighting a colonial war in Indo-China. Improvement was slow in coming, and there were massive strikes in 1947 and 1948 at plants in Paris and throughout the Département du Nord.

## THE NEW ORDER

The Fourth Republic was founded in 1946, over the objections of General de Gaulle. He resigned from the provisional government that he had created in protest against a constitution that simply re-created the Third Republic. De Gaulle formed his own party, Rassemblement du Peuple Français, and spent the next thirteen years in opposition. During that time malaise, political conflict and colonial wars brought down governments on an average of every six months, until the Assembly finally was persuaded that the French must 'marry their century' after all. In 1958 they asked de Gaulle to form an emergency government, and empowered him to rule by decree for a period of six months.

The general began by setting his associate, Michel Debré, to write a new constitution with enhanced powers for the president. When it was finished, he took it to the people and received 80 per cent approval. After six months the Assembly elected de Gaulle president of the new Fifth Republic. He then made presidential election national by direct vote, the first of which took place in 1965. De Gaulle defeated future Socialist president, François Mitterrand, in a run-off.

## LOUIS-NAPOLÉON REDIVIVUS

De Gaulle going to the people, which he did frequently in his tenure as president, was reminiscent of Louis-Napoléon. The tactic failed him only once, in the aftermath of the great student uprising in Paris in 1968. De Gaulle was, in his way, the true heir of the Bonapartes. This was particularly evident in his foreign relations. Seeking to make France again a dominant European power, he introduced nuclear weapons, took France out of the North Atlantic Treaty Organization, denied Britain entry into the Common Market, and tried to drive '*les Anglo-Saxons*' (Britain and the United States) out of Europe. Louis-Napoléon would have understood both the motive and the tactics.

# *Colonial Troubles*

The Fourth Republic presided over the dissolution of the French colonial empire, save for Algeria. That was a problem no Fourth Republic premier could surmount. Charles de Gaulle, on the other hand, could and did.

## ALGERIA

Algerian nationalists were not prepared to wait to be given independence, and began a campaign of terrorism to drive the French out. By 1955 170,000 French troops were in Algeria, many of them disgruntled veterans of the Indo-China war, opposing about 15,000 FLN rebels. In 1956 Premier Guy Mollet proposed to negotiate with the rebels, to which the French *colons* (colonists) reacted violently. Policy was reversed and the government committed itself to 'keep Algeria French'. This was part of the justification that year for joining with Great Britain and the new state of Israel in a war with Egypt over the Suez Canal. Nationalist Egypt was thought to be aiding the Algerians. It was all in vain, for the United States threatened to intervene with force, and both Britain and France withdrew.

Parisians were divided on the Algerian issue. Costly colonial wars had much to do with French financial malaise, and French troops in Algeria were at least as brutal as FLN terrorists. However, the *colons* had many sympathizers, and when they revolted in 1958 over a rumour that Premier Pflimlin planned to negotiate with the FLN, thousands of Paris motorists created bedlam by tooting car horns to the beat of '*Al–gér–ie– Fran–çaise*'. It remained for Charles de Gaulle finally to end the situation, first by defusing a *colons'* revolt backed by paratroopers, and then by granting independence to Algeria. There was a personal price, however. Georges Bidault broke with de Gaulle over Algeria, and was forced to leave the country as a result. The two men remained bitter enemies.

## OAS

Independence for Algeria initiated another, and in its way more dangerous, crisis. Algeria gained independence in 1962, at which point nearly a million *colon* refugees entered France. They joined disgruntled army officers and disaffected Gaullists in forming the Organisation de l'Armée Secrète (OAS), the object of which was to assassinate de Gaulle and stage a coup. Much OAS activity took place in Paris, such as a nearly successful attempt on the president's life in August 1962 in the suburb of Petit-Clamart. 'OAS' and '*Algérie Française*' were written or painted on walls all over the city. Cinemas and theatres were bombed and individuals blown up with bombs pushed through letter-boxes. People were shot down in the streets, and on at least one occasion the Palais du Luxembourg was closed because of terrorist activities. This 'civil war' claimed more than 12,000 lives, and engaged French security forces in activities little different in kind or degree from those under-taken by the Gestapo during the occupation of Paris.

# *Intellectual Life*

Paris lost its leading place in music, ballet and art after the war, but took the lead in intellectual pursuits and film.

## THE WRITERS

Camus and Sartre continued to explore the permutations of exis-tentialism, the idea that as human existence is absurd, it is for the individual to make his or her own rules. Simone de Beauvoir worked her way through the feminist considerations that resulted in *Le deuxième Sexe*, and the writers of 'anti-novels' took their departure from all forms of literary convention. The ideal of *engagement* – social and political involvement – reversed itself in due course into *dégagement*, 'aloof, highly élitist, self-consciously experimentalist' in the manner of the 1920s.

Claude Lévi-Strauss's structuralism became the 'dominant intellec-tual fashion' of the 1960s in literary criticism, psychology, philosophy and historiography, among Left Bank literati and the faculty of the University of Paris. This was the idea that human beings are the object rather than the subject of forces over which they have no control. Post-structuralism followed in the 1970s, which Gordon Wright char-acterized as simple ideas 'dressed up in unintelligible jargon'. Parisian

The brasseries in the Boulevard Saint-Germain: the favourite haunts of Paris intellectuals such as Jean-Paul Sartre, Albert Camus and Simone de Beauvoir

intellectuals finally tired of such debates and returned to the rationalist humanism that was their heritage, having proved once more that Paris was among the world's 'most heated incubators of pure intellectualism'. Regrettably, not everyone followed them. Jacques Derrida's 'deconstructionist' methodology continues to obfuscate the efforts of literary critics in America.

## THE CINEMA

After the war, Parisian cinematography picked up where it had left off in the later 1930s. Jean de Baroncelli, *Le Monde* film critic, thought the reason might be that 'young creative people today [1959] have a cinematic instinct and the cinema is their first choice'. Styles varied: Marcel Carné's *Les Portes de la Nuit* (1946) was *film noir*, Jean Cocteau's *La Belle et la Bête* (1946) was lyrical, and Jacques Tati's comedy – *Jour de*

*Fête* (1949) and *Mon Oncle* (1958) – was, in the broadest sense, Chaplinesque. Of course, many directors succumbed to the lure of money, with colourful but uninspired commercial adaptations of such literary classics as Stendhal's *Le Rouge et le Noir*.

Much post-war cinema was avant-garde: *Belles de nuit* (René Clair, 1952), *Hiroshima Mon Amour* (Alain Resnais, 1959) and *L'Homme qui aimait les Femmes* (François Truffaut, 1977). Paris was the centre, and whatever the style French cinema resounded with the names of directors, screenwriters and actors who were Parisian or had come to live in Paris: Jean Renoir, Jean-Luc Godard, Roger Vadim, Leslie Caron, Yves Montand, Simone Signoret and Gérard Depardieu, to name only a few.

## THE PRESS

Journalism came back to life in Paris after liberation. *Le Monde*, the Paris equivalent of *The Times* of London, was established in 1944; so, too, was *Le Parisien Libéré*. *France-Soir* came the next year, and the news magazine *L'Express* opened in 1957. Today well over one hundred daily and weekly newspapers, and news, fashion and other magazines, are published in Paris.

# The 1960s

Post-war Paris clung to *vieux Paris* until the 1960s. Then the city truly began to 'marry its century'.

## DEMOGRAPHY

By 1962 migration from the countryside and central Paris gave the Département du Nord a population of 8.5 million, of which about 7 million lived in Greater Paris. The central city had declined to 2.7 million, down from 2.9 million in 1911. The rate of growth of Greater Paris was nearly double the national average, though slower than such provincial cities as Lyon and Marseille. Even with people moving out, the city centre remained overcrowded in 1962, with 143 people per acre as compared to 43 in London. Moreover, almost one-third of residential buildings were in a decayed or unsanitary condition. Some form of urban planning was in order.

PLANNING

In 1960 the *Plan d'Aménagement et d'Organisation Général de la Région Parisienne*, or PADOG, was published. The idea was to discourage population growth in both central and Greater Paris by limiting new jobs through curtailing additional offices and factories in the Paris region. The plan also called for extensive renovation of the inner city. However, it was immediately pointed out that to restrict new offices and factories would also limit economic growth. Planned (as opposed to *laissez-faire*) expansion was the appropriate compromise Paul Delouvrier suggested, and President de Gaulle agreed. The Schéma Directeur d'Aménagement et d'Urbanisme de la Région de Paris was formed in 1963 as the implementary body. It projected population trends, housing conditions, economic development, and other criteria necessary for urban planning.

The objective was to decongest the centre, make better use of the periphery, co-ordinate employment, dwelling and transportation, create more green space, and all the while carry out historic pre-servation. Decentralization was implicit, that is moving factories and population further away from the centre, a trend that had begun in the late 1950s. That meant developing *cités jardins* (garden cities) in such places as Plessis-Robinson and Vitry, similar to the 'garden city' movement in England. Light industry, cultural and educational opportunities distinct from the city of Paris were the idea – the Nan-terre campus of the University of Paris is an example of this trend. Pleasant surburban living conditions also were instituted, which accounts for the huge numbers of commuters among those who work in the city. The Paris of the 1990s is to some extent the result of Schéma Directeur planning, and while hardly perfect it is an improvement over that of the 1960s.

SKYSCRAPERS

Whether improvement included building skyscrapers was a matter of opinion. The idea was broached around the turn of the century by

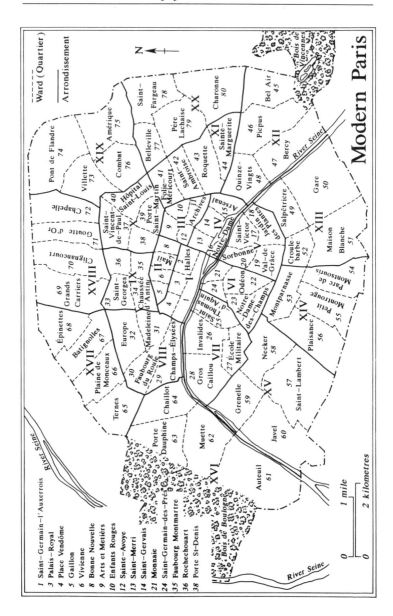

Modern Paris

Ward (Quartier)

Arrondissement

N

*River Seine*

1 mile
2 kilometres
0
0

1 Saint–Germain–l'Auxerrois
3 Palais–Royal
4 Place Vendôme
5 Gaillon
6 Vivienne
8 Bonne Nouvelle
9 Arts et Metiers
10 Enfants Rouges
12 Sainte–Avoye
13 Saint–Merri
14 Saint–Gervais
21 Monnaie
24 Saint–Germain–des–Prés
35 Faubourg Montmartre
36 Rochechouart
38 Porte St–Denis

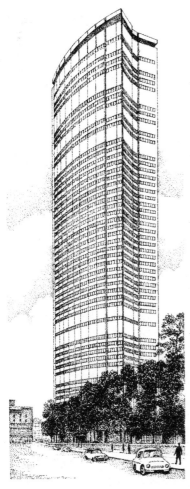

The Montparnasse Tower

Auguste Perret, among others, in part because land in Paris was becoming extremely expensive. However, critics protested the idea of 'our capital surrounded by a belt of enormous buildings'. An American argued that 'a nervous Frenchman would go into spasms if he were suddenly shot skyward from the ground to the 20th storey in one of our improved modern electric elevators'. Architect Le Corbusier was a skyscraper advocate between the wars, pointing out that by concentrating activity on a small ground space, the skyscraper was a way 'to have air, light and greenery all around us again'.

In the 1960s the Schéma Directeur, noting that even Communist Saint-Denis was building what for a time was the highest skyscraper in Europe, embraced the concept and limited building by height only according to existing buildings and vistas. La Défense, the University of Paris Science Faculty and the Maine-Montparnasse tower are only a few examples of the 'upward trend' which then began.

## TRANSPORTATION AND ITS COMPLICATIONS

After the war, cars greatly complicated the already complex problem of getting around Paris. Taxis were too few, too expensive and too unreliable, particularly at lunch- and dinner-time when they were most needed. American columnist Art Buchwald complained that 'in New York or London taxis drive their clients towards their destination; in Paris, you accompany the *chauffeur* towards his garage or his restaurant'. They also tended not to know street names or one-way street systems, which wasted time. Working-class Parisians used the *Métro* and the bus as well. This was not ideal, as an older worker pointed out. 'Every day of my life I spend four hours in public transport! It's simply inhuman.'

Between 1950 and 1970 the annual passenger load of public transport dropped from 450 million to 180 million. The car became more affordable and took over: 1 million in 1961, over 2 million in 1965 and 2.5 million in 1970. However, as John Ardagh noted, there was a problem. '[A] few broad roads masking a honeycomb of narrow ones, ill served with exit routes and ill-adapted for the building of modern traffic islands' made driving in Paris more and more a nightmare. Available street surface was only 10 per cent greater in 1970 than in 1900.

Attempts to deal with the problem had limited success. Traffic lanes were expanded at the expense of pavements, along such thoroughfares as the boulevards Montparnasse, Malesherbes, Haussmann and Magenta, which did little to improve traffic flow but greatly inconvenienced pedestrians. New surface roads were built in connection with slum clearance projects, such as the Boulevard Vercingetorix leading south from Montparnasse, begun in 1976 and subsequently downgraded to a 'rue'. Underground roads, first projected in 1928, continued to be discussed but not implemented. The Boulevard Périphérique (ring road) was completed in 1973, and was soon producing one accident per kilometre per day. New roads were laid along the Seine embankments, to their ruination in the opinion of *vieux Paris* diehards. One-way street systems were laid out, the *Métro* was expanded, and a suburban railway, the Réseau Express Régional (RER), was developed in co-ordination with the *Métro*, all in hopes of encouraging people to train into Paris and leave their cars at home. For example, one may now travel via RER and the *Métro* from Charles de Gaulle airport to Place de l'Odéon on a single ticket purchased at the airport.

More cars also meant proportionately less parking. The revolutionary flame that burns within every Parisian repudiated the parking meter from the start and never looked back (although that day may come). The inevitable solution was underground parking garages – beneath Avenue George V, Place Vendôme and Place du Parvis de Nôtre-Dame Cathedral, to mention only three. They did not solve the problem, but that did not dampen Parisians' love affair with their cars.

## CLEANING UP THE CITY

In the 1950s, quite without being told, Parisians began modernizing and cleaning up shopfronts in such commercial quarters as the area around the Rue Lafayette and the Gare Saint-Lazare. In 1958 Minister of Construction Pierre Sudreau encouraged the process, for aesthetic and structural reasons. 'Phased' rent increases were allowed, so long as some of the money was devoted to cleaning up façades and courtyards and making other repairs. The process worked despite initial scepticism. Public opinion embraced it and the State committed itself to spend 10 million francs on cleaning up public buildings. Sand-blasting or pressurized water jets removed decades of sooty patina, bringing forth the original cream or tan colour of l'Opéra, Notre-Dame, the Louvre, Les Invalides and other historic structures. Paris began to look old and new at the same time. It remains an interesting phenomenon.

## THE UNIVERSITY OF PARIS

In 1968 160,000 students matriculated at the university, many of them at such suburban centres such as Orsay and Nanterre. Increasing numbers meant overcrowding and reduced quality: a 500-seat lecture hall might have to accommodate 1,000 students; crammed laboratories sometimes led to failed science exams; lodgings were hard to come by, and meals in student canteens, though affordable, often meant waiting in long queues. Many students simply gave up and quit because of such conditions. On average, only thirty out of 100 students in the Arts and Law faculties were graduating by 1968. Meanwhile the professors lived an ivory-tower existence, scorning the 'real' world around them, and being shocked whenever one of their number, such as Raymond Aron, appeared on radio or television, or wrote for the popular press. A.J.P.

Taylor would have been more of a renegade at the Sorbonne than ever he was in Oxford.

Students grew frustrated, and when other factors brought their inherent 1960s radicalism to a head, Paris exploded.

## MAY 1968

What happened in May 1968 should have come as no surprise. The uprising began with students at Nanterre, and soon engaged independent workers' movements. Overcrowding, stuffy professors, and such silly bureacratic rules as requiring Nanterre students to go to central Paris to buy tickets for their swimming pool, created the atmosphere. The causes were the authoritarian Gaullist regime, the Vietnam War – demonstrators in the Latin Quarter often chanted 'John–son, as–sa–ssin', a reference to President Lyndon Johnson, as they battled police – and disenchantment with the traditional Left in favour of Maoism,Trotskyism and anarchism. It probably did not help that the buildings at Nanterre were ugly stone blocks.

The rising was referred to as *les événements*. It was led, so far as it was led by anyone, by 'Danny the Red' Cohn-Bendit, a German sociology student at Nanterre. It all began when an American Express office was blown up in March and the perpetrator, a Nanterre student, was arrested. Students demonstrated on behalf of this 'victim of imperialism'; teach-ins, strikes and clashes with the police followed. On 3 May the Nanterre campus was closed, and the agitators immediately moved operations to the Sorbonne.

Over the next week, riots, demonstrations, students throwing stones and Molotov cocktails, and police brutalizing students with clubs and tear gas, were featured on the television news. Parisians and others were shocked and dismayed, especially since de Gaulle had so recently averred that in a time of upheavals France would continue to 'offer an example of effectiveness in the conduct of affairs'. On 13 May spontaneous strikes began at factories in Nantes and Rouen, and spread to Paris, until some 750,000 workers were involved. The students' rising was the excuse; but these workers were mainly frustrated over low wages, unemployment, obdurate employers and repressive measures taken against strikers. However, they were not supported by either the

CGT or mainstream Communists. Nor were the students, whom Communist leaders called 'fascist provocateurs', 'mindless anarchists', or simply 'adventurers'. On 30 May President de Gaulle broadcast an appeal for popular support against the rising and the people responded. 100,000 Gaullists demonstrated in the Champs-Élysées, and *les événements* were over.

It was over for Charles de Gaulle as well. He resigned as president the next year, after a national referendum went against him, partly because of failed policies associated with the May rising. He died in 1970. A national memorial service was held at the Arc de Triomphe, and Place de l'Étoile was renamed Place Charles de Gaulle in his honour. Nothing was named for 'Danny the Red', at least not officially.

## *The Contemporary City*

Most trends from the 1960s continued into the 1970s and beyond. Between 1968 and 1975 the city lost 500,000 inhabitants, with the I$^{er}$ *arrondissement* alone, an area undergoing extensive renovation, reduced by 33 per cent. Greater Paris was just shy of 10 million in 1976: 2,299,830 people lived in the central city, while the suburbs accounted for 7,578,694. Meanwhile concern for the quality of urban life continued to illuminate efforts to maintain continuity and initiate change in Paris.

### QUALITY OF LIFE

Most post-war urban problems were of long standing, including residential neighbourhoods defined as *îlots insalubres*, or 'unhealthy islets', which lacked adequate sanitation facilities of all kinds; and the suburban housing shortage, complicated by post-war population increases. These kinds of conditions were addressed on the periphery through projects called *grand ensemble*, and in the central city through renovation.

A *grand ensemble* contained from 8,000 to 10,000 dwelling units, in large uniform blocks. They were anything but attractive or pleasant; the most infamous was Sarcelles beyond the Porte de la Chapelle, which was described and decried as 'this dormitory city, this great barracks, this concentration camp where we are locked in rabbit cages ... in one of the worst catastrophes our society has ever invented'. By 1969 one person in six in Greater Paris lived in such blocks. What was gained in sanitation was perhaps lost in the decline of mental health, or at least many thought so. However, the price of more pleasant dwellings within the central city, and of individual detached or semi-detached houses in the suburbs, was, and remains, prohibitive for many Parisians.

Renovation in the central city was also an imperfect solution. An area near Place d'Italie in the XIII$^e$ *arrondissement* was typical: a 'dingy, lower-class neighbourhood, notably lacking in picturesqueness or remnants of faded grandeur,' where 'leprous exteriors ... augur badly for the interior comfort. . . .' Old apartment buildings, shops, bars, and so forth, were torn down and replaced with modern, clean, high-rise apartments. The Rue Nationale, which ran through the area, was widened. When all was complete, neither street nor quarter were recognizable. Moreover, the renovation was accompanied by a sharp rise in rents; now only the comfortable bourgeoisie could afford to live in the Rue Nationale. The traditional inhabitants ended up in such suburban *grands ensembles* as Sarcelles. Whether the new residents could re-create the sense of community that had existed in the old neighbourhood, or would want to, was problematic. This pattern was repeated in varying degrees in Montmartre and Riquet.

The Marais and Île Saint-Louis were also at issue. However, being historic areas they were approached differently. Buildings in the South Marais identified as having true historic value were restored rather than renovated. Restoration followed traditional architectural styles, and hoped to preserve as well the traditional artisan activities of the area – jewellery-making, leather-work and toy-making. However, as with other urban renewal schemes, restoration raised the cost of living, and at least some of the working-class population had to follow their compatriots from the Rue Nationale and the Place d'Italie quarter to the suburbs. The eastern Île Saint-Louis was treated in similar fashion. On the western side, however, the *quais*, which had become fashionable in the seventeenth century, continued to be so into the late twentieth. The *hôtels* in that quarter were well maintained throughout, and were never close to qualifying as *îlots insalubres*.

Other renovations of note include the 1961 decision, after much debate, to remove Les Halles and build a new produce market at

Rungis, south of the city. This project began in 1969 and was completed soon after. Meanwhile, redevelopment of the Les Halles site began in the 1970s, amid the usual controversy over what it all meant. It ended when a series of glass and iron-roofed shopping centres was completed. They were complemented, if that is the word, by the 'high tech' modern art and culture museum, Centre Georges Pompidou, immediately to the east of Les Halles, and I.M. Pei's controversial glass and steel *pyramide* which has covered the underground entrance to the Musée du Louvre since 1989. The Centre Georges Pompidou by English architect Richard Rogers is, in appearance, the Lloyd's building of London, also by Rogers, lying on its side. To many critics the Pei *pyramide* defies classification.

## *Paris Today*

The present population of Greater Paris is well over 12 million, and that of the central city just over 2.15 million. Not all are what Richard Bernstein's cab driver would call Parisians.

FOREIGNERS

Some 350,000 'foreigners' live in Paris. This is nothing new: since the time of Julius Caesar Paris has been a magnet for what Parisians are pleased to term *les étrangères*. In 1891 180,000 of them lived in the city; that number had grown to 342,000 in 1990, which does not include expatriate North Americans, British, Germans and other western Europeans. They live in some forty 'communities' in such central areas as the district around the Gare du Nord and Gare de l'Est quarters, and in such suburbs as Belleville, Saint-Denis and Pantin. There are, among others, 2,700 Haitians, 3,500 Pakistanis, 4,500 Mauritians, 120,000 Algerians, Moroccans and Tunisians, thousands of Chinese and Vietnamese, and enough Armenians to make that Paris community the second-largest Armenian city in the world. In short, the present city is a polyglot of national, ethnic and racial minorities, who contribute a pleasing diversity in cuisine, fashion and some forms of entertainment. 'To be sure, as Bernstein's cab driver made clear, not all Parisians are happy about this diversity, and increasingly so as regards the rising numbers of North African immigrants to whom are attributed all manner of extremist Islamic activities.

## HAUTE COUTURE

High fashion has been part of the Paris image for a long time. The House of Worth was the first great Paris fashion house and, as fashion designer for the Empress Eugénie in the Second Empire, may be said to have 'invented' *haute couture*. Worth dominated for years. After the First World War, Gabrielle 'Coco' Chanel and Elsa Schiaparelli were perhaps the best known among the many designers who made Paris the indisputable twentieth-century capital of *haute couture*. Chanel popularized the casual, sporty look of bobbed hair and no corsets, developed designer perfumes, and 'lived fast' in the manner of the 1920s *beau monde*. Schiaparelli designed with an eye towards the bold and sophisticated, with accessories that hinted at the surreal. Both charged a great deal for their work. Chanel 'hated Schiaparelli, whom she referred to, nastily, as "that Italian artist who makes clothes"'.

After the Second World War, the most famous names were Christian Dior, Yves Saint-Laurent and André Courrèges. Dior, in his own words, 'drew women-flowers, soft shoulders, flowering busts, fine waists like liana and wide skirts like corolla'. He was soon a household word; when he died in 1957 his assistant, Yves Saint-Laurent, took over the House of Dior. The next year he introduced the 'trapeze' look, youthful and easy-fitting. In due course he left Dior and opened his own house, and remains the premier *couturier* in Paris. André Courrèges is best remembered for the 'mini' skirt, which he claimed to invent. That claim did not go unchallenged in London.

The principal houses of *haute couture* are to be found in Avenue Montaigne between Place d'Alma and Rond Point des Champs-Élysées. Take lots of money.

## EURODISNEY

Paris has appealed to tourists since the early nineteenth century. The attractions included historic sights, new structures of unusual dimension, theatres, restaurants, museums, shopping and a skyline unique in Europe. In very recent times Eurodisney at Marne La Vallée, 20 miles east of the city, has been added to the list. First broached in the 1980s, this European version of Disneyworld in Florida was supported by the Mitterrand government as, hopefully, a boost to the national economy; it was opposed by culture minister Jack Lang and the Paris cultural élite, which decried it as an invasion of American 'non-culture'. However, the Disney Corporation and President Mitterrand persisted, and Eurodisney opened on 12 April 1992.

The French economy is still waiting to reap projected benefits. Perhaps that will come, now that Disney Corporation has bent the knee to European custom and allowed the consumption of alcoholic beverages on the premises.

## CONTINUITY

Skyscrapers 'encircle' Paris because building regulations a century old prevent their construction in the central city; rush-hour traffic on the Champs-Élysées moves at about the same speed as it did when Henry IV was assassinated, but the *Métro* glides underground comfortingly and swiftly on rubber tyres; a cup of *café au lait* at a pavement table in the Boulevard Saint-Germain, or in a bistro in Montmartre, remains the pleasure it was a century ago; and diversity of race, nationality and point of view is everywhere, as to some degree it has been from Julian the Apostate to the present. So, too, are the vagabonds, street urchins and those who live by their wits in *Métro* stations, the steps leading to Sacré-Coeur, and the back streets of every quarter. François Villon would recognize them without an instant's hesitation. There are also sports hooligans, well known in British, German and Dutch football circles for years, but only recently a phenomenon at the Parc des Princes sports ground in Paris. On the other hand there were hooligans by definition every time there was a public disturbance, probably even in Julian's day.

A blend of past and present is the key to Paris. There is much that is new and much that is old, and some that is very old. Neither *vieux Paris* nor *Paris nouveau* have triumphed altogether, and that is as it should be. Otherwise the fabled City on the Seine might have faded into obscure and decayed quaintness, or else become unrecognizable, a 'Manhattan on the Seine', as one skyscraper critic phrased it. Either way, the result would have been deplorable. Above all it would not have been Paris.

# Chronology of Major Events

**B.C.**

53 — Julius Caesar makes Lutetia his headquarters

**A.D.**

ca.1–50 — First stone bridges built connecting the Île de la Cité with the river banks

ca.245 — Saint Denis founds the Christian Church in Lutetia

261 — Saint Denis martyred

ca.280 — The Left Bank burned by Germanic invaders

357 — Julian the Apostate becomes governor of Lutetia

422 — Geneviève, patron saint of Paris, born in Nanterre, now a Paris suburb

ca.550 — Cathedral of Saint-Étienne built on the site of the present Cathedral of Notre-Dame

560 — Saint-Germain-l'Auxerrois begun opposite the Cour Carrée; this became the parish church for the kings of France

613 — Queen Brunhild executed where Rue Saint-Honoré meets Rue de l'Arbre Sec

630 — Dagobert rebuilds Sainte-Geneviève's church at Saint-Denis, and establishes it as the 'royal necropolis'; he established the Saint-Denis fair in 635

845–85 — Paris repeatedly sacked by Vikings

1147 — The Knights Templar settle in Paris and build the Temple

1163 — Bishop Maurice de Sully begins Notre-Dame Cathedral

1181–3 — Les Halles built

1185 — Haraclius, patriarch of Jerusalem, celebrates mass at Notre-Dame Cathedral

1186 — Philip II begins paving the main thoroughfares

1190–1205 — Philip builds a new city wall

1200 — Philip charters the University of Paris

1204 — Philip starts building the Louvre

| | |
|---|---|
| 1217 | Benedictines (Jacobins) established in Paris |
| 1246–9 | Louis IX (Saint-Louis) builds Sainte-Chapelle |
| 1253 | Robert de Sorbon, Louis IX's chaplain, founds the college of the Sorbonne |
| 1301–13 | Philip IV builds the Conciergerie Palace on the Île de la Cité |
| 1307 | Jacques de Molay and other Templars are burnt in Paris |
| 1309 | Sire de Joinville writes *Histoire de Saint-Louis* |
| 1355–6 | Étienne Marcel, *Prévôt des Marchands*, seizes control of Paris; he was then murdered in the name of future King Charles V |
| 1380–3 | The Bastille built |
| 1413 | Pont Notre-Dame becomes the first Paris bridge to receive a name |
| 1420–36 | Paris directly under English rule |
| 1461 | François Villon writes *Le Testament* |
| 1470 | Work begins on the Hôtel de Ville |
| 1499 | The wooden Pont Notre-Dame collapses and carries all its houses and shops into the river 'with a fearful crash' |
| 1518 | Budé's *L'Institution du Prince* published |
| 1532–64 | François Rabelais publishes *Gargantua* and *Pantagruel* |
| 1534 | Ignatius Loyola and Francis Xavier meet with fellow students in the crypt of the old church at Montmartre to found the Society of Jesus |
| 1536 | Day of the Placards when anti-Protestant riots grip Paris |
| 1546 | Francis I begins renovating the Louvre, the work planned by Pierre Lescot |
| 1554 | Jean Crespin's *Book of Martyrs* |
| 1564 | Philbert Delorme begins Tuileries Palace for Marie de' Medici |
| 1572 | 24 August, the St Bartholomew's Day massacre in which thousands of Protestants were slaughtered in Paris |
| 1588 | Catholic League of Sixteen seize control of Paris |
| 1603 | Pont-Neuf built |
| 1607 | Place Dauphine laid out |
| 1610 | Henry IV assassinated while traffic-jammed in his carriage in the Rue de la Ferronnerie |
| 1612 | First public posters appear in Paris |
| 1614 | Last meeting of the Estates General prior to the Revolution of 1789 |
| 1615 | Marie de' Medici orders the Palais du Luxembourg (originally the Palais d'Orléans) and its attendant Luxembourg Gardens |
| 1617, 1673 | Tariffs established for sedan chairs and carriages |
| 1620 | A series of paintings by Peter Paul Rubens extolling the life of Marie de' Medici hung in the Palais du Luxembourg |

| | |
|---|---|
| 1631 | First newspaper, *Gazette de France*, founded by Théophraste Renaudot |
| 1632 | Pierre Corneille writes *Le Cid* |
| 1634 | Académie Française founded by Cardinal Richelieu; Louis XIV becomes its protector in 1672 |
| 1648 | Royal Academy of Painting and Sculpture; reorganized under Colbert in 1664 |
| 1648–53 | Paris occupied by soldiers of the Fronde uprising |
| 1660 | Boileau's *Les Embarras de Paris* |
| 1662 | Gobelins tapestry factory moved to its present site |
| 1665 | *Journal des Savants* founded |
| 1666 | Academy of Science founded |
| 1667 | Paris Observatory opened; the first municipal street-lighting system inaugurated |
| 1672 | The first daily newspaper, *Le Journal de La Ville de Paris*, started |
| 1677 | Jean Racine writes *Phèdre* |
| 1700 | Population of Paris reaches 560,000 |
| 1718 | Palais de l'Élysée begun by Mollet for the count d'Évreux |
| 1728 | Gabriel and Aubert begin the building which presently houses the Musée Rodin |
| 1751 | First volume of Diderot's *Encyclopédie* |
| 1759 | Voltaire writes *Candide* |
| 1776 | *Journal de Paris* begins |
| 1778–84 | Caron de Beaumarchais creates *Le Mariage de Figaro* |
| 1782–4 | Palais-Royal arcade built |
| 1785 | David paints *Le Serment des Horaces* |
| 1789 | The French Revolution begins in Paris with the fall of the Bastille; population of Paris reaches 600,000 |
| 1793 | Louvre transformed into a National Museum, and royal tombs in Abbey of Saint-Denis destroyed; Louis XVI (condemned by the National Assembly as Louis Capet, recalling the first king of France) and Queen Marie-Antoinette are executed; the Reign of Terror begins in Paris |
| 1799 | Napoléon Bonaparte's *coup d'état* at Saint-Cloud |
| 1802 | René Chateaubriand writes *Le Génie du Christianisme* |
| 1804 | Napoléon crowns himself emperor at Notre-Dame Cathedral; Père Lachaise cemetery established |
| 1808 | Arc de Triomphe du Carrousel completed; Paris placed under jurisdiction of the Prefect of the Seine |
| 1809 | At the Tuileries palace Josephine de Beauharnais agrees to divorce Napoléon I |
| 1814 | Gas street lamps installed |
| 1820 | Alphonse de Lamartine writes *Méditations poétiques* |
| 1824 | *Le Globe* newspaper opens |

| | |
|---|---|
| 1828 | First omnibus established |
| 1829–48 | Honoré de Balzac writes his multi-volume *La Comédie humaine* |
| 1830 | Revolution in Paris |
| 1831 | Stendhal writes *Le Rouge et le Noir* |
| 1833 | Hector Berlioz marries Harriet Simpson in what is now the dining-room of the British embassy, Rue du Faubourg Saint-Honoré; William Thackeray was also married there three years later |
| 1834 | La Ville de Paris, precursor of the department store, opens |
| 1836 | Public gaming houses closed |
| 1837 | First French railway opens from Paris to Saint-Germain |
| 1840–5 | Last Paris wall completed |
| 1844 | Alexandre Dumas *père* writes *Les Trois Mousquetaires* |
| 1846 | George Sand writes *La Mare au diable*; Paris population reaches 1 million |
| 1848 | Revolution in Paris |
| 1851 | Louis-Napoléon's coup |
| 1855 | First Paris Exposition; others followed in 1867, 1889, 1900 and 1937 |
| 1857 | Gustave Flaubert writes *Madame Bovary*; Charles Baudelaire writes *Les Fleurs du mal* |
| 1863 | Salon des Refusés opens in Paris, featuring Manet's *Déjeuner sur l'Herbe* |
| 1870–1 | Paris besieged first by Prussians, then by French government forces trying to put down the Paris Commune rising |
| 1872–1912 | Sacré-Coeur-de-Montmartre built; consecrated in 1919 |
| 1875 | Palais Garnier (Paris Opéra) completed |
| 1876 | Stéphane Mallarmé writes *L'Après-midi d'un faune*; Au Bon Marché, the first true department store, opens in the Rue de Bac |
| 1880 | Émile Zola writes *Nana* |
| 1889 | Eiffel Tower completed for the Exposition; Gyp writes *Bob à l'Exposition* as criticism of the tower; Moulin Rouge opens in Boulevard de Clichy |
| 1891 | French Open Tennis tournament, now part of the Grand Slam tennis tour which includes Wimbledon, the US Open and the Australian Open, is played for the first time, in Paris. |
| 1893 | Maxim's Restaurant opens |
| 1895 | Confédération Général du Travail organized |
| 1898 | Action Française founded; Marie Curie discovers radium; Zola writes *J'Accuse* on behalf of Dreyfus |
| ca.1900 | Paris population passes 2 million |
| 1902 | Debussy's *Pelléas et Mélisande* premières |
| 1911 | Harry's New York Bar opens at 5 Rue Daunou |

| | |
|---|---|
| 1913 | Riotous first performance of Stravinsky's *Sacre du Printemps* |
| 1913–28 | Marcel Proust completes *A la recherche du temps perdu* |
| 1914 | Battle of the Marne saves Paris in early months of the First World War |
| 1919 | Peace conferences to end the war meet in Paris |
| 1922 | Paul Valéry writes *Charmes* |
| 1928 | Committee for Managing the Paris Region created in conjunction with the Ministry of the Interior |
| 1933 | André Malraux writes *La Condition humaine* |
| 1937 | Last segments of the 1845 wall demolished; last Paris exposition held |
| 1940 | Germans occupy Paris |
| 1944 | Paris liberated from German occupation; *Le Monde* and *France-Soir* established; Jean-Paul Sartre's *Huis-Clos* opens at Vieux Colombier theatre |
| 1947 | Albert Camus writes *La Peste* |
| 1949 | Simone de Beauvoir writes *Le Deuxime Sexe* |
| 1958 | Charles de Gaulle called upon to form emergency government; Fifth Republic formed |
| 1962 | Attempt to assassinate President de Gaulle at Petit-Clamart outside Paris nearly succeeds |
| 1968 | Student riots in Paris lead to the retirement of President de Gaulle |
| 1973 | Montparnasse Tower, the tallest skyscraper in Europe, completed |
| 1976 | Centre Georges Pompidou completed |
| 1977 | Office of Mayor of Paris revived |
| 1989 | Paris celebrates bicentennial of the French Revolution; I.M.Pei's controversial Louvre *pyramide* completed; l'Opéra de la Bastille opens |
| 1992 | Eurodisney opens at Marne La Vallée, near Paris |
| 1993 | Premier Pierre Bérégovoy commits suicide; Oscar de la Renta becomes the first American to head a French fashion house, the House of Pierre Balmain |
| 1994 | The Eurotunnel connecting England and France under the English Channel, opens for business |
| 1995 | France resumes nuclear weapons testing against world wide protest; Marie Curie becomes the first woman to be entombed in the Panthéon among the 'great men' of France |
| 1996 | François Mitterand, the longest-serving president in French history, dies |
| 1997 | Fire in Channel Tunnel caused £250 million in damages |

# Presidents and Heads of Governments

## THIRD REPUBLIC

### Presidents

Adolphe Thiers *1871–1873*
Patrice de MacMahon *1873–1879*
Jules Grévy *1879–1887*
Sadi Carnot *1887–1894*
Jean Casimir-Périer *1894–1895*
Félix Faure *1895–1899*
Émile Loubet *1899–1906*
Armand Fallières *1906–1913*
Raymond Poincaré *1913–1920*
Paul Deschanel *February–September 1920*
Alexandre Millerand *1920–1924*
Gaston Doumergue *1924–1931*
Paul Doumer *1931–1932*
Albert Lebrun *1932–1940*

### Heads of Government

Louis-Jules Trochu *1870–1871*
Eugène Chevandier de Valdrôme *1870–1871* (The Bordeaux Government)
Adolphe Thiers *February 1871–February 1875*
Louis Buffe *March 1875–February 1876*
Jules Dufaure *February–December 1876*
Jules Simon *December 1876–May 1877*
Albert de Broglie *May–November 1877*
Gaëtan de Grimaudet de Rochebouet *November–December 1877*
Jules Dufaure *December 1877–January 1879*

William H. Waddington *February–December 1879*
Charles de Freycinet *December 1879–September 1880*
Jules Ferry *September 1880–November 1881*
Léon Gambetta *November 1881–January 1882*
Charles de Freycinet *January–July 1882*
Charles Duclerc *August 1882–January 1883*
Armand Fallières *January–February 1883*
Jules Ferry *February 1883–March 1885*
Henri Brisson *March–December 1885*
Charles de Freycinet *January–December 1886*
René Goblet *December 1886–May 1887*
Maurice Rouvier *May–November 1887*
Pierre Tirard *December 1887–March 1888*
Charles Floquet *April 1888–February 1889*
Pierre Tirard *February 1889–March 1890*
Charles de Freycinet *March 1890–February 1892*
Émile Loubet *February–November 1892*
Alexandre Ribot *December 1892–April 1893*
Charles Dupuy *April–November 1893*
Jean Casimir-Périer *December 1893–May 1894*
Charles Dupuy *May 1894–January 1895*
Alexandre Ribot *January–October 1895*
Léon Bourgeois *November 1895–April 1896*
Jules Méline *May 1896–June 1898*
Henri Brisson *June–October 1898*
Charles Dupuy *October 1898–June 1899*
René Waldeck-Rousseau *June 1899–May 1902*
Émile Combes *June 1902–January 1905*
Maurice Rouvier *January 1905–March 1906*
Ferdinand Sarrien *March–October 1906*
Georges Clemenceau *October 1906–July 1909*
Aristide Briand *July 1909–February 1911*
Ernest Monis *March–June 1911*
Joseph Caillaux *June 1911–January 1912*
Raymond Poincaré *January 1912–January 1913*
Aristide Briand *January–March 1913*
Louis Barthou *March–December 1913*
Gaston Doumergue *December 1913–June 1914*
René Viviani *June 1914–October 1915*
Aristide Briand *October 1915–March 1917*
Alexandre Ribot *March–September 1917*
Paul Painlevé *September–November 1917*
Georges Clemenceau *November 1917–January 1920*

Alexandre Millerand *January–September 1920*
Georges Leygues *September 1920–January 1921*
Aristide Briand *January 1921–January 1922*
Raymond Poincaré *January 1922–June 1924*
Frédéric François-Marsal *June 1924*
Édouard Herriot *June 1924–April 1925*
Paul Painlevé *April–November 1925*
Aristide Briand *November 1925–July 1926*
Raymond Poincaré *July 1926–November 1929*
André Tardieu *November 1929–February 1930*
Camille Chautemps *February 1930*
André Tardieu *March–December 1930*
Théodore Steeg *December 1930–January 1931*
Pierre Laval *January 1931–February 1932*
André Tardieu *February–May 1932*
Édouard Herriot *June–December 1932*
Joseph Paul-Boncour *December 1932–January 1933*
Édouard Daladier *January–October 1933*
Albert Saraut *October–November 1933*
Camille Chautemps *November 1933–January 1934*
Édouard Daladier *January–February 1934*
Gaston Doumergue *February–November 1934*
Pierre-Étienne Flandin *November 1934–May 1935*
Ferdinand Bouisson *June 1935*
Pierre Laval *June 1935–January 1936*
Albert Sarraut *January–June 1936*
Léon Blum *June 1936–June 1937*
Camille Chautemps *June 1937–March 1938*
Léon Blum *March–April 1938*
Édouard Daladier *April 1938–March 1940*
Paul Reynaud *March–June 1940*
Philippe Pétain *June–July 1940*

## VICHY

Philippe Pétain *1940–1944*
Pierre Laval *1942–1944*

## FOURTH REPUBLIC

### *Presidents*

Vincent Auriol (Soc.) *1947–1954*
René Coty (Cons.) *1954–1958*

### *Heads of Government*

Charles de Gaulle (provisional) *September 1944–January 1946*
Félix Gouin (Soc.) *January–June 1946*
Georges Bidault (Chr. Dem.) *June–November 1946*
Léon Blum (Soc.) *December 1946–January 1947*
Paul Ramadier (Coalition) *January–November 1947*
Robert Schuman (Coalition) *November 1947–July 1948*
André Marie (Coalition) *July–August 1948*
Robert Schuman (Coalition) *August–September 1948*
Henri Queille (Coalition) *September 1948–October 1949*
Georges Bidault (Coalition) *October 1949–June 1950*
Henri Queille (Coalition) *June–July 1950*
René Pleven (Coalition) *July 1950–February 1951*
Henri Queille (Coalition) *March–July 1951*
René Pleven (Coalition) *August 1951–January 1952*
Edgar Faure (Coalition) *January–February 1952*
Antoine Pinay (Cons.) *March–December 1952*
René Mayer (Coalition) *January–May 1953*
Joseph Laniel (Coalition) *June 1953–June 1954*
Pierre Mendès-France (Coalition) *June 1954–February 1955*
Edgar Faure (Coalition) *February 1955–January 1956*
Guy Mollet (Socialist) *January 1956–May 1957*
Maurice Bourgès-Manoury (Radical) *June-September 1957*
Félix Gaillard (Radical) *November 1957–April 1958*
Pierre Pflimlin (Chr. Dem.) *May 1958*

## FIFTH REPUBLIC

### *Presidents*

Charles de Gaulle (Gaullist) *1959–1969*
Georges Pompidou (Gaullist) *1969–1974*

Valéry Giscard d'Estaing (Cons.) *1974–1981*
François Mitterand (Soc.) *1981–1995*
Jaques Chirac (Gaullist) *1995–*


### Heads of Government

Charles de Gaulle (Gaullist) *June 1958–January 1959*
Michel Debré (Gaullist) *1959–1962*
Georges Pompidou (Gaullist) *1962–1968*
Maurice Couve de Murville (Gaullist) *1968–1969*
Jacques Chaban-Delmas (Gaullist) *1969–1974*
Jacques Chirac (Cons.) *1974–1976*
Raymond Barre (Cons.) *1976–1981*
Pierre Mauroy (Soc.) *1981–1984*
Laurent Fabius (Soc.) *1984–1986*
Jacques Chirac (Cons.) *1986–1988*
Michel Rocard (Cent.) *1988–1991*
Edith Cresson (Soc.) *1991–1992*
Pierre Bérégovoy (Soc.) *1992–1993*
Édouard Balladur (Gaullist) *1993–1995*
Alain Juppé (Gaullist) *1995–1997*
Lionel Jospin (Soc.) *1997–*

# Notre-Dame Cathedral

France has many Notre-Dames, but there is only one **Notre-Dame de Paris**, *the* national symbol. The Place du Parvis in front of the church contains (in addition to a bad equestrian statue of Charlemagne) a stone slab from which all distances from Paris to the furthest corner of France are measured.

The site on the Île de la Cité was holy ground with a specifically female orientation since before recorded history. Where Notre-Dame stands, Druids sacrificed virgins, Romans worshipped the Great Mother, and Merovingians built a cathedral to Saint-Étienne, with a church next-door called Notre-Dame which honoured the Virgin Mary. The progression to Bishop Maurice de Sully's 'Our Lady' cathedral, begun in 1163, was both continuous and logical.

## Medieval Cathedral Builders

Notre-Dame was built from stone quarried on the Butte Saint-Jacques, and in Bagneux, Arcueil and Montrouge. The quarrymen were skilled craftsmen who knew how to cut to best advantage. The stone travelled by cart and barge to Paris, where it was shaped and dressed by journeyman stone-masons for building blocks, columns and *colonnettes* (thin columns used for decoration and window support), wedge-shaped voussoirs for the arches, and the elaborate keystones without which the arches could not have stood. Master masons carved the delicate, lace-like window tracery, and the hundreds of decorative madonnas, patriarchs, kings, saints and gargoyles for the exterior. Rubble and mortar for the space within the walls between the blocks of dressed stone was left to apprentices. Meanwhile skilled carpenters built scaffolding, carved and installed tie-beams, plates and rafters, and devised wheel-windlasses to heave stones into place, all from timbers felled where the Gare de l'Est now stands. Finally the master builder, who oversaw the entire project as a combination architect, general contractor and foreman, was an artisan who had risen from the ranks through his abilities. He dressed in finery, and carried, but did not wear, mason's gloves, as a symbol that he had risen above his origins. The master builder who probably started Notre-Dame was known simply as 'Richard the Mason'.

Artisans were guild members who jealously guarded their rights. A story in the *Chansons de geste* describes a penitent nobleman who, to atone for his sins, worked for practically nothing in one of the many workshops which fed the rising structure. The guild members regarded him as a scab, and finally beat him to death when he would not leave.

## Funding

Louis VII contributed substantially to Notre-Dame, in order to have 'a church worthy of his capital city'. Other funding came from private individuals in

Notre-Dame

exchange for the promise of burial within the Cathedral, from Paris guilds as an act of city patriotism, from church communities as far afield as Hungary and Scotland, to which expeditions of clerics went to solicit funds, and from the sale of indulgences – a cash advance for forgiveness of sin, to put it in modern terms. This was unfortunate, because nothing was more subject to abuse than selling salvation in advance, as Martin Luther pointed out later with considerable effect.

## The Cathedral

The cornerstone was laid in 1163 by Pope Alexander III. The remainder required two centuries to complete. The chancel (choir), 170 feet long by 157 wide and 100 foot high, was finished in 1182. The ceiling is vaulted and supported by pillars, transverse arches and triangular ribbing, the effect of which is both practical and pleasing to the eye. Four tiers of stained-glass windows bathe the interior in sapphire, ruby, emerald and topaz-coloured light. Light was essential to Bishop de Sully, for he believed it symbolized the fundamental uplifting truth of Christianity. This, like the building itself, was central to the concept of the Gothic.

The transepts followed, built between 1182–98. The arm of the north transept was extended in 1250. The nave was completed with its twin towers about 1245. It is supported by flying buttresses, those exterior stone supports that seem almost to float in space, and which give Notre-Dame its characteristically Gothic appearance. The Galerie des Chimières (gallery of chimneys) runs along the base of the towers, 238 steps above ground level. Double aisles start in the chancel and proceed through the length of the church. However, when the lines of uniform round shafts that support the chancel reach the nave, they become lines of columns in which pillars encased in *colonnettes* alternate with single shafts. The western façade features three great portals topped by two flat-topped towers. The central and largest is the Last Judgement, finished in 1230 and covered with carvings appropriate to the theme; the right and left portals, Saint Anne and the Virgin, were both finished in 1220 and appropriately decorated with carvings devoted to the sanctification of the subject-matter.

The rose windows, one each on the west, north and south sides, are among the most famous Gothic features of the structure. The weight of their great size was allowed for by arranging *colonnettes* like the spokes of a wheel all around the central oculus. These connect to a second set of *colonnettes* through a series of trefoiled arches. The effect is breathtaking.

Notre-Dame is also famous for its bells, added over time, most of which have survived the centuries. They are named of course, as was customary in the middle ages: Guillaume, Gabriel, Pugnese, Pasquier, Thibault, Jean, Claude, Nicolas and François are in the north tower; the south contains Jacqueline, later called Emmanuel, which weighs in at 25,000 pounds. Of all the bells, only Marie, formerly Emmanuel's partner in the south tower, no longer exists. It was smelted down in the 1790s to make cannon during the revolutionary wars.

Notre-Dame underwent much restoration and some alteration over the centuries between being completed in the fourteenth century and cleaned in the 1980s. Chapels were added in the reign of Philip IV; Louis XII built an altar for the Lady Chapel in 1622. The seventeenth century saw many tombs removed in an effort to rid the church of what Molière was pleased to call 'barbarous Gothic'. That effort continued in the eighteenth, including Jacques-Germain Soufflot breaching the central portal in 1771 to accommodate the great canopies popular in the processions of the day.

The Romantic Age took a different view of Gothic, however. In the nineteenth century Victor Hugo championed medieval Notre-Dame in his book *Notre-Dame de Paris*, and Viollet-le-Duc did his best to restore aspects of the church, for example replacing destroyed sculpture by using sculpture from such Gothic cathedrals as Chartres, Reims and Amiens as stylistic models. The result was not displeasing. Meanwhile, from the seventeenth to the nineteenth centuries clearance projects removed the medieval warren that surrounded the cathedral and replaced it with green space that is far more pleasing to the eye, not to mention the nostrils.

## Great Events at Notre-Dame

Activity at Notre-Dame over the centuries reflects to some degree the history of both Paris and the nation. Albigensian heretic Count Raymond of Toulouse made his peace with the church there in 1229, during which he submitted to a ritual flogging before the high altar. The funeral mass of Charles VI was sung there in 1422, orchestrated by the duke of Bedford, English governor of occupied France. His sovereign, Henry VI, was crowned in Notre-Dame in 1431. The cathedral was desecrated by a Huguenot mob after the death of Francis I in 1547, and Henry of Navarre, who gave up Protestantism in order to become Henry IV, was married there. Notre-Dame was turned into a 'temple of Reason' early in the Revolution, and a storehouse later on. It was restored to religious function in time for the coronation of Napoléon I. Napoléon III was married there, some of the cathedral clergy were executed by Communards in 1871, Joan of Arc was canonized in a special ceremony in 1909, and the funeral mass of Marshal Foch, hero of the First World War, was held there in 1929. On 26 August 1944 a Te Deum celebrated the liberation of Paris; and in 1970 a funeral mass for Charles de Gaulle paid homage to the man most responsible for it. Huge crowds filled the square for both events, while dignitaries from around the world were seated in the cathedral.

# The Louvre

The **Louvre** is a museum that grew out of a fortress and a royal palace. In 1989 an underground entry-way was constructed and covered by a peculiar glass and steel pyramid, designed by Ieoh Ming Pei, a Chinese-American, which fits with its Renaissance surroundings rather as tennis shoes fit with a dinner suit.

## The Fortress

It began with a structure, probably a fort, built in the seventh century on the site of the Cour Carrée, where the Romans kept wolfhounds, and facing Saint-Germain-de-l'Auxerrois. 'Louvre' might derive from the Latin *lupara* (wolf-hunt kennel); more likely the origin is the old Saxon *lower* (fortress). In any case, while building the new city walls between 1204 and 1223, Philip Augustus turned the seventh-century structure into a castle. His Louvre consisted of four blocks built of yellow stone – the stone type used in all subsequent additions – linked in a rectangle around a donjon (free-standing tower), part of which he used as a prison. Between 1364 and 1380 Charles V's master builder, Raymond du Temple, extended the city wall westward. This reduced the necessity of the Louvre serving as a fortress, so he raised the two-storey Louvre walls another thirty feet, topped them with towers and terraces, and turned the castle into a royal palace. Charles VI used this palace for royal guests; he preferred to reside in the Palais de la Cité.

## The Palace

Francis I, the self-consciously Renaissance prince, was determined either to raze the Louvre or modernize it. His advisors persuaded him to choose the latter course. Work began with demolition of the donjon and outer wall, the latter replaced by a garden. In 1546 Pierre Lescot, canon of Notre-Dame and superintendent of royal palaces, began work on the palace itself. By 1549 a two-winged building ran along the south and east sides of the Cour Carrée quadrangle. Catherine de' Medici, widow of Henry II, carried forward with the

Palais de Tuileries west of the Louvre, begun in 1563, and the Grand Galerie (now called the Galerie du Bord de l'Eau) which faced the Seine and linked the Louvre to the Tuileries. It was started in 1565 and completed in 1595. This gallery burned down in 1661, but was rebuilt by Louis le Vau and Charles le Brun, with some stylistic changes, on the order of Louis XIV. In 1566 Catherine initiated the Petite Galerie, which ran north to the Pavillon de l'Horloge, rebuilt in 1855 as the Pavillon Sully by Hector-Martin Lefuel. Jacques Lemercier took over Louvre expansion in 1624, using Lescot's designs but quadrupling their extent. The west wing of the quadrangle soon extended to the Rue de Rivoli.

From 1624 until the mid-nineteenth century, some of the best of Paris artists and architects, such as Jean Goujon, Claude Perrault, François d'Orléans, le Vau, le Brun, Soufflot, Lefuel and Viollet-le-Duc among others, built pavilions and galleries, raised and modernized roofs, and added decorations, most famously in the 1670s to the buildings on the east side of the quadrangle, where a colonnade of twenty-eight paired Corinthian columns decorate a façade 570 feet long and 270 feet high, facing Saint-Germain-l'Auxerrois.

In 1678 Louis XIV moved to Versailles, whereupon the Louvre ceased to be a royal palace and much of it was turned into apartments and studios. It fell into disrepair thereafter, until a new round of restoration began in 1775. More additions and renovations followed, until a century later the Louvre Palace was finally completed as architects and builders from Lescot to Lefuel had envisioned it. It stretched nearly three-quarters of a mile along the Seine and the

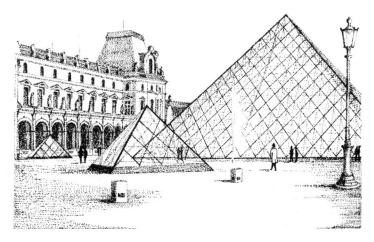

The Louvre with the new pyramid entrance

Rue de Rivoli in two wings that connected the Cour Carrée to the Tuileries Palace, incorporating the Place du Carrousel and the finance ministry along the way. Then came the Commune rising of 1871 and the Tuileries was destroyed, never to be rebuilt. The configuration of the Louvre was altered yet again.

There are eighteen pavilions in all, the exteriors decorated with medallions, such as the LA for Louis XIII and Anne of Austria on the Pavillon Marengo, reliefs, statuary, caryatids, columns, friezes and pediments. Interiors were equally ornamental, such as the Salle des Cariatides, famous for its caryatid statues, and the Galerie d'Apollon, where Eugène Delacroix painted the ceiling in 1848. In 1981 President Mitterrand inaugurated the 'grand Louvre project', designed to turn the entire complex into a museum. The finance ministry was relocated, a large reception area created beneath the Cour Napoléon, and the pyramid built which provides entrance to all departments of the museum.

# Historic Churches

## *Saint-Germain-des-Prés and Saint-Germain-l'Auxerrois*

The abbey church of Saint-Germain-des-Prés in the Boulevard Saint-Germain, and Saint-Germain-l'Auxerrois opposite the Louvre, were the inspiration of Bishop Germain (Germanus) of Paris. The first, founded in 542 by King Childebert to house his piece of the True Cross and later his remains, was built under the supervision of the bishop. The latter was started by the bishop himself in 560, to honour the memory of Bishop Saint-Germain of Auxerre.

First called after Saint-Vincent, **Saint-Germain-des-Prés** was the dominant church in Paris prior to the founding of Notre-Dame Cathedral. It received its present name in 754 when Bishop Germain was canonized. The three Romanesque bell towers, nave and transepts were built between 990 and 1100 after Vikings had sacked the church on four occasions. Saint-Germain-des-Prés has more Romanesque features than any church in Paris. However, there is also a Gothic chancel and flying buttresses, constructed in the twelfth century, and stained-glass windows installed in the thirteenth.

The Chapel Saint-Symphorien was built in the seventeenth century. Meanwhile, part of the nave was being renovated and vaulting installed in the west tower, along with a Romanesque-style bell chamber. The pointed spire was added in the nineteenth century, at the same time that Hyppolite Flandrin was painting a series of mediocre murals on the interior walls. A number of seventeenth-century worthies are entombed in the chapels: John Casimir, king of Poland before becoming a Benedictine monk, William Douglas, 10th earl of Angus, and his grandson, Lord James Douglas, and the philosopher, René Descartes. The Merovingian royal tombs were taken away during the Revolution, at which time the church was used as a saltpetre factory.

**Saint-Germain-l'Auxerrois** had deteriorated and was rebuilt in the eighth century – just in time for the Vikings to capture it and turn it into a fortress. In the early eleventh century Robert the Pious returned the church to its original function, rebuilding it in Romanesque style. Philip II later made the structure part of his wall. Much of the present church is Gothic and Renaissance, built between the thirteenth and sixteenth centuries. The central portal is from 1220, the nave with flying buttresses and inner aisles from the fourteenth century, the porch was finished in 1439, and the flanking portals in the sixteenth century. The inner bay near the south transept, and which is the base of the south clock tower, is a Romanesque survival.

Saint-German-l'Auxerrois became the parish church for the kings of France when they moved permanently to the Louvre. A bell, ringing to celebrate the wedding of Henry of Navarre and Marguerite of Valois at Notre-Dame, inadvertently sent the signal that began the massacre of Huguenots on St Bartholomew's day in 1572. On a happier note, the church came to be known as the 'Saint-Denis of Genius and Talent', because of the many architects buried there who participated in Louvre renovations, particularly in the seventeenth and eighteenth centuries. Also artist Adolphe Willette, who died in 1929, left a proviso in his will that artists would assemble in the church on the first Sunday in Lent to pray for artists who will die in the coming year.

## Saint-Denis

The **Basilica of Saint-Denis**, the necropolis of French kings (Clovis I, Dagobert, Louis XII and Francis I, among many others), is in the drab, industrial suburb of Saint-Denis. Built in the twelfth and thirteenth centuries, it was the inspiration of Abbot Suger, who wanted to renovate the dilapidated Carolingian church that had stood on the site for four centuries. Construction began in 1137, with Suger himself serving as master builder. The first step was to restore the nave, tear down the western apse and add a façade with twin towers and three portals. The second, begun in 1140, was to rebuild the choir, which Suger covered with a cross-ribbed vault and pointed arches, and sur-rounded with a double ambulatory containing nine chapels, each with a pair of tall windows. 'The entire sanctuary is thus pervaded by a wonderful and continuous light entering through the most sacred windows,' he wrote. That was the idea: for Suger (like Bishop de Sully of Notre-Dame later) light was metaphysical, an emanation of divinity, spirit, intelligence and understanding.

Suger associated many miracles with the new choir, such as that the Pontoise quarry contained exactly the right stone, that a nearby forest contained exactly enough trees for the roof, that certain rubies, sapphires, emeralds and other gems owned by Henry I of England found their way into his hands to ornament the huge crucifix, and that the church survived a violent storm while buildings all around it were blown down.

The choir and altar, beneath which rest the relics of Saint-Denis, were consecrated in 1144, in the presence of King Louis VII and Queen Eleanor of Aquitaine, among other notables. What they saw was breathtaking. Even Bernard, the dour abbot of Clairvaux, reformer of clerical abuses and suspicious of all earthly things, intoned: 'This man builds for God alone.' In his renovated nave and choir, Suger had constructed a church that glorified God with its sheer beauty. His unprecedented use of mosaics, glass and stone, towering arches and other architectural innovations, bridged the gap between Romanesque and Gothic.

Suger did not live to see the rest of his dream materialize. That was left to thirteenth-century master builder Pierre de Montreuil, about whom little is known.

## Sainte-Chapelle

Built with unusual speed between 1245–8 by Louis IX, **Sainte-Chapelle** is 'a jewel of Gothic architecture'. Once thought to be the work of Pierre de Montreuil, experts now believe it was probably the unknown master builder of Amiens Cathedral. It was Louis's private chapel – linked then at the upper level to the royal apartments in the Palais de la Cité – and a house for relics he had obtained from Venetian merchants, relics now kept in Notre-Dame Cathedral. The betrothal of Richard II of England and Isabel of France in 1396 is the only significant historical event associated with the chapel. Charles VIII did some renovating and made alterations in 1485, including the west rose window. Other changes were introduced in the nineteenth century, including the garish interior decorations by Émile Boeswillwald. The chapel survived a fire in 1776, escaped demolition during the Revolution, and was rescued when the Communards of 1871 wanted to burn it. Presently, Christopher Turner finds 'a sense of emptiness' in the chapel, for the altar and organ have been removed, and only one mass is said there each year, by invitation only, on the feast day of Saint Yves in May. Otherwise Sainte-Chapelle serves as a concert hall and museum.

The building is on two levels. The lower served as a chapel for royal household servants, the upper as the royal chapel, which is reached by means of a spiral staircase. The reliquary stood on a rostrum at the east end of the upper chapel. A cross-ribbed vault supports the roof, which in turn is supported by 60-foot-high pillars and columns. These are interspersed with 50-foot windows in such profusion that the walls themselves appear to be made of stained glass. This glass is from the original building and is among the oldest in Paris. Sainte-Chapelle is more than 100 feet long by 50 wide, and the single spire in the centre rises to a height of 246 feet. The walls are supported by light buttresses which frame the tall windows.

## La Basilique du Sacré-Cœur

This basilica of gleaming white domes and campanile sits atop the hill of Montmartre on the Right Bank, near Place du Tertre, famous as the haunt of Montmartre commercial artists and the tourists who patronize them. **Sacré-**

Sacré-Cœur

**Cœur** was built to commemorate the martyrs of the Commune Rising of 1871. Whether that meant those killed on the hill by Communards when the rising began, or those executed on the hill by government troops as it was being put down, depends upon who is asked. That Sacré-Cœur is a church of reparation is symbolized by the painting that covers the dome of the apse, which includes the figure of Christ and an image of the Sacred Heart above the Latin motto *Gallia Paenitens* (France Penitent). Funded both privately and publicly, this controversial project began in 1873 to a design by Paul Abadie. Technical difficulties (such as how to make such a building secure on top of a hill composed of soft, loamy soil), along with political opposition, made the work progress slowly. It was completed before the First World War but consecrated only in 1919.

Throughout this long period of construction and well after it, Sacré-Cœur was attacked by Republicans and workers in Paris who saw it as only a symbol of persecution. It was supported by thousands of others devoted to the cult of the Sacred Heart. The cornerstone ceremony in 1875 was kept low-key in order to avoid incidents. In 1880 Parisian radicals proposed that a 'colossal statue of *Liberty*', like that given to the Americans in 1876, be raised in front of it. This did not happen. Then, in 1881 and 1897, the Chamber of Deputies entertained motions to rescind public funding for the church. This also did not happen. All the same, controversy has continued into recent times. On the centennial (1971) of the Commune Rising, demonstrators took refuge in the basilica claiming to occupy a church 'built upon the bodies of communards. . .'. They were expelled with considerable brutality by police. In 1976 a bomb damaged one of the domes of the basilica.

Sacré-Cœur combines a Romanesque and Byzantine style. The exterior is gleaming, cream-white stone, the brightness of which is in stark contrast to the dark interior, which is decorated with mosaics, murals and statuary. The campanile was designed by Lucien Magne and completed in 1904. Its bell weighs 19 tons, one of the largest in the world. The truly penitent can suffer the long, arduous climb up the steps from Place Saint-Pierre to Sacré-Cœur. The rest may take the *funiculaire* and reach the church breath intact.

# Historic Buildings

## Le Palais de Justice and La Conciergerie

On the Île de la Cité and behind the gilt gates that open on to the Boulevard du Palais lies the **Palais de Justice**, a complex of buildings comprising the Paris law courts. Their function continues a tradition that dates from the first century, when Roman governors both lived and administered law on the site. Kings of Gaul and France occupied the same site and performed similar functions. Francis I was the last monarch to reside in what was then called the Palais de la Cité, which he gave to the *Parlement de Paris* when he removed permanently to the Louvre in 1528. The name was changed to Palais de Justice during the revolution, when the government moved to the Tuileries and left the Cité to the law courts. The Préfecture de Police is near by.

Owing to fires and renovations, much of the present complex is of modern construction, regardless of style. The Cour de Cassation, for example, appears Renaissance but in its present form dates from 1868. There are notable exceptions. In the thirteenth century Louis IX built the Tour Bonbec, so called because prisoners were tortured there until they became babbling idiots, or *bonbecs*. The Tour d'Argent and its twin, the Tour de César, are part of the **Conciergerie**, added to the complex by Philip IV between 1301–13. Jean le Bon built the Tour de l'Horloge about 1353. The Salles des Pas-Perdus is a 1618 reconstruction of a fourteenth-century Great Hall, and at 240 by 90 feet is among the largest rooms to be found anywhere. Finally, the Première Chambre Civile, much renovated over time, was built by Louis IX as a royal apartment. Later it became the Grande Chambre of the *Parlement*, where Louis XIV declared, riding crop in hand, *'L'état, c'est moi'* (I am the state). During the Terror (1793–4) Tribune Fouquier-Tinville condemned some 2,700 Parisians to the guillotine in this room, including Queen Marie-Antoinette.

When Charles V moved to the Louvre in 1358, he put a concierge in charge of Philip IV's addition, which henceforth came to be known as the Conciergerie. This structure is best recalled as one of the main prisons for the condemned during the Terror. Prisoners received their last toilet in a cell near

The Conciergerie, with the Pont au Change in the foreground

the Galerie des Prisonniers, then to the tumbrels waiting below in the Cour du Mai. Female prisoners such as Charlotte Corday and Madame Roland took their last exercise in the Cour des Femmes. There is an expiatory chapel in the cell where Marie-Antoinette was imprisoned before her trial and execution in 1793.

## *Les Invalides and L'École Militaire*

The **Hôtel des Invalides**, ordered by Louis XIV and designed by Libéral Bruant, was built between 1671–6 as a military retirement home on the Plaine de Grenelle, then outside Paris proper. It was the inspiration of Louis's war secretary, François Louvois, who recognized the needs of this aspect of a state perpetually at war. 100,000 square feet in extent, the *hôtel* was constructed around a military chapel, and included a hospital and the veterans' living quarters. It is among the best examples of French classical style in Paris. The central dome emulates Saint Peter's in Rome.

In 1676 6,000 veterans and disabled soldiers moved in, accompanied by priests, doctors and nurses. Two churches, Saint-Louis des Invalides for the

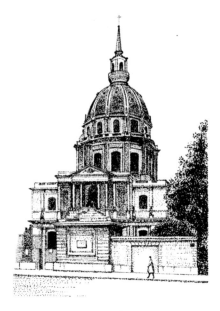

The Dôme des Invalides

soldiers and the Dôme des Invalides for the king, were added between 1677 and 1706, designed and largely built by Jules Hardouin-Mansart. There are fifteen enclosed courtyards, and one of the gateposts at the entrance to the complex features a sun face, in honour of Louis XIV as the '*roi du soleil*'. Presently the complex includes museums and some seventy pensioners, the National Institute, the Museum and Medical Department of the French army, and the tombs of Marshal Turenne, Joseph Bonaparte, Napoléon Bonaparte and his son, Marshal Foch and Marshal Lyautey.

The revolutionaries who stormed the Bastille on 14 July 1789 started by seizing Les Invalides and making off with 28,000 rifles from the arsenal. In 1837 the first performance of the Berlioz *Grande Messe des Morts* was held in the Dôme des Invalides, using a seventeenth-century organ; and in 1840, in an effort to gain the support of Bonapartists, Louis-Philippe presided over a grand ceremony that saw Napoléon I's remains, brought from St Helena, reburied beneath the dome in, as Orest Ranum described it, 'the most ostentatious tomb in the world, except perhaps for the Great Pyramid in Egypt'. One wonders if Louis would have approved such an addition.

The **École Militaire**, next door in Place Joffre, was built between 1751–72 as an officer training school. It was in part Madame de Pompadour's idea, for she thought Louis XV should have a building to rival Les Invalides. Louis reluctantly agreed but would not put up funds, which finally were provided by a tax on playing cards. Jacques-Ange Gabriel began the complex, which he designed in classical style with columns and a central dome. In addition to guard-rooms, courtyards, chapels and offices, the complex included a barracks to house 500 cadets, among whom was Napoléon Bonaparte. It opened in 1777.

A decade later, Louis XVI closed the training school and made the complex over into a depot and barracks for the Swiss Guard. The National Guard took it over in 1848, and the École Supérieure de Guerre in 1878. Thus its status as an officer training school was restored, which it remains to the present day.

## *Le Palais de l'Élysée and L'Hôtel de Ville*

The **Palais de l'Élysée** in the Rue du Faubourg Saint-Honoré, near both the British and US embassies, has been home to the presidents of France since 1873. The palace began as the Hôtel d'Evreux, owned by the miserly count of Evreux, in what was then a run-down quarter of the city. The duke of Orléans, regent to Louis XV, informed the count he would visit him, which compelled Evreux to spend a considerable sum turning his *hôtel* into a proper mansion. The renovation was completed in 1717. Three years later the count went insane and died, the result, it was said, of having had to part with so much money.

Thereafter the *hôtel* was residence to many notables. Madame de Pompadour bought and renovated the property in 1750, bequeathing it to Louis XV. The palace passed to Louis XVI, who gave it to his cousin, Bathilde of Orléans. She renamed it the Palais de l'Élysée. It served as a restaurant and night club during the Revolution; Napoléon abdicated there a second time, after Waterloo; Louis-Napoléon was the first French president to reside there, until he moved into the Tuileries; and visiting royalty, including Queens Victoria and Elizabeth II of England, have stayed in the palace. The presidential office is the Salon Doré, decorated in 1861 by Louis Godon for the Empress Eugénie. A modern addition, fall-out perhaps from introduction of the *force de frappe* under the de Gaulle presidency, is the nuclear shelter in the basement. It was added by Georges Pompidou.

In 1977 Paris revived the office of mayor, and the **Hôtel de Ville** at the end of Avenue Victoria became the official residence. It is a position that can be nearly as important as president of the Republic, as Jacques Chirac demonstrated during his tenure. Paris city administration first occupied this site in the Maison aux Piliers, beginning in 1357. That building was replaced in the sixteenth century by Francis I, using the Italian architect Domenico da Cortona; subsequent additions and renovations were made in the eighteenth century. The design and construction of the present building, undertaken between 1873–82 to replace the building burnt by Communards in 1871, was overseen by Théodore Ballu, architect under Baron Haussmann who also designed the belfry for Saint-Germain-l'Auxerrois. The result is as near a replication of the Renaissance original as a Victorian architect could manage. Philip Bibert Hamerton claimed in 1883 that 'the Parisian Hôtel de Ville seems the most perfectly beautiful of modern edifices...'

Louis XVI was brought to the Hôtel de Ville from Versailles in July 1789 and made to don the red, white and blue cockade; Robespierre sought refuge there without success when the Convention overthrew him in 1794; and when Napoléon put municipal power into the hands of the Prefect of the Seine in 1808, the *hôtel* became the official residence. It remained so until the office of mayor was revived.

## Le Panthéon

Built between 1759-90 at the end of Rue Soufflot, the **Panthéon** was inspired by Louis XV and designed by Jacques-Germain Soufflot as a commemorative church to Sainte Geneviève, patron saint of Paris. However, the Revolution intervened before it was completed and its function was changed. In 1791 the marquis of Villette proposed that the building become a necropolis for great Frenchmen, and Quatramère de Quincy, appointed to superintend the process, renamed it the *Panthéon français*.

Much toing and froing followed. In 1806 Napoléon I decreed it become a church once more; in 1823 Louis XVIII rededicated it to Sainte Geneviève; Louis-Philippe secularized it again in 1831; Louis-Napoléon made it the 'national basilica' in 1851; and in 1871 it served briefly as headquarters of the Paris Commune. Its present status as the 'national necropolis' dates from 1885, when Victor Hugo was interred there. Meanwhile Sainte Geneviève presumably remains next door in the church of Saint-Étienne-du-Mont, where she has been since the fifteenth century, along with playwright Jean Racine, philosopher Blaise Pascal and murdered revolutionary Jean-Paul Marat.

The Panthéon reflects the high point of eighteenth-century neo-classicism in architecture, wherein elements of Gothic 'lightness' and support columns were combined with the purity of Greek and Roman form. Soufflot's design included a Greek cross, central dome, and decorated triangular frieze fronting a portico roof supported by 72-foot-high columns. The dome was to equal St Paul's in London, but was scaled back as work progressed. Just as well: in 1780, when the drums over which it was built were being constructed, one of the support pillars cracked. Soufflot died the next year, supposedly from stress brought on by fear that the whole structure would collapse. His pupil, Rondelet, carried on, adding solid walls and pilasters for support. Elsewhere, columns rather than walls bear structural weight almost exclusively. An exterior catwalk around the dome at the base of the support columns provides a spectacular view of Paris in all directions; an interior catwalk allows visitors to look down on nineteenth-century murals by Paul Chenavard and Puvis de Chavannes, and other decorations.

The crypt contains the remains of the heroes (not military, for the most part) of France. Among the most famous are Soufflot himself, Voltaire, the first to be installed, Jean-Jacques Rousseau, Émile Zola, Victor Hugo and Jean Jaurès.

## *L'Opéra Garnier*

The neo-Baroque **Opéra Garnier** stands at the end of the Avenue de l'Opéra. It is *the* theatre of the Second Empire period, modelled by Charles Garnier after Victor Louis's opera house in Bordeaux. The avenue was laid out by Baron Haussmann specifically to enhance the theatre. Both are part of the larger Haussmann plan for rebuilding central Paris. The theatre was built between 1862–75, and when Empress Eugénie complained that it had no discernible style, Garnier replied, 'It is the Napoléon III style.' That, one supposes, meant both gaudy and imperial. Certainly critic Ian Nairn thought so; when Marc Chagall's ceiling painting of scenes from ballet and opera was unveiled in 1964, he observed that its modernistic design fitted badly with the imperial theatre: 'a flute where trumpets are needed,' he wrote.

At 118,400 square feet the Opéra is the largest theatre in the world; the space is not all seating, however. Half of the theatre is taken up by the entry foyer, decorated with a Venetian mosaic arch that leads to the staircase, the staircase itself, with 32-foot-wide marble steps and onyx banisters, and the Grand Foyer, more than 160 feet long and decorated with mirrors and allegorical frescoes. There are a mere 2,158 seats – compared to 3,600 at La Scala in Milan. There are five tiers of loggias, many of which provide a poor view of the stage; on one occasion the duke of Brunswick gave up trying to watch a performance of *Le Mariage de Figaro* and played a chess match instead. On the other hand loggia occupants are easily seen by other theatre-goers, and perhaps that is the point. This theatre was built for an Imperial élite, and even today it is used for presidential galas and balls as much as for artistic performance.

Copies of the famous Jean Baptiste Carpeaux sculptures, *Poetry, Music, Drama* and particularly *The Dance* (the originals are now in the Louvre) flank the approach. The basement is a vast grotto of mirrors reflecting fountains, pools, and anyone who walks through; Gaston Leroux derived the idea of *The Phantom of the Opera* from this cavern. In the auditorium a six-tonne chandelier hangs from the ceiling and the stage is closed by a painted curtain. In all respects, the Opéra is the perfect symbol of Second Empire Paris. L'Opéra Garnier now houses the Académie Nationale de Musique et Dance, and performance is limited mainly to ballet. Opera in Paris is performed largely in the Opéra de la

Bastille in the Place de la Bastille, completed in 1989 by Carlos Ott to mark the bicentenary of the French Revolution. This modernistic hall boasts two auditoriums which seat 2,700 and 1,200 respectively.

# Monuments to Modernity

## La Tour Eiffel

The **Eiffel Tower** was constructed for the 1889 Paris Exposition, after a design by Gustave Eiffel, a bridge builder from Dijon. However: 'We come . . . to protest . . . the useless and monstrous Eiffel Tower, which public hostility . . . has already baptized the "tower of Babel",' began a letter in *Le Temps* in 1887, signed by such of the Parisian arts establishment as Charles Gounod, Jules Massenet and Alexandre Dumas *fils*. They opposed the 984-foot tower as unsafe, unaesthetic and an insult to Paris. The writer Gyp (Countess Martel de Janville) added her criticism in *Bob à l'exposition*, where her cheeky title character noted that the machines exhibited were at least useful, but: 'Darn it all! . . . what does it do, an Eiffel Tower?' Of course, Eiffel had his own view: 'I think, myself, that the tower will be beautiful,' noting the attraction of size and that it provided 'striking proof of the progress realized in this century by the art of the engineers'.

The tower was constructed, the city of Paris took ownership after twenty years, and instead of pulling it down added a radio antenna. It has become one of the most familiar landmarks in the world. The Eiffel Tower weighs 7,000 tonnes; its girders are hollow, there are 12,000 replaceable component parts held in place by 2.5 million rivets, and on hot days the metal expands to increase the height by as much as six inches. Forty tons of paint are required for each septennial repainting (most recently in 1988), and there are 1,652 steps to the top, for anyone wishing to eschew the lift, with two stages in between where restaurants are available. From the top it is possible on a very clear day to see Chartres Cathedral, some 55 miles distant. The 150 millionth visitor 'spun the turnstile' on 30 August 1993. Appropriately, it was a Parisian, Jacqueline Martinez.

## Le Métropolitain

Ideas for an urban rail system were first advanced in 1845, then again in 1872 with actual plans for putting it underground. Two decades of bickering

273

The Eiffel Tower looming over the rooftops of Paris

between the Paris City Council, the Département du Seine and a number of *vieux Paris* preservationists delayed any definitive action being taken. The fact that another world fair was being planned for 1900 finally got *Le Métropolitain* under way.

In 1896, a plan was drawn up whereby the City would build tunnels and platforms, and private companies would lay track, provide access stations and buy rolling stock. This was put in the form of law in 1898. A Belgian firm headed by Baron Empain won the contract to build the system. They organized the Compagnie du Chemin de Fer Métropolitain de Paris (CMP) to implement it. Work began the same year, under the supervision of a Paris civil engineer, Fulgence Bienvenüe, who may properly be regarded as the father of the Paris *Métro*.

The first line, from Porte de Vincennes in the east to Porte Maillot in the west, opened on 19 July 1900. Ten three-car trains, powered by electricity, operated exclusively underground, save for passing over Saint-Martin canal just before arriving at the Bastille station. This first line was an amazing success; it carried 1.8 million passengers in August and 4 million in December. Expansion went forward at once, surpassing all expectations in speed of completion. The second line, Étoile to Trocadéro, opened on 2 October 1900, and the third, Étoile to Porte Dauphine, on 13 December. Each of these, and others built over the next decade, were extended until by 1914 ten lines criss-crossed Paris. Still more lines have been added and existing ones expanded over the three-quarters of a century since, and they have been interconnected through station links with the Réseau Express Régional (RER).

During the 1950s the system experienced a decline, the result of over-crowding during the German occupation that made underground travel a nightmare, and rapid post-war proliferation of affordable cars available to Parisians who were moving to the suburbs. However, urban congestion plus modernization of the system soon restored *Métro* popularity, and by 1960 the system was carrying 1.2 billion passengers annually. That number has only increased since.

Of the glass and iron-canopied station entrances designed in Art Nouveau style by Hector Guimard around the turn of the century for part of the Paris

Le Métro

*Métro*, some eighty-two survive, though none of them occupy their original sites. Most have been replaced by streamlined modern concrete blocks. Even so, the Guimard canopies symbolize the leap into the modern age that, like the Eiffel Tower, the *Métro* represented. Ironically, Gustav Eiffel proposed that entrances be built of stone and gilt in classical style, a far remove from the style of his famous tower.

Presently, more than 300 stations on thirteen lines, operating above and below ground, constitute the *Métro* city network exclusive of the RER. Trains 'whoosh' through tunnels on rubber tyres, the 'pneu', or pneumatic, rolling stock that was introduced in 1951. Platform television monitors carry advertising and news bulletins, and advise on interrupted service and travel delays. Platforms have been modernized with cheerful colours, bright lights, wall advertisements and decorations, such as in the Louvre station which displays copies of exhibits in the museum above. Escalators have been added in many stations. The longest, at Place des Fêtes, is 73 feet, and the shortest, at Chaussée d'Antin, is a mere 12 feet. Travolators also exist in some of the large interconnecting stations; the longest is the triple-bank travolator at Montparnasse-Bienvenüe, opened in 1968. Any station that is at least 39 feet below the street, such as La Cité, is served by a lift.

## Unesco

The headquarters of the United Nations Educational, Scientific and Cultural Organization (UNESCO) was completed in 1958 on the Place de Fontenoy, not far from the École Militaire. One French and one American architect, Bernard Zehrfuss and Marcel Breuer respectively, and an Italian engineer, Pier Nervi, designed this building with curved walls in the shape of a Y. The trapezoid-shaped Assembly Hall, the walls and roof of which resemble a vegetable slicer, was added later. Only eight storeys high, the building is relatively unobtrusive amongst eighteenth- and nineteenth-century surroundings despite its modernistic form and style. On the west side are an Alexander Calder mobile, a Henry Moore reclining figure and a Joan Miró mural. On the east side is Isamu Noguchi's Japanese garden. A large Picasso mural decorates an interior wall.

## La Tour Montparnasse

Built next to and overlooking the Gare Montparnasse complex between 1969 and 1973, the **Montparnasse Tower** is also the result of Franco-American collaboration. Collins, Tuttle and Company of New York were in overall charge, firms from New York and Chicago were consulted, and the French raised the money and did part of the architectural design. According to Wylie Tuttle, the Americans were involved because 'Paris needs a skyscraper and the

The UNESCO headquarters, which were completed in 1958

competition here isn't as strong'. Planning for the project began in 1934 as part of Montparnasse redevelopment. A tower was to be the focal point. However, the Second World War got in the way and planning did not resume until the 1950s.

The result was a black obelisk rising 656 feet (56 storeys) above the streets of Paris. Save for the colour, it much resembles Centrepoint Tower in Tottenham Court Road, London. When completed, the Tour Montparnasse came in for much criticism, on the grounds that it lacked architectural distinction, was too close to the city centre and was visually distracting. *Vieux Parisiens* might have preferred that renovators had limited themselves to smartening up the old quarter, including perhaps restoring the old Montparnasse railway station where in August 1944 General von Choltitz, German commander of Paris, encountered General Leclerc, head of the French army of liberation. President Giscard d'Estaing was sympathetic. After his election in 1974 he slowed down the Montparnasse type of expansion, claiming that 'the city must remain familiar to all'. Perhaps he was influenced by the American student who, viewing the city from atop the Arc de Triomphe, remarked: 'This isn't quite what I expected, but I guess you can't stop progress.'

## La Défense

At the west end of Avenue Charles de Gaulle is **La Défense**, the 'Manhattan-style' district 'with its architectural landscape expressing the rivalry of commercial firms'. In other words, an enormous skyscraper-complex devoted to business and high-rise apartments, and with an infrastructure of autoroutes (the Boulevard Circulaire connecting to Boulevard Périphérique), underground parking for about 32,000 cars, and public transportation lines (bus and train), including an extension of the new RER.

Like every publicly controlled Paris modernization project from Haussmann onwards, La Défense was controversial. The first plan, approved in 1964, called for thirty towers, the highest to be just over 600 feet and the others 300, with residential buildings limited to eight storeys. This plan was criticized for banality of design. The second and ultimate plan was initiated after 1968. It allowed for much larger buildings, including residential towers matching the 25–45 storeys of the office structures. This time the aesthetic argument took second place to complaints that the towers would mar the perspective looking west from the Louvre towards the Arc de Triomphe. However, former Prefect of the Seine Paul Delouvrier disagreed in an article written for *Le Monde*. 'Let the sky show behind the Étoile a new quarter of Paris, a modern Paris of big business. . . . I myself find nothing to criticize.' Moreover, he reminded his readers, 'it is eight kilometres from Carrousel to La Défense, and five kilometres from the Étoile to the new quarter: with the sky of Paris often murky even in good weather, the towers will frequently blur in the distance.' President Georges Pompidou agreed with Delouvrier, arguing among other things that 'the French prejudice, and particularly that of Parisians, against height is, to my eyes, completely retrograde'.

Construction of La Défense was directed by a government agency, the Établissement Public pour l'Aménagement de la Défense (EPAD). The site covers almost 1,000 hectares. Like London's Barbican, which is a similar kind of complex, the name refers to a fortification, in this case from the war of 1870–1. Building began in the 1970s, and continued into the 1980s, with towers ranging from a mere twenty-five to as much as forty-two storeys. Among the more interesting are the oldest, Tour Roussel-Nobel and Groupe des Assurances Nationales, then Tour Fiat and its 1980s twin, Tour Elf, and Union des Assurances de Paris. The most recent towers include Aurore, with bronze-tinted glass layers, Porte Sud and Les Miroirs, twin towers and small at a mere

La Grande Arche

sixteen storeys. There are decorations as well, such as Alexander Calder's last work, *The Spider*, and many fountains, gardens and courtyards. Meanwhile building goes on with an eye, as President Mitterrand has suggested, 'resolutely oriented towards the twenty-first century'. This includes the Grande Arche, completed in 1989, which is more than 330 feet high and consists of three cubes around an open middle.

## Centre Georges Pompidou

In the eleventh century Beaubourg on the Right Bank was a village; in the twelfth it was incorporated into Paris behind Philip Augustus' new wall; by the twentieth it was a slum much in need of renovation. The area was included in the scheme to redevelop Les Halles which began in the 1960s. In 1969 President Pompidou, encouraged by his art patron wife, pushed for building a contemporary arts museum on a cleared area alongside Rue Beaubourg. English architect Richard Rogers, with Italian Renzo Piano collaborating, won the design competition. Work began in 1972 and the **Centre Georges Pompidou** was completed in 1976.

The finished product is, to be kind, peculiar. A five-storey 'parallelepiped' of glass and steel without towers or skyline feature save for ventilation shafts, and the exterior is covered with scaffold-like steel pipes. Much of it is brightly painted in reds, greens, blues and yellows. Anthony Glyn has catalogued jokes about the structure, which include: 'Why did they have to put an oil refinery in the middle of Paris?' 'When are they going to take the scaffolding down?' 'So this is where the *Titanic* sank,' and so on. Glyn contends, however, that at least 'the building has personality. It is not just another glass egg-box.' Perhaps: others contend that when Rogers returned to London, he took the Centre Georges Pompidou concept and turned it on end, creating the Lloyd's Building. This edifice thrusts skyward like a tower and is among the most breathtaking monuments to 'high tech' architecture in existence. For some, one works and one does not.

All the same, the Centre Georges Pompidou contributes greatly to public culture in Paris. Each of the five storeys covers 90,000 square feet, which provides ample space for the Bibliothèque Publique d'Information, the Musée National d'Art Moderne, and the Institut de Recherche et de Coordination Acoustique/Musique. An op-art portrait of Pompidou by Vasarély hangs on the ground floor, outside which, in the Place Georges Pompidou, a variety of jugglers, sleight-of-hand magicians and other entertainers amuse onlookers much in the manner of Covent Garden.

# *Paris Parks*

## Bois de Boulogne

The 2,000-acre **Bois de Boulogne** on the western edge of the city was once a private hunting forest for Valois kings. It first opened to the public in the reign of Louis XIV, who ordered construction of the Allée de Longchamps and Allée de la Reine Marguerite. The forest provided firewood during the Revolution, and was a camp ground for English and Russian troops after Waterloo. When Louis-Napoléon saw the Bois de Boulogne in 1848 he called it an 'arid promenade', and Galignani's *Guide* noted that it was used mainly for 'duelling and suicides'. In 1852 Emperor Napoléon III transferred the wood to the city of Paris, and the following year Prefect Haussmann brought to Paris a gifted engineer from Bordeaux, Adolphe Alphand, who set to work transforming the *bois* into the present park.

As a start, the last remnant of the old city wall, along the east side of the wood, was torn down. Over the next half-dozen years lakes and grottoes were created, trees planted, restaurants built – today, Armenonville, the Pré Catalan and Château de Madrid continue the tradition of elegant dining in the *bois* – and the Longchamps racecourse was constructed. The Boulevard l'Empératrice (Avenue Foch) between l'Étoile and Porte Dauphine was designed to provide access, and Alphand created 43 miles of curved carriage roads and bridle paths within the park, as well as many footpaths, some of which Napoléon himself staked out.

In the twentieth century Roland Garros tennis stadium was added to house the French Open Championships each May. The Jardin d'Acclimatation was also constructed; with its small zoo, doll's house and miniature car track, this garden is primarily for children.

## Bois de Vincennes

Napoléon III did not want it thought that he was ignoring the poorer inhabitants of the eastern faubourgs. Therefore Alphand gave similar treatment to the **Bois de Vincennes**, east of the city beyond the Porte Dorée (Porte de Picpus), where Saint-Louis used to take the air after mass and listen to petitions from his subjects. This *bois* was actually larger than Bois de Boulogne, but a sixth of it was reserved for military use. All the same, the cost of its development was three times as great as the Bois de Boulogne. When work was finished in the early 1860s, Bois de Vincennes had three small lakes, some artificial streams, miles of new paths and roadways, grottoes, cascades, restaurants and cafés, and a racetrack with large grandstand. There were many tree and lawn plantings as well. Presently the *bois* also incorporates a zoological garden and a velodrome.

## Parc Buttes–Chaumont

Alphand took 62 acres in the working-class La Villette and Belleville areas where once a gibbet stood, and which was a rubbish dump until 1849, and designed the **Parc Buttes-Chaumont**. He created a mountain landscape, bringing in top soil to support trees, lawns and shrubs, and pumped water from the Canal de l'Ourcq to the north for streams, a lake with an island in the middle and a 100-foot waterfall. Once again there were restaurants and cafés. Parc Buttes-Chaumont was the most difficult project of all the parks. It cost twice as much as the Bois de Boulogne, even though it was one-twentieth of the size.

## Parc Monceau

Alphand's next job, in 1860, was the **Parc Monceau** along the Boulevard de Courcelles, which is named for a vanished village. It was built north-east of l'Étoile, out of a private park created in 1778 for Philippe-Égalité, the duke of Orléans. The duke's park was first known as Folies de Chartres, and lay alongside the 'farmers' wall' constructed in 1785. There were toll houses, done in neo-classical style by Claude Ledoux, where roads went through the wall. Alphand made no effort to preserve them. Parc Monceau received the usual treatment: new lawns, flowerbeds, trees, shrubs, a lake, a grotto and a waterfall, and space for pony rides and other amusements for children.

## Parc Montsouris

In 1867, on thirty-nine deserted acres on the hill of Montsouris, a mile and a half south of the Jardin du Luxembourg, Alphand built **Parc Montsouris**. He created pleasure gardens with bridges, pathways for strollers, three broad lawns, and plantings to hide the railway tracks that ran through the park. A large lake was laid out in the centre of one lawn; this time, however, there was neither a waterfall nor a grotto. War interrupted the work in 1870 and it was not completed until 1878. In June 1912 Vladimir Lenin, leader of the Russian bolsheviks, decided to leave Paris for Switzerland, and it was at the Pavillon du Lac in Parc Montsouris that he bade his Paris comrades goodbye.

## *Jardin du Luxembourg*

The largest green space on the Left Bank, the **Jardin du Luxembourg**, was laid out in Renaissance style in 1612, and between 1615–31 the Palais du Luxembourg, now the home of the French Senate, was built in the middle of it. The Fontaine de Médicis was installed in 1624, but most of the statues decorating it are nineteenth-century. The same is true of the statues of French queens and other prominent women which decorate the terrace around the south pond. These were designed originally for the park of the rebuilt Château Sceaux in the upper Seine valley.

Part of the Jardin du Luxembourg was taken away to build the Avenue de l'Observatoire in the early nineteenth century. Later Napoléon III created a furor when he wanted to take still more to build other streets. In the light of much opposition, he cut back the original expropriation to only ten acres taken from the nursery south of the present Rue Auguste Comte. While this pleased no one, at least it quieted the uproar.

## *Parc Champ-de-Mars*

The rectangular **Parc Champ-de-Mars** is the open area between the Eiffel Tower and the Place Joffre in front of the École Militaire. It is characterized by perfectly symmetrical lawns, walks and crossroads, the design of J.C. Formigé between 1908–28. The park is primarily of historic interest. The space was laid out in 1767 as a military parade ground where market gardens once had been. It was opened to the public in 1780, and three years later the first scientifically designed balloon was released there. It flew for forty-five minutes before landing, appropriately, near the present Le Bourget airport. Thinking it was a monster local peasants attacked it. In 1790 300,000 people celebrated Bastille Day on the Champ-de-Mars, and in the nineteenth century a racecourse and five world fairs occupied the site.

## *Jardin des Tuileries*

The **Jardin des Tuileries** (with the Jardin du Carrousel) is 63 acres of trees, ponds, fountains, statues (mostly copies of seventeenth- and eighteenth-century work) and pigeons, but little grass. It extends more than a half mile from the Place de la Concorde east to the Place du Carrousel. The garden was laid out for the new Tuileries palace in 1564, and redone in the seventeenth century by André Le Nôtre for Louis XIV and his principal minister, Jean-Baptiste Colbert. Le Nôtre also designed the Terrasse du Bord de l'Eau and the Terrasse des

Feuillants which flank the sides of the garden. The name Tuileries derives from kilns for the manufacture of tiles, or *tuiles*, which occupied the site before the palace was built. Many of Louis XVI's Swiss guards were massacred in the gardens when mobs stormed the Tuileries on 10 August 1792. The garden has been a popular place for strolling and promenading for more than two centuries.

## Jardin des Plantes

This complex of botanical gardens, zoo and natural history exhibits on the Left Bank near Gare d'Austerlitz has been described as the Paris equivalent of London's Kew Gardens and Regent's Park. Founded in 1626 as the royal herb garden, **Jardin des Plantes** was extended in the eighteenth century to its present 60-acre area. The public were admitted from 1650 onwards. Among other notable items is the false acacia planted in 1636 and thought to be the oldest tree in Paris; a cedar of Lebanon brought from Kew Gardens in 1734; and a cross-section from a 2,000-year-old California Sequoia with rings appropriately marked to indicate historical events that took place at various stages of the tree's growth.

## Parc de la Villette

The 137-acre site of **Parc de la Villette** was a livestock market and slaughterhouse between 1867 and 1974. In 1970 the City of Paris gave the land to the French government, which subsequently built a 'park of the future'. Bernard Tschumit designed the park, beginning in 1983; it is particularly appealing to children who account for 70 per cent of the visitors.

Some of the original structures remain. The nineteenth-century Maison de la Villette houses exhibitions. La Grande Halle for exhibitions and trade fairs was once the cattle market, while the Cité des Sciences et de l'Industrie started as the abattoir. It was adapted in 1980 by Adrien Fainsilber to become, as President Giscard d'Estaing phrased it, the 'supermarket of the future', featuring display, documentation, communication and research. Most other structures – the Planetarium, Géode, Zénith (a venue for rock concerts mainly) and La Cité de la Musique were created specifically to serve the park.

# Bridges on the Seine

## Pont au Change and Petit Pont

These two bridges have the longest history; their earliest manifestations were Roman bridges built of stone. The **Grand Pont** connected the Île de la Cité with the Right Bank, the **Petit Pont** with the Left. Soon Parisians were building houses and shops on them. The Petit Pont became the domain of philosophers and merchants, and the Grand Pont of goldsmiths and money-changers from the ninth century on. Both bridges were damaged repeatedly by fire, flood and Viking raids. After the great flood of 1296 they were rebuilt in wood. At that time the Grand Pont was rebuilt east of the original and was called the Pont aux Changeurs which simply acknowledged the business conducted there. It was rebuilt in 1859 as the **Pont au Change**. The present Petit Pont was built in 1853.

Meanwhile the Pont des Planches de Mibrai, a 'poor wooden thing', was constructed on the original site of the Grand Pont following the 1296 flood. It lasted until 1406, and was replaced by the **Pont Notre-Dame** in 1413.

## Pont Saint-Michel, Pont Notre-Dame and Pont-Neuf

**Pont Saint-Michel**, the first new rather than merely reconstructed bridge to span the Seine since Roman times, was built in 1378 by prison labour, which may explain why it took nine years to complete. The bridge housed everything from spurmakers to booksellers, and was repeatedly damaged by ice and flood. It was replaced in 1857 by the first bridge to be constructed out of Portland cement.

The 1413 **Pont Notre-Dame**, funded from public subscription, contained grain mills and beautiful houses, the first in Paris to have numbers. The citizens successfully sued the city when ice wrecked the bridge in 1499, and the city had to pay for rebuilding it. This bridge was completely reconstructed between 1853 and 1913.

**Pont-Neuf**, built between 1578–1607, is 'one of the wonders of Paris', and the only Seine bridge to survive, despite renovations, more or less in its original form. From its inception Pont-Neuf was a central attraction, and Parisians claimed: 'You cannot cross the Pont-Neuf without seeing a monk, a harlot, or a white horse.' Peddlers, musicians, a hydraulic pump, La Samaritaine, towering three storeys above the second arch on the north side, and medicine shows were among the main attractions. Shopkeepers' stalls were removed only in 1854.

## Pont Marie, Pont-au-Double and Pont Royal

Development on the Île Saint-Louis in the seventeenth century included the **Pont Marie**, built of stone and wood between 1614–34 and named for the first would-be developer of the island, engineer and bridge-builder Jean-Christophe Marie. The bridge sloped upward to a sharp peak in the centre as it connected the island with the Right Bank. Over the years Pont Marie suffered periodic damage from floods and ice, and habitation on the bridge was forbidden after the great flood of 1740 threatened the entire structure. In 1859 the central peak was levelled to ease the traffic flow. Roofed niches in the façade, and triangular stone piers around which the river flows, are all that remain of the original bridge.

The **Pont-au-Double** between the Cité and the Left Bank was built in 1634 as a toll-bridge where horsemen had to pay double, hence the name. The toll was abolished in 1789. The bridge was also occupied by a wing of the Hôtel-Dieu. When a flood destroyed the bridge in 1709 it was replaced exactly as it had been. Because of the hospital, it was also exempt until 1835 from a general decree of 1769 that removed all houses from all bridges. Pont-au-Double was taken down altogether in 1845, and rebuilt of iron, the present structure, in 1882.

Louis XIV ordered the **Pont Royal** in 1685 to replace a wooden bridge that burned in 1656. It is classic in form, bare of ornamentation, and depends upon harmonic use of material to define its beauty, including the river in which reflections of the five arches seem to be part of the design. Contrary to popular belief, the bridge was not funded by a lottery.

## Pont de la Concorde, Pont des Arts, Pont d'Iéna and Pont d'Arcole

Built between 1788–91, **Pont de la Concorde** was built of stone just in time to be renamed for the Revolution. Napoléon I sought to decorate it with statues of war heroes, and the Restoration put up statues of national heroes. These were all removed in 1857, leaving the structure with its present appearance. Since 1791 the bridge has been the scene of riots, fighting between Germans and the *Résistance*, strikes and demonstrations.

Opened in 1803, the **Pont des Arts** was the first Seine footbridge in Paris. It was also the first iron bridge, and attracted some 60,000 spectators to its inauguration. However, its location near the Pont-Neuf created difficulties for barges navigating the Seine, and the bridge suffered repeated damage from collisions. It has been rebuilt in recent years with attention paid to the original design, save for a reduction in the number of arches which once were its most attractive feature. Pavement artists now abound on the bridge, and the view from the Pont des Arts of the Île de la Cité, the Pont-Neuf and other features of central Paris are spectacular.

**Pont d'Iéna** was dedicated in 1814, emblazoned with imperial eagles. After Waterloo the allies occupied Paris and 'when [Marshal] Blücher saw the bridge and heard its name, his German blood boiled, his Prussian mustaches quivered and his Junker honour screamed in his Teutonic bones'. However, he was not allowed to blow up the bridge, however much he wanted to. Horse statuary was installed at the two ends in 1852, and there is a stairway with broad steps leading from the bridge down to the river, which is ideal for sunbathing.

Not until 1828 did a bridge connect the Hôtel de Ville with Notre-Dame, and that was the **Pont de Grève**, a pedestrian bridge. It is a suspension bridge, of interest mainly for being a battleground in the Revolution of 1830 and the struggle against the Germans in 1944, and for the legend surrounding its present name. A revolutionary who forced his way on to the bridge during a battle on 28 July 1830, and raised the tricolour on the central suspension tower, had called upon his fellow revolutionaries to remember his name 'Arcole' – or perhaps he shouted something about Napoléon I at a bridge in Arcole in Italy. In any event, 'it was something about Arcole, they all swore to that'. When the Revolution of 1830 was over, the bridge was renamed **Pont d'Arcole**.

## Pont National and Pont de Tolbiac

These bridges, built respectively in 1858 and 1895, are neither beautiful, ugly, nor historically interesting. All the same, each has a claim to fame. **Pont National** is the first bridge crossing the Seine within the city gates to the east, the direction from which the Seine flows; and the 'uninspired' **Pont de Tolbiac**, the name taken from a Merovingian battle site which historians cannot actually find, has the distinction of being the least-crossed bridge in Paris.

## Pont Alexandre III, Pont Mirabeau and Pont de la Tournelle

Built between 1897–1900 of moulded steel and stone balustrades, **Pont Alexandre III** spans the Seine in a single arch. It is almost excessively decorated, including rows of lamps on either side in a sort of Art Nouveau style, and larger lamps at either end surrounded by dancing cupids, which is why it is sometimes referred to as the 'tattooed lady' of Paris bridges. Wielding a gold and ivory trowel, Tsar Nicholas II laid the first stone and named the bridge after his father. This bridge, Blake Ehrlich wrote with utter accuracy, 'bespeaks the ingenuity, exuberance, optimism and sensuality that abounded in France at the turn of the century'.

**Pont Mirabeau**, opened in 1895, was a serious engineering project employing steel. Like Pont Alexandre III two years later, it was turned into a gaudy display of exuberant decoration: larger-than-life naked females blowing silver trumpets and brandishing torches rise above the parapet. Otherwise, it is distinguished only by being the last bridge one encounters before leaving Paris toward the west.

The **Pont de la Tournelle**, on the other hand, is in the middle of Paris, connecting the Île Saint-Louis with the Left Bank. Four wooden bridges spanned this spot of river, beginning in the seventeenth century; all were destroyed by ice and flood. The present bridge was erected in 1928, a single arch of what appears to be stone but is actually reinforced concrete. Its claim to fame lies in being one of the very few Paris bridges to be conceived and constructed entirely in the twentieth century.

# Cemeteries

By the end of the eighteenth century Paris cemeteries were stretched beyond the breaking point. Skeletons protruded from churchyard burial grounds, and in 1786 the greatly ·overcrowded **Cimetière des Innocents** 'exploded', so to speak, spewing corpses into the basement of an adjacent apartment building and an asphyxiating odour throughout the neighbourhood. That was the last straw. The government closed all existing church and city grounds to further burials and set about acquiring new public space for the purpose. Meanwhile excess bones were collected from existing cemeteries and removed to a quarry south of Paris.

## Père Lachaise

The largest of the new cemeteries, at 118 acres, the Cimetière de l'Est next to Belleville, was opened in 1804 on Napoléon's orders, in the week of his coronation. It was later renamed **Père Lachaise** after Louis XIV's confessor, and to whom the site once belonged. The land is on the west side of a slope that begins at Boulevard de Ménilmontant. It was purchased from Baron Desfontaines by Nicolas Frochot in 1795 at a bargain price. Père Lachaise is often called a 'garden cemetery', which is curious because it is criss-crossed by stone-lined roads bearing street markers.

The cemetery is final resting place for a great variety of people, by no means all Parisian or even French. Among the most.famous, and certainly the oldest, are Abélard and Héloïse, the tragic medieval lovers of Paris legend; they were transferred to Père Lachaise from Paraclete in 1817. A 'well-known path, worn by generations of unhappy lovers,' leads to their grave – or so it is said. Their tomb depicts the couple at prayer and is covered by a gazebo in ornate style. Baron Haussmann, who once planned to abolish Père Lachaise as part of his urban renovation scheme, occupies a mausoleum with a rusty door.

Other well-known inhabitants include: artists Alfred de Musset, Jacques-Louis David and Eugène Delacroix; writers La Fontaine, Molière and Colette; composers Frédéric Chopin, Georges Bizet and Georges Enesco; Ferdinand de Lesseps, builder of the Suez Canal; James Douglas Morrison, lead singer for the

Père Lachaise Cemetery

American rock group The Doors, who may or may not actually be dead, and actually buried in the grave topped by his pop-art bust; the French Rothschilds, famous for banking and great Bordeaux wines; Auguste Comte, the Positivist philosopher; and Prince Talleyrand, perhaps the most enigmatic statesman in French history. There are hundreds more, some with grave covers that reflect their lives in a bizarre manner. Victor Noir, for example, who was shot for publicly criticizing Napoléon III's cousin Pierre, is depicted by a horizontal statue on his grave cover just as he appeared moments after the shooting, complete with top hat lying at his side.

The Avenue Circulaire on the east side of the cemetery is lined with memorials to holocaust victims, slain *Résistance* fighters, and deported French workers from World War II. Modern sculptures pay tribute to the former inmates of Oranienburg, Sachsenhausen, Buchenwald-Dora and other concentration camps. A wall, the Mur des Fédérés, commemorates Paris Communards executed in the cemetery in 1871.

## Montmartre

Cimetière du Nord, later called **Cimetière de Montmartre**, opened around 1806 on 28 acres at the east end of Avenue Rachel, not far from Sacré-Coeur. Like Père Lachaise it has the appearance of a small city. Famous residents here include writers Henri Murgur, Stendhal, Heinrich Heine and Alexandre Dumas *fils*; artist Edgar Degas; composers Hector Berlioz, Jacques Offenbach and Adolphe-Charles Adam; dancer Vaslav Nijinsky; film-maker François Truffaut; and social philosopher Charles Fourier. As in Père Lachaise, there are also many little-known residents.

## Saint-Vincent, Passy and The Catacombs

These small cemeteries date from the nineteenth century, are small, one to three acres, and contain interesting statuary. A doll's house with faces peeking out decorates **Saint-Vincent**, for example. Painter Maurice Utrillo is the only famous inhabitant. Saint-Vincent lies half-way between Cimetière du Montmartre and Sacré-Coeur. **Passy**, in the shadow of the Eiffel Tower, boasts a sculpture of a dog waiting patiently on its master's tomb. Composers Claude Debussy and Gabriel Fauré, painter Édouard Manet and writer Jean Giraudoux are among the best-known to have been buried here.

   **The Catacombs** in the Avenue Denfert-Rochereau, unlike their Roman counterpart, offer only a grisly reminder of the way of all flesh. Count Mirabeau is interred here, but mostly there is only a collection of skulls and bones, moved here from the Cimetière des Innocents in 1786.

## Montparnasse

This 45-acre site, opened in 1824 as Cimetière du Sud and renamed **Cimetière de Montparnasse** later, is best known for the four-poster bed monument over the tomb of M. and Mme Charles Pigeon – inventor of the Pigeon lamp – which includes a sculpture of the tomb's occupants. It is also famous for some of those buried within the precincts: composers Camille Saint-Saëns and César Franck; philosopher Jean-Paul Sartre; American actress Jean Seberg; Vichy premier Pierre Laval, who was executed as a traitor to France in 1945; and writers Guy de Maupassant and Charles Baudelaire. Alfred Dreyfus, victim of the Dreyfus affair, also lies here.

## La Chapelle Expiatoire

In 1797 many guillotined aristocrats and others, including Louis XVI and Marie-Antoinette, were buried in large trenches with quick-lime to hasten their decomposition, in land on Rue Pasquier and what became Boulevard

Haussmann. This land was purchased by Olivier Desclozeaux, a closet royalist. At the Restoration he sold it with its grisly contents to Louis XVIII, who raised La Chapelle Expiatoire on the site in 1826, in memory of the victims. Those honoured include the best and worst of the Revolution period: Madame du Barry, last mistress of Louis XV; 'Philippe-Égalité', cousin of Louis XVI; Girondiste Madame Roland; Charlotte Corday, who killed Marat; Jacques-René Hébert, extremist publisher of *Le Père Duchesne*; General Armand-Louis Custine, who forbade circulation of Hébert's paper; Jacques-Pierre Brissot, who argued against the execution of the king; and, of course, the royal couple.

# Museums and Galleries in Paris

## The Louvre

The **Louvre** is the closest equivalent in Paris to the British Museum. Visitors number in excess of two million annually. However, unlike its London counterpart the Louvre became a museum only after long service as a fortress and royal palace.

The first royal collector for the Louvre was Charles V in the fourteenth century. Francis I carried the process much further in the sixteenth century, by patronizing such great artists of the day as Leonardo da Vinci, who brought the *Mona Lisa* to Paris with him. That masterpiece is now shown from behind unbreakable glass in a security box with all manner of alarms built into it. Subsequent monarchs and ministers of state – Louis XIV, Richelieu, Mazarin, Colbert, Napoléon I – made their contributions to the Louvre as well, though Napoléon had to return most of his contributions since they had been looted from across Europe. Revolutionary governments after 1792 also looted, but since it was mostly from the Church and aristocracy, these works remained in the Louvre.

In 1747 a petition from Lafont de Saint-Yenne persuaded the superintendent of palaces to set aside a special room in the Louvre where artists could come to study the masters' work. Building upon what this arrangement suggested, 'Directeur des Bâtiments' the count of Angivillier in 1774 began turning the Louvre into the museum it has become. He purchased paintings of historic value and planned public exhibitions for the galleries. A decision of the Paris Convention in 1793 turned the Louvre Palace into a national museum, which merely confirmed what the count had started.

Today the Louvre contains six departments. Greek and Roman antiquities, organized in 1800, includes such famous works as the Venus de Milo and the Victory of Samothrace; Egyptian antiquities was organized in 1826, with Jean Champollion, discoverer of the Rosetta Stone (in the British Museum in London), as curator. The other departments include Oriental antiquities, Medieval, Renaissance, and Modern Sculpture and Art objects, Painting and

Drawing, and Christian antiquities. Among the famous paintings are Leonardo's *Mona Lisa*, no doubt the most famous Louvre possession, Raphael's *Portrait of Baldassare Castiglione*, Titian's *Man with a Glove*, van Dyck's *Portrait of Charles I of England*, Rembrandt's *Supper at Emmaus*, Michelangelo's *Slave*, Bartolommeo's *Marriage of Saint Catherine*, Vignon's *Young Choirboy*, Delacroix's *Abduction of a Young Woman*, and Corot's *Young Woman with Mandolin*, to mention only a few. There are tens of thousands of other works from every period.

## Museums

### ANTHROPOLOGY, ARCHAEOLOGY, CULTURE

The **Musée de l'Homme** in the Palais de Chaillot (Place du Trocadéro) deals with prehistoric and primitive cultures. Among the outstanding exhibits are a Cro-Magnon skeleton, the 'Hottentot Venus', copies of prehistoric wall paintings, and the extensive collection of pre-Columbian artifacts. The **Crypte Archéologique du Parvis Notre-Dame** and the **Musée de Notre-Dame de Paris**, both on the Cathedral grounds, display remains dating back to the Roman temple to Jupiter. The **Musée Guimet** (Place d'Iéna) and the **Musée Cernuschi** (Avenue Vélasquez) specialize in early and modern Asian art and artefacts. The Musée Guimet is linked to the Asian department at the Louvre.

Cultural exhibits come in many forms. The **Cabinet des Médailles et des Antiques** in the Bibliothèque Nationale (Rue de Richelieu) and the **Monnaie** (Quai Conti) galleries display historic coins from around the world as well as from France. Decorative arts and fashions from France and around the world, from ancient times to the present, are to be found in the **Musée de la Mode et du Costume** (Avenue Pierre), the **Musée des Arts Décoratifs** (Rue de Rivoli), and the **Musée Nissim de Camondo** (Rue de Monceau).

### ART AND ARCHITECTURE

The Louvre is the great art museum of Paris, but there are others. Paintings, enamels, porcelains, books, tapestries, drawings and furniture from antiquity to the Renaissance are located in the **Musée de Beaux Arts de la Ville de Paris** (Petit Palais), while the **Musée Cognacq-Jay** (Rue Elzévir) contains mainly eighteenth-century European paintings and furniture. The **Musée National des Monuments Français** (Palais de Chaillot), the inspiration of Viollet-le-Duc, traces the history of monumental architectural decoration from Romanesque to Classical; it features plaster casts of carved sections of buildings, and copies of stained glass and murals. The **Musée d'Orsay** (Rue de Bellechasse), which opened in 1986, houses the Impressionist and neo-Impressionist collections formerly in the Jeu de Paume, the Palais de Tokyo in Avenue du President Wilson, and the Louvre. Twentieth-century abstractionists – Utrillo,

Léger, Kandinsky, Picasso, Miró, Matisse, Delaunay, Braque, Mondrian, Chagall, Dali, Warhol and Lichtenstein, to mention only a few – are housed in the **Musée National d'Art Moderne** (Centre Georges Pompidou).

## PARIS

Roman ruins and medieval art and artefacts pertinent to Paris are found in the **Musée de Cluny** (Place Paul Painlevé). Such early twentieth-century Paris School painters as Dufy, Modigliani and Matisse are displayed in the **Musée d'Art Moderne de la Ville de Paris** (Palais de Tokyo). The **Musée Carnavalet** (Rue de Sévigné) is the municipal museum of the city of Paris, with exhibits devoted to its history.

## PERSONALITIES

Most Paris museums devoted to individuals concern artists. **Maison de Victor Hugo** (Place des Vosges) is an exception; there the writer penned part of *Les Misérables*, and there is much Hugo memorabilia. The same is true of **Maison de Balzac** (Rue Raynouard); and of **Lenin's Flat** (4 Rue Marie-Rose), a museum dedicated to the maker of the 1917 Bolshevik Revolution in Russia. Otherwise the **Musée Marmottan** (Rue Louis Boilly) is devoted to Claude Monet, and includes the Wildenstein collection of 13th–14th-century Flemish illuminated manuscripts and miniatures. Rodin's pupil, Antoine Bourdelle, is the featured artist of the **Musée Bourdelle** (Rue Antoine-Bourdelle). **Musée de la Serrure** (Rue de la Perle), sometimes referred to as **Musée Bricard**, is devoted to the collection of locks and decorative hardware assembled by Bricard in the nineteenth century. Romantic painter Eugène Delacroix is featured in **Musée Delacroix** (Place de Fürstemberg), Pablo Picasso in **Musée Picasso** (Rue de Thorigny), and Auguste Rodin in **Musée Rodin** (Rue de Varenne).

## SCIENCE AND TECHNOLOGY

The **Palais de la Découverte** (Avenue Franklin D. Roosevelt) is the science museum of Paris, featuring a planetarium and public demonstrations and lectures; research also is carried on here. The **Centre de Création Industrielle** (Centre Georges Pompidou) considers such aspects of contemporary life as noise. The history of public health care in Paris is displayed in the **Musée de l'Assistance Publique** (Rue des Bernardins); and pre-industrial French life, labour, dress and folklore are the subject of the **Musée National des Arts et Traditions Populaires** (Route du Mahatma-Gandhi).

## WAR

Since Les Invalides was created as a soldiers' retirement home, it is fitting that it houses as well the **Musée de l'Armée**, with collections ranging from the middle ages to the Second World War; and the **Musée de l'Ordre de** la **Libération**, emphasizing the 1940–4 period. The **Musée de la Marine** in the Palais de Chaillot contains much of interest to naval history enthusiasts.

MISCELLANY

Not everything fits into an easy category, which is the situation with the **Musée Grévin** (Boulevard Montmartre), the Paris version of Madame Tussaud's in London. Its nineteenth-century founder was a caricaturist. The **Musée de la Chasse et de la Nature** (Rue des Archives) features paintings, hunting weapons, and stuffed game birds and animals. The history of communications over the ages is featured in the **Musée de la Poste** (Boulevard de Vaugirard); for the philatelist there is a complete collection of French postage stamps from 1849 and a model stamp-making machine. The communication balloon used in the Paris siege of 1870 is also here. The **Musée de Montmartre** (Rue Cortot) houses examples of Montmartre porcelain, and otherwise is devoted to the memory of writers and painters who lived and worked in Montmartre.

## *Galleries*

Paris is full of art and exhibition galleries, great and small. Some, very small but very chic, are to be found in the back streets of the Latin Quarter. Others are better known. The **Grand Palais** and **Petit Palais** (both Avenue Winston Churchill) feature some short-term exhibits ranging from antiquities to science displays. **Galerie Lambert** (Rue Saint-Louis-en-l'Île) sometimes shows artists who have or do live on the island. The **Musée de l'Orangerie** (Jardin des Tuileries) usually displays only contemporary expressionist art on a short-term basis, though it does possess permanent Impressionist and Modernist exhibits. Short-term exhibits also characterize the **Musée du Luxembourg**; the annual Salon des Femmes Peintre is held here, while the annual Salon de Mai is exhibited in **Espace Cardin** (Avenue Champs-Élysées). Finally, the Centre Georges Pompidou is the home of the **Galeries Contemporaines**, which features several different exhibits annually. The **Salle d'Art Graphique** does the same.

# The Environs of Paris

**Notre-Dame de Chartres** is as celebrated a cathedral as is Notre-Dame de Paris, and even more a work of art. It crowns a hilltop in the town of Chartres, some fifty-five miles south-west of Paris, and is perhaps the best example of medieval church architecture, decoration and atmosphere in the world. Émile Mâle and Henry Adams agreed that it contained the essence of the medieval mind. Mâle wrote: 'The cathedral is the visible expression of medieval thought: nothing important has been left out.' Adams wrote *Chartres Cathedral* to make precisely the same point. Chartres was the context for Joris-Karl Huysman's novel *La Cathédrale*, and Charles Péguy made a pilgrimage there from Paris on foot in 1912, in order to be in the right frame of mind to write poetry about the cathedral.

The town of Chartres is successor to the Carnutic Gaul town of Autricum. Located at a crossroads in the fertile Beauce region, it has a long history of commercial prosperity. Religious buildings have occupied the site of the Gothic cathedral since at least the fourth century. The present structure was started by Abbot Fulbert in 1020, after fire destroyed its predecessor; it was consecrated in 1037. Another fire in 1194 took everything but the façade and towers of Fulbert's church. Reconstruction began at once and was completed in 1260. Additions since include the elaborately decorated choir screen (started in 1514), the 'Flamboyant' spire on the north tower (ca. 1510), and a metal frame for the roof (1836), and restoration of the stained glass (20th century).

The exterior is characterized by two strikingly dissimilar towers and spires, an elaborately decorated triple portal in the façade, hundreds of carvings, and Gothic flying buttresses. The interior is in perpetual twilight, the main illumination being provided by the stained-glass windows. This is by design, for it heightens the aura of medieval sanctity which so impressed Henry Adams and Émile Mâle. Two hundred sculptures adorn the 270-foot choir-screen in a series of scenes depicting the story of Christ. More than 21,500 square feet of stained glass fill the windows. The glass in the three west windows dates from the twelfth century, the rest is later. The Rose de France window, a gift from Louis IX and Blanche of Castile, and the Notre-Dame de la Belle-Verrière are among the most beautiful. Altogether, inside and out, there are 10,000 painted and sculpted figures in the cathedral. Neither the master builder nor the artists who created the windows are known by name.

About thirty miles to the south-east of Paris lies **Fontainebleau**, a palace which Napoléon I called 'the house of the centuries'. The name probably derives from Fontaine-Belle-Eau, or 'fountain of good water'. Fontainebleau is surrounded by the parkland and forests which were a favourite hunting area for French kings back to Hugh Capet, who made the old château a second capital of their domain. The present buildings date from Francis I. He did to Fontainebleau what he did to the Louvre: that is, he hired Italian architects and artists, principally Fiorentino Rosso and Primaticcio di Bologna, to modernize a medieval castle. Henry II, Catherine de' Medici and Henry IV also made contributions, employing the likes of Philibert Delorme and Jean Bullant for the work.

The history of Fontainebleau after Francis is filled with famous associations. Louis XIV signed the Revocation of the Edict of Nantes here, though he lived at Versailles. He improved the gardens, however, adding that task to André Le Nôtre's Versailles responsibilities. Louis XV and Marie Leszczyńska were married here, and Jean-Jacques Rousseau stayed in the palace in 1754 and organized the first performance of his pastoral play, *Le Devin du Village*. Napoléon I imprisoned Pope Pius VII at Fontainebleau for having dared to excommunicate him, signed his abdication there in 1814, and departed for Elba.

Fontainebleau is a series of buildings loosely organized around six courtyards, the largest of which is the Cour du Cheval Blanc. The Louis XV and Francis I wings, and a connecting building which is entered by climbing Jean Androuet du Cerceau's famous 'horseshoe staircase' (1630), are grouped around it. Other notable courtyards include the Cour de la Fontaine, flanked by the Reines-Mères and Belle Cheminée wings, the Cour Ovale, with the royal apartments and the Salle de Bal, and the Cour des Offices, which is lined with structures built in Henry IV's reign. Gardens also abound, most famously the Jardin Anglais and the Jardin de Diane. There is also a large canal commissioned by Henry IV, nearly a kilometre long, which is the lifeline of the parkland.

The interior is elaborately decorated with paintings, panelling, tapestry and furniture from three centuries. The Galerie François I is one of the most beautiful rooms. Decorated by Fiorentino, it features elegantly carved panels and sculptures, murals, and a *parquet à points de Hongrie* (herring-bone pattern) wooden floor. Many of the royal apartments are decorated with Empire furnishings (Bonapartist), and the Salle des Tapisseries features Gobelins tapestries from Louis XIV's reign.

Historically, the town of Fontainebleau has existed more or less because of the château, and features a number of aristocrats' *hôtels*. Writer Katherine Mansfield lived here until her death in 1923.

Twelve miles west of Paris are the town and **Palais de Versailles**. The town has many elegant houses, but the palace, now a national museum, is 'a world of its own'. It dates from the reign of Louis XIV, who took a late medieval château and built a palace around it that was the wonder of Europe. Work began in 1661 under Le Nôtre (the grounds), and Le Vau and Le Brun (the buildings). They had created Nicolas Fouquet's château at Vaux-le-Vicomte. The Salon d'Apollon (the throne room) and the Salon de la Guerre are among the outstanding interior rooms. The most notable, however, is the 240-foot-long Galerie des Glaces, created by Jules Hardouin-Mansart, whose flat-topped roofs are one of the most characteristic features of French baroque architecture. Seventeen large windows open on to the Parterre d'Eau (water garden), and are reflected on the opposite side of the room by seventeen mirrors. Mansart also designed the Orangerie, which contained 1,300 trees. The chapel was built by Robert le Cotte, just in time for Louis's death. The palace is filled with paintings and other decorations from several centuries, including some of David's best-known works from the Empire period.

The palace contains 10,000 rooms and as many windows, with apartments for everyone from the royals to household servants. Construction was carried on for nearly thirty years, employing 36,000 workers and 6,000 horses, at a cost of more than 65 million livres. When it was completed in 1690, Louis moved the court, government, administration and the leading nobles to the town and palace, in order to keep them in line. He never forgot the Fronde of 1648. There the centre of France remained until well into the eighteenth century. Louis's successors added to the palace only nominally. Louis XV built the Petit Trianon for Madame Pompadour, but the most famous (or infamous) addition was the *hameau* (hamlet) where Marie-Antoinette played at being a milkmaid.

History at Versailles, though brief compared to Fontainebleau, is nevertheless rich. Louis XIV made it the seat of government; Marie-Antoinette practised the homely arts there and became a laughing-stock; revolution in 1789 brought a mob on foot from Paris, which forced the royal family to come to the Tuileries Palace; Louis-Philippe made Versailles a national museum in the 1830s; the Prussians proclaimed the German Empire there in 1871 and the peace which ended war with that empire was signed at Versailles in 1919, both in the Galerie des Glaces; and the government of the Third Republic, fearful of Paris after the Commune rising of 1871, sat there from 1871–9, before returning to Paris.

# Further Reading

AMANN, PETER *Revolution and Mass Democracy: The Paris Club Movement in 1848* (Princeton, 1975)

ARDAGH, JOHN *The New French Revolution* (New York, 1968)

ARTZ, FREDERICK W. *France under the Bourbon Restoration, 1814–1830* (Cambridge, Mass., 1931)

BEACH, VINCENT W. *Charles X of France: His Life and Times* (Boulder, 1971)

BERLANSTEIN, LENARD R. *The Working People of Paris, 1871–1914* (Baltimore, 1984)

BERNARD, LEON *The Emerging City* (Durham, NC, 1970)

BERNSTEIN, RICHARD, *Fragile Glory: A Portrait of France and the French* (New York, 1990)

BLOCH, MARC *Strange Defeat: A Statement of Evidence Written in 1940* (New York, 1968)

BLUMENSON, MARTIN *Liberation* (Alexandria, 1978)

BOOTHE, CLARE *Europe in the Spring* (New York, 1940)

BRERETON, GEOFFREY *A Short History of French Literature* (Baltimore, 1954)

BROGAN, DENIS *The Development of Modern France*, 2 vols. (New York, 1966)

BROWN, BERNARD *Anatomy of a Revolt* (Morristown, 1975)

COBB, RICHARD *French and Germans, Germans and French* (Hanover, 1983)

COLLINS, LARRY, and LAPIERRE, DOMINIQUE *Is Paris Burning?* (New York, 1965)

CRONIN, VINCENT *Paris on the Eve: 1900–1914* (London, 1989)

CULBERTSON, JUDI, and RANDALL, TOM *Permanent Parisians* (Chelsea, 1986)

DANOS, JACQUES, and GIBELEN, MARCEL *June '36: Class Struggle and the Popular Front in France* (London, 1986)

DARK, SIDNEY *Paris* (New York, 1941)

DELAPORTE, FRANÇOIS *Disease and Civilization: The Cholera in Paris, 1832* (Cambridge, Mass., 1986)

DIEFENDORF, BARBARA *Beneath the Cross: Catholics and Huguenots in Sixteenth-Century Paris* (New York, 1991)

DILL, MARSHALL *Paris in Time* (New York, 1975)

DRUKS, HERBERT, and LACETTI, SILVIO R. *Cities in Civilization: The City in Western Civilization* (New York, 1971)

DRUON, MAURICE *The History of Paris from Caesar to Charlemagne* (London, 1969)

DUBLY, HENRI-LOUIS *Ponts de Paris: A Travers Les Siècles* (Paris, 1957)

DUVAL, G. *Shadows of Old Paris* (Philadelphia, 1911)

EDWARDS, STEWART, ed. *The Communards of Paris, 1871* (London, 1973)

EGBERT, VIRGINIA WYLIE *On the Bridges of Medieval Paris* (Princeton, 1974)

EHRLICH, BLAKE *Paris on the Seine* (New York, 1962)

EVENSON, NORMA *Paris: A Century of Change, 1878–1978* (New Haven, 1979)

FUCHS, RACHEL G. *Poor and Pregnant in Nineteenth-Century Paris* (New Brunswick, 1992)

GALLAHER, JOHN G. *The Students of Paris and the Revolution of 1848* (Carbondale, 1980)

GENET (JANET FLANNERY) *Paris Journal, 1944–1971*, 2 vols. (New York, 1965 and 1971)

GEREMEK, BRONISLAW *The Margins of Society in Late Medieval Paris* (New York, 1987)

GOOCH, BRISON D. *Napoleon III: Man of Destiny* (New York, 1963)

GOUBERT, PIERRE *The Course of French History* (New York, 1988)

HARDY, BRIAN *Paris Metro Handbook* (Middlesex, 1988)

HARSIN, JILL *Policing Prostitution in Nineteenth-Century Paris* (Princeton, 1987)

HARVEY, DAVID *Consciousness and the Urban Experience* (Baltimore, 1985)

HAUSE, STEVEN C. *Hubertine Auclert: The French Suffragette* (New Haven, 1987)

HORNE, ALISTAIR *A Savage War of Peace: Algeria, 1954–1962* (New York, 1977)

HORNE, ALISTAIR *The Fall of Paris: The Siege and the Commune, 1870–71* (New York, 1965)

HORNE, ALISTAIR *The French Army and Politics, 1870–1970* (New York, 1984)

HORNE, ALISTAIR *To Lose a Battle: France 1940* (London, 1969)

IRVINE, WILLIAM *The Boulanger Affair Reconsidered* (New York, 1989)

ISHERWOOD, CHRISTOPHER *Farce and Fantasy: Popular Entertainment in Eighteenth-Century Paris* (Oxford, 1986)

JAMES, HENRY *Parisian Sketches* (New York, 1957)

KAPLOW, JEFFRY, *The Names of Kings: The Parisian Laboring Poor in the Eighteenth Century* (New York)

KRAMER, LLOYD S. *Threshold of a New World: Intellectuals and the Exile Experience in Paris, 1830–1848* (Ithaca, 1988)

LANOUX, ARMAND, *Bonjour, Monsieur Zola* (Paris, 1962)

LANOUX, ARMAND *Paris in the Twenties* (New York, 1960)

LE GALLIENNE, RICHARD *From a Paris Scrapbook* (New York, 1938)

LITTLEWOOD, IAN *Paris: A Literary Companion* (London, 1987)

LOTTMAN, HERBERT *Colette: A Life* (Boston, 1991)

LOTTMAN, HERBERT *The Fall of Paris: 1940* (New York, 1992)

LOTTMAN, HERBERT *Flaubert: A Life* (Boston, 1989)

LOTTMAN, HERBERT *The Left Bank: Writers, Artists, and Politics from the Popular Front to the Cold War* (Boston, 1982)

McMILLAN, JAMES F. *Dreyfus to De Gaulle: Politics and Society in France, 1898–1969* (London, 1985)

McMILLAN, JAMES F. *Housewife or Harlot: The Place of Women in French Society, 1870–1940* (New York, 1981)

MAY, GITA *Madame Roland and the Age of Revolution* (New York, 1970)

MAY, GITA *Stendhal and the Age of Napoleon* (New York, 1977)

MELZER, SARA E., and RABINE, LESLIE W. *Rebel Daughters: Women and the French Revolution* (Oxford, 1992)

MERCIER, LOUIS SEBASTIEN *The Picture of Paris Before & After the Revolution* (New York, 1929)

MERRIMAN, JOHN M. *1830 in France* (New York, 1975)

MILLER, MICHAEL *The Bon Marché: Bourgeois Culture and the Department Store, 1869–1920* (Princeton, 1981)

MILLER, RUSSELL *The Resistance* (Alexandria, 1979)

MOOTE, LLOYD *Louis XIII, The Just* (Berkeley, 1989)

MOSES, CLAIRE GOLDBERG *French Feminism in the 19th Century* (Albany, 1984)

NORD, PHILIP G. *Paris Shopkeepers and the Politics of Resentment* (Princeton, 1986)

OKEY, THOMAS *The Story of Paris* (New York, 1919)

PERRAULT, GILLES, and AZEMA, PIERRE *Paris under the Occupation* (New York, 1989)

PESSIS, JACQUES, and CRÉPINEAU, JACQUES *The Moulin Rouge* (New York, 1989)

PINKNEY, DAVID *The French Revolution of 1830* (Princeton, 1972)

PINKNEY, DAVID *Napoleon III and the Rebuilding of Paris* (Princeton, 1958)

QUÉTEL, CLAUDE *Escape from the Bastille* (New York, 1990)

RANUM, OREST *Paris in the Age of Absolutism: An Essay* (New York, 1968)

REFF, THEODORE *Manet and Modern Paris* (Chicago, 1982)

REYNOLDS, Quentin *The Wounded Don't Cry* (New York, 1940)

RICE, HOWARD C. *Thomas Jefferson's Paris* (Princeton, 1976)

ROCHE, DANIEL *The People of Paris, an Essay on Popular Culture in the 18th Century* (Berkeley, 1987)

ROE, F.C. *Modern France: An Introduction to French Civilization* (New York, 1961)

RUDÉ, GEORGE *The Crowd in the French Revolution* (Oxford, 1959)

SALVADORI, RENZO *Architect's Guide to Paris* (London, 1990)

SCHERWAN, KATHERINE *The Birth of France* (New York, 1987)

SEIGEL, JERROLD *Bohemian Paris* (New York, 1986)

SOBOUL, ALBERT *The Parisian Sans-Culottes and the French Revolution, 1793–4* (Oxford, 1964)

SOUCY, ROBERT *French Fascism: The First Wave, 1924–1933* (New Haven, 1986)

STEEL, VALERIE *Paris Fashion: A Cultural History* (New York, 1988)

SUTCLIFFE, ANTHONY *The Autumn of Central Paris* (Montreal, 1971)

TANNAHILL, REAY, ed. *Paris in the Revolution: A Collection of Eye-Witness Accounts* (London, 1967)

THOMPSON, GUY LLEWELYN *Paris and its People Under English Rule, 1420–1436* (Oxford, 1991)

TOMBS, ROBERT *The War Against Paris, 1871* (Cambridge, 1981)

VIZETELLY, ERNEST ALFRED *Paris and Her People Under the Third Republic* (New York, 1971)

WALTER, JAKOB *The Diary of a Napoleonic Foot Soldier* (New York, 1991)

WEISZ, GEORGE *The Emergence of Modern Universities in France, 1863–1914* (Princeton, 1983)

WILLIAMS, ROSALIND H. *Dream Worlds: Mass Consumption in Late Nineteenth-Century France* (Berkeley, 1982)

WINSTON, RICHARD and CLARA *Notre-Dame de Paris* (New York, 1971)

YOUNG, ARTHUR *Travels in France* (London, 1890)

# Index

# *Interlink's Bestselling Travel Publications*

## The Traveller's History Series

| | |
|---|---|
| *A Traveller's History of China* (2nd ed.) | $14.95 pb |
| *A Traveller's History of England* (3rd ed.) | $14.95 pb |
| *A Traveller's History of France* (4th ed.) | $12.95 pb |
| *A Traveller's History of Greece* (3rd ed.) | $14.95 pb |
| *A Traveller's History of India* | $14.95 pb |
| *A Traveller's History of Ireland* (3rd ed.) | $14.95 pb |
| *A Traveller's History of Italy* (4th ed.) | $14.95 pb |
| *A Traveller's History of Japan* (2nd ed.) | $14.95 pb |
| *A Traveller's History of London* | $13.95 pb |
| *A Traveller's History of North Africa* | $14.95 pb |
| *A Traveller's History of Paris* (2nd ed.) | $14.95 pb |
| *A Traveller's History of Russia* (3rd ed.) | $14.95 pb |
| *A Traveller's History of Scotland* (3rd ed.) | $13.95 pb |
| *A Traveller's History of Spain* (3rd ed.) | $14.95 pb |
| *A Traveller's History of Turkey* (3rd ed.) | $14.95 pb |

## The Traveller's Wine Guides

| | |
|---|---|
| *A Traveller's Wine Guide to France* | $17.95 pb |
| *A Traveller's Wine Guide to Germany* | $17.95 pb |
| *A Traveller's Wine Guide to Italy* | $17.95 pb |
| *A Traveller's Wine Guide to Spain* | $17.95 pb |

*Available at good bookstores everywhere.*
*We encourage you to support your local bookseller.*

To order or request our complete catalog,
please call us at **1-800-238-LINK** or write to:
**Interlink Publishing**
46 Crosby Street, Northampton, MA 01060